Rudolf Lindau

The Philosopher's Pendulum

And other stories

Rudolf Lindau

The Philosopher's Pendulum
And other stories

ISBN/EAN: 9783744751445

Printed in Europe, USA, Canada, Australia, Japan

Cover: Foto ©Thomas Meinert / pixelio.de

More available books at **www.hansebooks.com**

THE PHILOSOPHER'S PENDULUM

THE

PHILOSOPHER'S PENDULUM

AND OTHER STORIES

BY

RUDOLPH LINDAU

WILLIAM BLACKWOOD AND SONS
EDINBURGH AND LONDON
MDCCCLXXXIII

CONTENTS.

THE PHILOSOPHER'S PENDULUM:

A TALE FROM GERMANY.

I.

During many long years Hermann Fabricius had lost sight of his friend Henry Warren, and had forgotten him.

Yet when students together they had loved each other dearly, and more than once they had sworn eternal friendship. This was at a period which, though not very remote, we seem to have left far behind us—a time when young men still believed in eternal friendship, and could feel enthusiasm for great deeds or great ideas. Youth in the present day is, or thinks itself, more rational. Hermann and Warren in those days were simple-minded and ingenuous; and not only in the moment of elation, when they had sworn to be friends for ever, but even the next day, and the day after that, in sober earnestness, they had vowed that nothing should separate them, and that they would remain united through life. The delusion had not lasted long. The pitiless machinery of life had caught up the young men as soon as they left the university, and had thrown one to the right, the other to the left. For a few months they had exchanged long and frequent letters; then they had met once, and finally they had parted, each going his way. Their letters had become more scarce, more brief, and at last had ceased altogether.

It would really seem that the fact of having interests in common is the one thing sufficiently powerful to prolong and keep up the life of epistolary relations. A man may feel great affection for an absent friend, and yet not find time to write him ten lines, while he will willingly expend daily many hours on a stranger from whom he expects something. None the less he may be a true and honest friend. Man is naturally selfish; the instinct of self-preservation requires it of him. Provided he be not wicked, and that he show himself ready to serve his neighbour—after himself—no one has a right to complain, or to accuse him of hard-heartedness.

At the time this story begins, Hermann had even forgotten whether he had written to Warren last, or whether he had left his friend's last letter unanswered. In a word, the correspondence which began so enthusiastically had entirely ceased. Hermann inhabited a large town, and had acquired some reputation as a writer. From time to time, in the course of his walks, he would meet a young student with brown hair, and mild, honest-looking blue eyes, whose countenance, with its frank and youthful smile, inspired confidence and invited the sympathy of the passer-by. Whenever Hermann met this young man he would say to himself, "How like Henry at twenty!" and for a few minutes memory would travel back to the already distant days of youth, and he would long to see his dear old Warren again. More than once, on the spur of the moment, he had resolved to try and find out what had become of his old university comrade. But these good intentions were never followed up. On reaching home he would find his table covered with books and pamphlets to be reviewed, and letters from publishers or newspaper editors asking for "copy"—to say nothing of invitations to dinner, which must be accepted or refused; in a word, he found so much *urgent* business to despatch, that the evening would go by, and weariness would overtake him, before he could make time for inquiring about his old friend.

In the course of years, the life of most men becomes so regulated that no time is left for anything beyond "necessary work." And, indeed, the man who lives only for his own pleasure—doing, so to speak, nothing—is rarely better off in this respect than the writer, the banker, and the *savant*, who are overburdened with work.

One afternoon, as Hermann, according to his custom, was returning home about five o'clock, his porter handed him a letter bearing the American post-mark. He examined it closely before opening it. The large and rather stiff handwriting on the address seemed familiar, and yet he could not say to whom it belonged. Suddenly his countenance brightened, and he exclaimed, "A letter from Henry!" He tore open the envelope, and read as follows:—

"MY DEAR HERMANN,—It is fortunate that one of us at least has attained celebrity. I saw your name on the outside of a book of which you are the author. I wrote at once to the publisher; that obliging man answered me by return of post, and, thanks to these circumstances, I am enabled to tell you that I will land at Hamburg towards the end of September. Write to me there, *Poste Restante,* and let me know if you are willing to receive me for a few days. I can take Leipzig on my way home, and would do so most willingly if you say that you would see me again with pleasure.—Your old friend,

HENRY WARREN."

Below the signature there was a postscript of a single line: "This is my present face." And from an inner envelope Hermann drew a small photograph, which he carried to the window to examine leisurely. As he looked, a painful impression of sadness came over him. The portrait was that of an old man. Long grey hair fell in disorder over a careworn brow; the eyes, deep sunk in their sockets, had a strange and disquieting look of fixity; and the mouth, surrounded by deep furrows, seemed to tell its own long tale of sorrow.

"Poor Henry!" said Hermann; "this, then, is your present face! And yet he is not old; he is younger than I am; he can scarcely be thirty-eight. Can I, too, be already an old man?"

He walked up to the glass, and looked attentively at the reflection of his own face. No! those were not the features of a man whose life was near its close; the eye was bright, and the complexion indicated vigour and health. Still, it was not a young face. Thought and care had traced their lines round the mouth and about the temples, and the general expression was one of melancholy, not to say despondency.

"Well, well, we have grown old," said Hermann, with a sigh. "I had not thought about it this long while; and now this photograph has reminded me of it painfully." Then he took up his pen and wrote to say how happy he would be to see his old friend again as soon as possible.

The next day, chance brought him face to face in the street with the young student who was so like Warren. "Who knows?" thought Hermann; "fifteen or twenty years hence this young man may look no brighter than Warren does to-day. Ah, life is not easy! It has a way of saddening joyous looks, and imparting severity to smiling lips.

"As for me, I have no real right to complain of my life. I have lived pretty much like every-body—a little satisfaction, and then a little dis-appointment, in turns, and often small worries: and so my youth has gone by, I scarcely know how."

On the 2d of October Hermann received a telegram from Hamburg announcing the arrival of Warren for the same evening. At the ap-pointed hour he went to the railway station to meet his friend. He saw him get down from the carriage slowly, and rather heavily, and he watched him for a few seconds before accosting him. Warren appeared to him old and broken-down, and even more feeble than he had ex-pected to see him from his portrait. He wore a travelling suit of grey cloth so loose and wide that it hung in folds on the gaunt and stoop-ing figure; a large wideawake hat was drawn down to his very eyes.

The new-comer looked right and left, seeking no doubt to discover his friend; not seeing him, he turned his weary and languid steps towards the way out. Hermann then came forward. Warren recognised him at once; a sunny youthful smile lighted up his countenance, and, evidently much moved, he stretched out his hand.

An hour later, the two friends were seated opposite to each other before a well-spread table in Hermann's comfortable apartments.

Warren ate very little; but, on the other hand, Hermann noticed with surprise and some anxiety that his friend, who had been formerly a model of sobriety, drank a good deal. Wine, however, seemed to have no effect on him. The pale face did not flush; there was the same cold fixed look in the eye; and his speech, though slow and dull in tone, betrayed no embarrassment.

When the servant who had waited at dinner had taken away the dessert and brought in coffee, Hermann wheeled two big arm-chairs close to the fire, and said to his friend—

"Now, we will not be interrupted. Light a cigar, make yourself at home, and tell me all you have been doing since we parted."

Warren pushed away the cigars. "If you do

not mind," he said, "I will smoke my pipe. I am used to it, and I prefer it to the best of cigars."

So saying, he drew from its well-worn case an old pipe, whose colour showed it had been long used, and filled it methodically with moist, blackish tobacco. Then he lighted it, and after sending forth one or two loud puffs of smoke, he said, with an air of sovereign satisfaction—

"A quiet, comfortable room — a friend — a good pipe after dinner — and no care for the morrow;—that's what I like."

Hermann cast a sidelong glance at his companion, and was painfully struck at his appearance. The tall, gaunt frame in its stooping attitude; the greyish hair, and sad fixed look; the thin legs crossed one over the other; the elbow resting on the knee and supporting the chin,—in a word, the whole strange figure, as it sat there, bore no resemblance to Henry Warren, the friend of his youth. This man was a stranger, a mysterious being even. Nevertheless, the affection he felt for his friend was not impaired; on the contrary, pity entered into his heart. "How ill the world must have used him," thought Hermann, "to have thus disfigured him!" Then he said aloud—

"Now, then, let me have your story, unless you prefer to hear mine first."

He strove to speak lightly, but he felt that the effort was not successful. As to Warren, he went on smoking quietly, without saying a word. The long silence at last became painful. Hermann began to feel an uncomfortable sensation of distress in presence of the strange guest he had brought to his home. After a few minutes, he ventured to ask for the third time, "Will you make up your mind to speak, or must I begin?"

Warren gave vent to a little noiseless laugh. "I am thinking how I can answer your question. The difficulty is that, to speak truly, I have absolutely nothing to tell. I wonder now—and it was that made me pause—how it has happened that, throughout my life, I have been so much bored by—nothing. As if it would not have been quite as natural, quite as easy, and far pleasanter, to have been amused by that same nothing—which has been my life.

"The fact is, my dear Hermann, that if I have had no deep sorrow to bear, neither have I been happy.

"I have not been extraordinarily successful, and have drawn none of the prizes of life. But

I am well aware that, in this respect, my lot resembles that of thousands of other men.

"I have always been obliged to work. I have earned my bread by the sweat of my brow. I have had money difficulties; I have even had a hopeless passion—but what then? every one has had that. Besides, that was in bygone days; I have learned to bear it, and to forget. What pains and angers me is, to have to confess that my life has been spent without satisfaction and without happiness."

He paused an instant, and then resumed, more calmly—"A few years ago I was foolish enough to believe that things might in the end turn out better. I was a professor with a very moderate salary at the school at Elmira. I taught all I knew, and much that I had to learn in order to be able to teach it—Greek and Latin, German and French, mathematics and physical sciences. During the so-called play-hours I even gave music lessons. In the course of the whole day there were few moments of liberty for me. I was perpetually surrounded by a crowd of rough, ill-bred boys, whose only object during lessons was to catch me making a mistake in English. When evening came, I was quite worn out; still I could always find time to dream for half an hour or so with my eyes open before going to bed. Then all my desires were accomplished, and I was supremely happy. At last I had drawn a prize! I was successful in everything; I was rich, honoured, powerful—what more can I say? I astonished the world—or rather, I astonished Ellen Gilmore, who for me was the whole world.

"Hermann, have you ever been as mad? Have you, too, in a waking dream, been in turn a statesman, a millionaire, the author of a sublime work, a victorious general, the head of a great political party? Have you dreamed nonsense such as that? I, who am here, have been all I say—in dreamland. Never mind; that was a good time.

"Ellen Gilmore, whom I have just mentioned, was the elder sister of one of my pupils, Francis Gilmore, the most undisciplined boy of the school. His parents, nevertheless, insisted on his learning something; and as I had the reputation of possessing unwearying patience, I was selected to give him private lessons. That was how I obtained a footing in the Gilmore family. Later on, when they had found out that I was somewhat of a musician—you may remember, perhaps, that for an amateur I was a tolerable performer on the piano—I went every day to the house to teach Latin and Greek to Francis, and music to Ellen.

"Now, picture to yourself the situation, and then laugh at your friend as he has laughed at himself many a time. On the one side — the Gilmore side—a large fortune and no lack of pride; an intelligent, shrewd, and practical father; an ambitious and vain mother; an affectionate but spoilt boy; and a girl of nineteen, surpassingly lovely, with a cultivated mind and great good sense. On the other hand, you have Henry Warren, aged twenty-nine; in his dreams the author of a famous work, or the commander-in-chief of the Northern armies, or, it may be, President of the Republic—in reality, Professor at Elmira College, with a modest stipend of seventy dollars a-month. Was it not evident that the absurdity of my position as a suitor for Ellen would strike me at once?

"Of course it did. In my lucid moments, when I was not dreaming, I was a very rational man, who had read a good deal, and learned not a little; and it would have been sheer madness in me to have indulged for an instant the hope of a marriage between Ellen and myself. I knew it was an utter impossibility—as impossible as to be elected President of the United States; and yet, in spite of myself, I dreamed of it. However, I must do myself the justice to add that my passion inconvenienced nobody. I would no more have spoken of it than of my imaginary command of the Army of the Potomac. The pleasures which my love afforded me could give umbrage to no one. Yet I am convinced that Ellen read my secret. Not that she ever said a word to me on the subject; no look or syllable of hers could have made me suspect that she had guessed the state of my mind.

"One single incident I remember which was not in accordance with her habitual reserve in this respect. I noticed one day that her eyes were red. Of course I dared not ask her why she had cried. During the lesson she seemed absent; and when leaving she said, without looking at me, 'I may perhaps be obliged to interrupt our lessons for some little time; I am very sorry. I wish you every happiness.' Then, without raising her eyes, she quickly left the room.

"I was bewildered. What could her words mean? And why had they been said in such an affectionate tone?

"The next day Francis Gilmore called to inform me, with his father's compliments, that he was to have four days' holidays, because his sister had just been betrothed to Mr Howard, a wealthy New York merchant, and that, for the occasion, there would be great festivities at home.

"Thenceforward there was an end of the dreams which up to that moment had made life pleasant. In sober reason I had no more cause to deplore Ellen's marriage than to feel aggrieved because Grant had succeeded Johnson as President. Nevertheless you can scarcely conceive how much this affair—I mean the marriage—grieved me. My absolute nothingness suddenly stared me in the face. I saw myself as I was—a mere schoolmaster, with no motive for pride in the past, or pleasure in the present, or hope in the future."

Warren's pipe had gone out while he was telling his story. He cleaned it out methodically, drew from his pocket a cake of Cavendish tobacco, and after cutting off with a penknife the necessary quantity, refilled his pipe and lit it. The way in which he performed all these little operations betrayed long habit. He had ceased to speak while he was relighting his pipe, and kept on whistling between his teeth. Hermann looked on silently. After a few minutes, and when the pipe was in good order, Warren resumed his story.

"For a few weeks I was terribly miserable; not so much because I had lost Ellen—a man cannot lose what he has never hoped to possess—as from the ruin of all my illusions. During those days I plucked and ate by the dozen of the fruits of the tree of self-knowledge, and I found them very bitter. I ended by leaving Elmira, to seek my fortunes elsewhere. I knew my trade well. Long practice had taught me how to make the best of my learning, and I never had any difficulty in finding employment. I taught successively in upwards of a dozen States of the Union. I can scarcely recollect the names of all the places where I have lived—Sacramento, Chicago, St Louis, Cincinnati, Boston, New York; I have been everywhere—everywhere. And everywhere I have met with the same rude schoolboys, just as I have found the same regular and irregular verbs in Latin and Greek. If you would see a man thoroughly satiated and saturated with schoolboys and classical grammars, look at me.

"In the leisure time which, whatever might be my work, I still contrived to make for myself, I indulged in philosophical reflections. Then it was I took to the habit of smoking so much." . . .

Warren stopped suddenly, and looking straight before him, appeared plunged in thought. Then, passing his hand over his forehead, he repeated, in an absent manner, "Yes, of smoking so much. . . . I also acquired another habit," he added, somewhat hastily—"but that has nothing to do with my story. The theory which especially occupied my thoughts was that of the oscillations of an imaginary instrument, to which, in my own mind, I gave the name of the *Philosopher's Pendulum*. To this invention I owe the quietude of mind which has supported me for many years, and which, as you see, I now enjoy.

"I said to myself that my great sorrow—if I may so call it without presumption—had arisen merely from my wish to be extraordinarily happy. When, in his dreams, a man has carried presumption so far as to attain to the heights of celebrity or to being the husband of Ellen Gilmore, it is not wonderful if, on awaking, he sustains a heavy fall before reaching the depths of reality. Had I been less ambitious in my desires, their realisation would have been easier, or, at any rate, the disappointment would have been less bitter. Starting from this principle, I arrived at the logical conclusion that the best means to avoid being unhappy is to wish for as little happiness as possible. This truth was discovered by my philosophical forefathers many centuries before the birth of Christ, and I lay no claim to being the first finder of it; but the outward symbol which I ended by giving to this idea is—at least I fancy it is—of my invention.

"Give me a sheet of paper and a pencil," he added, turning to his friend, "and with a few lines I can demonstrate clearly the whole thing."

Hermann handed him what he wanted without a word. Warren then began gravely to draw a large semicircle, open at the top, and above the semicircular line a pendulum, which fell perpendicularly and touched the circumference at the exact point where on the dial of a clock would be inscribed the figure VI. This done, he wrote on the right-hand side of the pendulum, beginning from the bottom and at the place of the hours V, IV, III, the words, *Moderate Desires—Great Hopes, Ambition—Unbridled Passion, Mania of Greatness.* Then, turning the paper upside down, he wrote on the opposite side, where on a dial would be marked VII, VIII, IX, the words, *Slight Troubles—Deep Sorrow, Disappointment—Despair.* Lastly, in the place of No. VI, just where the pendulum fell, he sketched a large black spot, which he shaded off with great care, and above which he wrote, like a scroll, *Dead Stop, Absolute Repose.*

THE PHILOSOPHER'S PENDULUM.

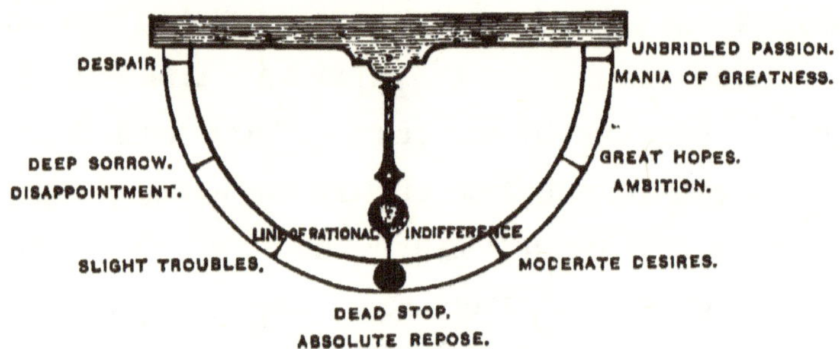

Having finished this little drawing, Warren laid down his pipe, inclined his head on one side, and raising his eyebrows, examined his work with a critical frown. "This compass is not yet quite complete," he said; "there is something missing. Between *Dead Stop* and *Moderate Desires* on the right, and *Slight Troubles* on the left, there is the beautiful line of *Calm and Rational Indifference.* However, such as the drawing is, it is sufficient to demonstrate my theory. Do you follow me?"

Hermann nodded affirmatively. He was greatly pained. In lieu of the friend of his youth, for whom he had hoped a brilliant future, here was a poor monomaniac!

"You see," said Warren, speaking collectedly, like a professor, "if I raise my pendulum till it reaches the point of *Moderate Desires,* and then let it go, it will naturally swing to the point of *Slight Troubles,* and go no further. Then it will oscillate for some time in a more and more limited space on the line of *Indifference,* and finally it will stand still without any jerk on *Dead Stop, Absolute Repose.* That is a great consolation!"

He paused, as if waiting for some remark from Hermann; but as the latter remained silent, Warren resumed his demonstration.

"You understand now, I suppose, what I am coming to. If I raise the pendulum to the point of *Ambition* or *Mania of Greatness,* and then let it go, that same law which I have already applied will drive it to *Deep Sorrow* or *Despair*. That is quite clear, is it not?"

"Quite clear," repeated Hermann, sadly.

"Very well," continued Warren, with perfect gravity; "for my misfortune, I discovered this fine theory rather late. I had not set bounds to my dreams and limited them to trifles. I had wished to be President of the Republic, an illustrious *savant*, the husband of Ellen. No great things, eh? What say you to my modesty? I had raised the pendulum to such a giddy height that when it slipped from my impotent hands it naturally performed a long oscillation, and touched the point *Despair*.

"That was a miserable time. I hope you have never suffered what I suffered then. I lived in a perpetual nightmare—like the stupor of intoxication." He paused, as he had done before, and then, with a painfully nervous laugh, he added, "Yes, like intoxication. I drank." Suddenly a spasm seemed to pass over his face, he looked serious and sad as before, and he said, with a shudder, "It is a terrible thing to see one's self inwardly, and to know that one is fallen."

After this he remained long silent. At last,

raising his head, he turned to his friend and said, "Have you had enough of my story, or would you like to hear it to the end?"

"I am grieved at all you have told me," said Hermann; "but pray go on; it is better I should know all."

"Yes; and I feel, too, that it relieves me to pour out my heart. Well, I used to drink. One takes the horrid habit in America far easier than anywhere else. I was obliged to give up more than one good situation because I had ceased to be *respectable.* Anyhow, I always managed to find employment without any great difficulty. I never suffered from want, though I have never known plenty. If I spent too much in drink, I took it out of my dress and my books.

"Eighteen months after I had left Elmira, I met Ellen one day in Central Park, in New York. I was aware that she had been married a twelvemonth. She knew me again at once, and spoke to me. I would have wished to sink into the earth. I knew that my clothes were shabby, that I looked poor, and I fancied that she must discern on my face the traces of the bad habits I had contracted. But she did not, or would not, see anything. She held out her hand, and said in her gentle voice—

"'I am very glad to see you again, Mr Warren. I have inquired about you, but neither my father nor Francis could tell me what had become of you. I want to ask you to resume the lessons you used to give me. Perhaps you do not know where I live? This is my address,' and she gave me her card.

"I stammered out a few unmeaning words in reply to her invitation. She looked at me, smiling kindly the while; but suddenly the smile vanished, and she added, 'Have you been ill, Mr Warren? You seem worn.'

"'Yes,' I answered, too glad to find an excuse for my appearance—'yes, I have been ill, and I am still suffering.'

"'I am very sorry,' she said, in a low voice.

"Laugh at me, Hermann—call me an incorrigible madman; but believe me when I say that her looks conveyed to me the impression of more than common interest or civility. A thrilling sense of pain shot through my frame. What had I done that I should be so cruelly tried? A mist passed before my eyes; anxiety, intemperance, sleeplessness, had made me weak.

I tottered backwards a few steps. She turned horribly pale. All around us was the crowd—the careless, indifferent crowd.

"'Come and see me soon,' she added hastily, and left me. I saw her get into a carriage, which she had doubtless quitted to take a walk; and when she drove past, she put her head out and looked at me with her eyes wide open—there was an almost wildly anxious expression in them.

"I went home. My way led me past her house—it was a palace. I shut myself up in my wretched hotel-room, and once more I fell to dreaming. Ellen loved me; she admired me; she was not for ever lost to me! The pendulum was swinging, you see, up as high as *Madness.*

"Explain to me, if you can, how it happens that a being perfectly rational in ordinary life should at certain seasons, and, so to speak, voluntarily, be bereft of reason.

"To excuse and explain my temporary insanity, I am ready to admit that the excitement to which I gave way may have been a symptom of the nervous malady which laid hold of me a few days later, and stretched me for weeks upon a bed of pain.

"As I became convalescent, reason and composure returned. But it was too late. In the space of two months, twenty years had passed over my head. When I rose from my sick-bed I was as feeble and as broken-down as you see me now. My past had been cheerless and dim, without one ray of happiness; yet that past was all my life! Henceforward there was nothing left for me to undertake, to regret, or to desire. The pendulum swung idly backwards and forwards on the line of *Indifference.*

"I wonder what are the feelings of successful men—of men who *have* been victorious generals, prime ministers, celebrated authors, and that sort of thing! Upheld by a legitimate pride, do they retire satisfied from the lists when evening comes, or do they lay down their arms as I did, disappointed and dejected and worn out with the fierce struggle? Can no man with impunity look into his own heart and ask himself how his life has been spent?"

Here Warren made a still longer pause than before, and appeared absorbed in gloomy thought. At last he resumed in a lower tone—

"I had not followed up Ellen's invitation. But in some way she had discovered my address, and knew of my illness. Do not be alarmed, my dear Hermann; my story will not become romantic. No heavenly vision appeared to me during my fever; I felt no gentle white hands laid on my burning brow. I was nursed at the hospital, and very well nursed too; I figured there as 'Number 380,' and the whole affair was, as you see, as prosaic as possible. But on quitting the hospital, and as I was taking leave of the manager, he handed me a letter, in which was enclosed a note for 500 dollars. In the envelope there was also the following anonymous note :—

"'An old friend begs your acceptance, as a loan, of the enclosed sum. It will be time enough to think of paying off this debt when you are strong enough to resume work, and you can then do it by instalments, of which you can yourself fix the amount, and remit them to the hospital of New York.'

"It was well meant, no doubt, but it caused me a painful impression. My determination was taken at once. I refused without hesitation. I asked the manager, who had been watching me with a friendly smile while I read the letter, whether he could give the name of the person who had sent it. In spite of his repeated assurances that he did not know it, I never doubted for a single instant that he was concealing the truth. After a few seconds' reflection I asked if he would undertake to forward an answer to my unknown correspondent; and on his consenting to do so, I promised that he should have my answer the next day.

"I thought long over my letter. One thing was plain to me—it was Ellen who had come to my help. How could I reject her generous aid without wounding her, or appearing ungrateful? After great hesitation I wrote a few lines, which, as far as I can recollect, ran thus:—

"'I thank you for the interest you have shown me, but it is impossible for me to accept the sum you place at my disposal. Do not be angry with me because I return it. Do not withdraw your sympathy; I will strive to remain worthy of it, and will never forget your goodness.'

"A few days later, after having confided this letter to the manager, I left New York for San Francisco. For several years I heard nothing of Ellen; her image grew gradually fainter, and at last almost disappeared from my memory.

"The dark river that bore the frail bark which carried me and my fortunes was flowing smoothly and silently along towards the mysterious abyss where all that exists is engulfed. Its course lay through a vast desert; and the banks which passed before my eyes were of fearful sameness. Indescribable lassitude took possession of my whole being. I had never, knowingly, done evil; I had loved and sought after good. Why, then, was I so wretched? I would have blessed the rock which wrecked my bark so that I might have been swallowed up and have gone down to my eternal rest.

"Up to the day when I heard of Ellen's betrothal, I had hoped that the morrow would bring happiness. The long-wished-for morrow had come at last, gloomy and colourless, without realising any of my vague hopes. Thenceforward my life was at an end."

Warren said these last words so indistinctly that Hermann could scarcely hear them; he seemed to be speaking to himself rather than to his friend. Then he raised the forefinger of his right hand, and after moving it slowly from right to left, in imitation of the swing of a pendulum, he placed it on the large black dot he had drawn on the sheet of paper exactly below his pendulum, and said, "*Dead Stop, Absolute Repose.* Would that the end were come!"

Another and still longer interval of silence succeeded, and at last Hermann felt constrained to speak.

"How came you to make up your mind," he said, "to return to Europe?"

"Ah yes, to be sure," answered Warren, hurriedly; "the story—the foolish story—is not ended. In truth it has no end, as it had no beginning; it is a thing without form or purpose, and less the history of a life than of a mere journeying towards death. Still I will finish—following chronological order. It does not weary you?"

"No, no; go on, my dear friend."

"Very well. I spent several years in the United States. The pendulum worked well. It came and went, to and fro, slowly along the line of *Indifference,* without ever transgressing, as its extreme limits on either hand, *Moderate Desires* and *Slight Troubles.* I led obscurely a contemplative life, and I was generally considered a queer character. I fulfilled my duties, and took little heed of any one. Whenever I had an hour at my disposal, I sought solitude in the neighbouring woods, far from the town and from mankind. I used to lie down under the big trees. Every season in turn, spring and summer, autumn and winter, had its peculiar charm for me. My heart, so full of bitterness, felt lightened as soon as I listened to the rustling of the foliage overhead. The forest! There is nothing finer in all creation. A deep calm seemed to settle down upon me. I was growing old. I was forgetting. It was about this time that, in consequence of my complete indifference to all surroundings, I acquired the habit of answering 'Very well' to everything that was said. The words came so naturally that I was not aware of the continual use of them, until one day one of my fellow-teachers happened to tell me that masters and pupils alike had given me the nickname of 'Very well.' Is it not odd that one who has never succeeded in anything should be known as 'Very well'?

"I have only one other little adventure to relate, and I will have told all. Then I can listen to your story.

"Last year, my journeyings brought me to the neighbourhood of Elmira. It was holiday-time. I had nothing to do, and I had in my purse a hundred hardly earned dollars, or thereabout. The wish seized me to revisit the scene of my joys and my sorrows. I had not set foot in the place for more than seven years. I was so changed that nobody could know me again; nor would I have cared much if they had. After visiting the town and looked at my old school, and the house where Ellen had lived, I bent my steps towards the park, which is situated in the environs—a place where I used often to walk in company of my youthful dreams. It was September, and evening was closing in. The oblique rays of the setting sun sent a reddish gleam through the leafy branches of the old oaks. I saw a woman seated on a bench beneath a tree on one side of the path. As I drew near I recognised Ellen. I remained rooted to the spot where I stood, not daring to move a step. She was stooping forward with her head bent down, while with the end of her parasol she traced lines upon the gravel. She had not seen me. I turned back instantly, and retired without making any noise. When I had gone a little distance, I left the path and struck into the wood. Once there, I looked back cautiously. Ellen was still at the same place, and in the same attitude. Heaven knows what thoughts passed through my brain! I longed to see her closer. What danger was there? I was sure she would not know me again. I walked towards her with the careless step of a casual passer-by, and in a few minutes passed before her. When my shadow fell on the path, she looked up, and our eyes met. My heart was beating fast. Her look was cold and indifferent; but suddenly a strange light shot into her eyes, and she made a quick movement, as if to rise. I saw no more, and went on without turning round. Before I could get out of the park her carriage drove past me, and I saw her once more as I had seen her five years before in Central Park, pale, with distended eyes, and her anxious looks fixed upon me.

"Why did I not bow to her? I cannot say; my courage failed me. I saw the light die out of her eyes. I almost fancied that I saw her heave a sigh of relief as she threw herself back carelessly in the carriage; and she disappeared.

"I was then thirty-six, and I am almost ashamed to relate the schoolboy's trick of which I was guilty. I sent her the following lines—

'A devoted friend, whom you obliged in former days, and who met you yesterday in the park without your recognising him, sends you his remembrances.' I posted this letter a few minutes before getting into the train which was to take me to New York; and as I did so, my heart beat as violently as though I had performed an heroic deed. Great adventures, forsooth! And to think that my life presents none more striking, and that trifles such as these are the only food for my memory!

"A twelvemonth later I met Francis Gilmore in Broadway. The world is small—so small that it is really difficult to keep out of the way of people one has once known. The likeness of my former pupil to his sister struck me, and I spoke to him. He looked at me at first with a puzzled expression; but after a few moments of hesitation he recognised me, a bright smile lighted up his pleasant face, and he shook hands warmly.

"'Mr Warren,' he exclaimed, 'how glad I am to see you! Ellen and I have often talked of you, and wondered what could have become of you. Why did we never hear from you?'

"'I did not suppose it would interest you.'

I spoke timidly; and yet I owed nothing to the young fellow, and wanted nothing of him.

"'You wrong us by saying that,' replied Francis; 'do you think me ungrateful? Do you fancy I have forgotten our pleasant walks in former days, and the long conversations we used to have? You alone ever taught me anything, and it is to you I owe the principles that have guided me through life. Many a day I have thought of you, and regretted you sincerely. As regards Ellen, no one has ever filled your place with her; she plays to this day the same pieces of music you taught her, and follows all your directions with a fidelity that would touch you.'

"'How are your father and mother, and how is your sister?' I inquired, feeling more deeply moved than I can express.

"'My poor mother died three years ago. It is Ellen who keeps house now.'

"'Your brother-in-law lives with you, then?'

"'My brother-in-law!' replied Francis, with surprise; 'did you not know that he was on board the Atlantic, which was lost last year in the passage from Liverpool to New York?'

"I could find no words to reply.

"'As to that,' added Francis, with great composure—'between you and me, he was no great loss. My dear brother-in-law was not by any means what my father fancied he was when he gave him my sister as a wife. The whole family has often regretted the marriage. Ellen lived apart from her husband for many years before his death.'

"I nodded so as to express my interest in his communications, but I could not for worlds have uttered a syllable.

"'You will come and see us soon, I hope,' added Francis, without noticing my emotion. 'We are still at the same place; but to make sure, here is my card. Come, Mr Warren—name your own day to come and dine with us. I promise you a hearty welcome.'

"I got off by promising to write the next day, and we parted.

"Fortunately my mind had lost its former liveliness. The pendulum, far from being urged to unruly motion, continued to swing slowly in the narrow space where it had oscillated for so many years. I said to myself that to renew my intimacy with the Gilmores would be to run the almost certain risk of reviving the sorrows and the disappointments of the past. I was then calm and rational. It would be madness in me, I felt, to aspire to the hand of a young, wealthy, and much-admired widow. To venture to see Ellen again was to incur the risk of seeing my reason once more wrecked, and the fatal chimera which had been the source of all my misery start into life again. If we are to believe what poets say, love ennobles man and exalts him into a demigod. It may be so, but it turns him likewise into a fool and a madman. That was my case. At any cost I was to guard against that fatal passion. I argued seriously with myself, and I determined to let the past be, and to reject every opportunity of bringing it to life again.

"A few days before my meeting with Francis, I had received tidings of the death of an old relative, whom I scarcely knew. In my childhood I had, on one or two occasions, spent my holidays at his house. He was gloomy and taciturn, but nevertheless he had always welcomed me kindly. I have a vague remembrance of having been told that he had been in love with my mother once upon a time, and that on hearing of her marriage he had retired into the solitude which he never left till the day of his death. Be that as it may, I had not lost my place in his affections, it seems: he had continued to feel an interest in me; and on his deathbed he had remembered me, and left me the greater part of his not very considerable fortune. I inherited little money; but there was a small, comfortably furnished country-house, and an adjoining farm let on a long lease for £240 per annum. This was wealth for me, and more than enough to satisfy all my wants. Since I had heard of this legacy, I had been doubtful as to my movements. My chance meeting with Francis settled the matter. I resolved at once to leave America, and to return to live in my native country. I knew your address, and wrote to you at once. I trusted that the sight of my old and only friend would console me for the disappointments that life has inflicted on me—and I have not been deceived. At last I have been able to open my heart to a fellow-creature, and relieve myself of the heavy burden which I have borne alone ever since our separation. Now I feel lighter. You are not a severe judge. Doubtless you deplore my weakness, but you do not condemn me. If, as I have already said, I have done no good, neither have I committed any wicked action. I have been a nonentity—an utterly useless being; 'one too many,' like the sad hero of Tourgueneff's sad story. Before leaving, I wrote to Francis informing him that the death of a relative obliged me to return to Europe, and giving him your address, so as not to seem to be running away from him. Then I went on board, and at last reached your home. *Dixi!*"

Warren, who during this long story had taken care to keep his pipe alight, and had, moreover, nearly drained the bottle of port placed before him, now declared himself ready to listen to his friend's confession. But Hermann had been saddened by all he had heard, and was in no humour for talking; he remarked that it was getting late, and proposed to postpone any further conversation till the morrow.

Warren merely answered, "Very well," knocked the ashes out of his pipe, shared out the remainder of the wine between his host and himself, and raising his glass, said, in a somewhat solemn tone, "To our youth, Hermann!" After emptying his glass at one draught, he replaced it on the table, and said complacently,

"It is long since I have drunk with so much pleasure; for this time I have not drunk to forgetfulness, but to memory."

II.

Warren spent another week in Leipzig with his friend. No man was easier to live with: to every suggestion of Hermann's he invariably answered, "Very well"; and if Hermann proposed nothing, he was quite content to remain seated in a comfortable arm-chair by the fireside, holding a book which he scarcely looked at, and watching the long rolls of smoke from his pipe. He disliked new acquaintances; nevertheless the friends to whom Hermann introduced him found in him a quiet, unobtrusive, and well-informed companion. He pleased everybody. There was something strange and yet attractive in his person; there was a "charm" about him, people said. Hermann felt the attraction without being able to define in what it consisted. Their former friendship had been renewed unreservedly. The kind of fascination that Warren exercised over all those who approached him, often led Hermann to think that it was not unlikely that in his youth he had inspired a real love in Ellen Gilmore.

One evening Hermann took his friend to the theatre, where a comic piece was being performed. In his young days Warren had been very partial to plays of that kind, and his joyous peals of laughter on such occasions still rang in the ears of his friend. But the attempt was a complete failure. Warren watched the performance without showing the slightest interest, and never even smiled. During the opening scenes he listened with attention, as though he were assisting at some performance of the legitimate drama; then, as if he could not understand what was going on before his eyes, he turned away with a wearied air and began looking at the audience. When, at the close of the second act, Hermann proposed that they should leave the house, he answered readily—

"Yes, let us go; all this seems very stupid—we will be much better at home. There is a time for all things, and buffoonery suits me no longer."

There was nothing left in Warren of the friend that Hermann had known fifteen years before.

He loved him none the less; on the contrary, to his affection for him had been superadded a feeling of deep compassion. He would have made great sacrifices to secure his friend's happiness, and to see a smile light up the immovable features and the sorrowful dulness of the eye. His friendly anxiety had not been lost upon Warren; and when the latter took his leave, he said with emotion—

"You wish me well, my old friend. I see it and feel it; and, believe me, I am grateful. We must not lose sight of each other again—I will write regularly."

A few days later, Hermann received a letter for his friend. It was an American letter, and the envelope was stamped with the initials "E. H." They were those of Ellen Howard, the heroine of Warren's sad history. He forwarded the letter immediately, and wrote at the same time to his friend—"I hope the enclosed brings you good news from America." But in his reply Warren took no notice of this passage, and made no allusion to Ellen. He only spoke of the new house in which he had just settled himself—"to end," as he said, "his days"; and he pressed Hermann to come and join him.

The two friends at last agreed to pass Christmas and New Year's Day together; but when December came, Warren urged his friend to hasten his arrival.

"I do not feel well," he wrote, "and am often so weary that I stay at home all day. I have made no new acquaintances, and, most likely, will make none. I am alone. Your society would give me great pleasure. Come; your room is ready, and will be, I trust, to your liking. There is a large writing-table and tolerably well-filled book-shelves; you can write there quite at your ease, without fear of disturbance. Come as soon as possible, my dear friend. I am expecting you impatiently."

Hermann happened to be at leisure, and was able to comply with his friend's wish, and to go to him in the first week of December. He found Warren looking worn and depressed. It was in vain he sought to induce him to consult a physician. Warren replied—

"Doctors can do nothing for my complaint. I know where the shoe pinches. A physician would order me probably to seek relaxation and amusement, just as he would advise a poor devil whose blood is impoverished by bad food to strengthen himself with a generous diet and good wine. The poor man could not afford to get the good living, and I do not know what could enliven or divert me. Travel? I like nothing so well as sitting quietly in my arm-chair. New faces? They would not interest me—yours is the only company I prefer to solitude. Books? I am too old to take pleasure in learning new things, and what I have learned has ceased to interest me. It is not always easy to get what might do one good, and we must take things as they are."

Hermann noticed, as before, that his friend ate little, but that, on the other hand, he drank a great deal. The sincere friendship he felt for him emboldened him to make a remark on the subject.

"It is true," said Warren, "I drink too much; but what can I do? Food is distasteful to me, and I must keep up my strength somehow. I am in a wretched state; my health is ruined."

One evening, as the two friends were seated together in Warren's room, while the wind and sleet were beating against the window-panes, the invalid began of his own accord to speak about Ellen.

"We now correspond regularly," he said. "She tells me in her last letter that she hopes soon to see me. Do you know, Hermann, that she is becoming an enigma for me? It is very evident that she does not treat me like other people, and I often wonder and ask myself what I am in her eyes? What does she feel towards me? Love? That is inadmissible. Pity, perhaps? This, then, is the end of my grand dreams—to be an object of pity? I have just answered her letter to say that I am settled here with the fixed intention of ending my useless existence in quiet and idleness. Do you remember a scene in Henry Heine's 'Reisebilder,' when a young student kisses a pretty girl, who lets him have his own way and makes no great resistance, because he has told her—'I will be gone to-morrow at dawn, and I will never see you again'? The certainty of never seeing a person again gives a man the courage to say things that otherwise he would have kept hidden in the most secret depths of his being. I feel that my life is drawing to a close. Do not say no, my dear friend; my presentiments are certain. I have written it to Ellen. I have told her other things besides. What folly! All I have ever done has been folly or chimera. I end my life logically, in strict accordance with my whole Past, by making my first avowal of love on my deathbed. Is not that as useless a thing as can be?"

Hermann would have wished to know some particulars about this letter; but Warren replied, somewhat vaguely, "If I had a copy of my letter, I would show it to you willingly. You know my whole story, and I would not be ashamed to lay before you my last act of folly. I wrote about a fortnight ago, when I felt sure that death was drawing near. I was in a fever, not from fear—Death gains but little by taking my life—but from a singular species of excitement. I do not remember what were the words I used. Who knows? Perhaps this last product of my brain may have been quite a poetical performance. Never mind! I do not repent of what I have done; I am glad that Ellen should know at last that I have loved her silently and hopelessly. If that is not disinterested, what is?" he added with a bitter smile.

Christmas went by sadly. Warren was now so weak that he could scarcely leave his bed for two or three hours each day. Hermann had taken upon himself to send for a doctor, but this latter had scarcely known what to prescribe. Warren was suffering from no special malady; he was dying of exhaustion. Now and then, during a few moments, which became daily more rare and more brief, his vivacity would return; but the shadow of Death was already darkening his mind.

On New Year's eve he got up very late. "We will welcome in the New Year," he said to Hermann. "I hope it may bring you happiness; I know it will bring me rest." A few minutes before midnight he opened the piano, and played with solemnity, and as if it had been a chorale, a song of Schumann's, entitled, "To the Drinking-cup of a departed Friend." Then, on the first stroke of midnight, he filled two glasses with some old Rhenish wine, and raised his own glass slowly. He was very pale, and his eyes were shining with feverish light; he was in a state of strange and fearful excitement. He looked at the glass which he held, and repeated deliberately a verse of the song which he had just been playing, "The vulgar cannot understand what I see at the bottom of this cup." Then, at one draught, he drained the full glass.

While he was thus speaking and drinking, he had taken no notice of Hermann, who was watching him with consternation. Recovering himself at length, he exclaimed, "Another glass, Hermann! To friendship!" He drained this second glass, like the first, to the very last drop; and then, exhausted by the effort he had made, he sank heavily on a chair. Soon after, Hermann led him like a sleepy child, to his bed.

During the days that followed, he was unable to leave his room; and the doctor thought it right to warn Hermann that all the symptoms seemed to point to a fatal issue.

On the 8th of January a servant from the hotel in the little neighbouring town brought a letter, which, he said, required an immediate answer. The sick man was then lying almost unconscious. Herman broke the seal without hesitation, and read as follows:—

"My dear Friend,—A visit to Europe which my father had long planned, has at last been undertaken. I did not mention it to you, in order to have the pleasure of surprising you.

On reaching this place, I learn that the illness of which you spoke in your last letter has not yet left you. Under these circumstances, I will not venture to present myself without warning you of my arrival, and making sure that you are able to receive me. I am here with my brother, who, like myself, would not come so near to you without seeing you. My father has gone on to Paris, where Francis and I will join him in a few days. ELLEN."

Hermann, after one instant's thought, took up his hat and dismissed the messenger, saying he would give the answer himself. At the hotel he sent in his card, with the words, "From Mr Warren," and was immediately ushered into Ellen's presence.

She was alone. Hermann examined her rapidly. He saw an extremely beautiful woman, whose frank and fearless eyes were fixed on him with a questioning look.

Hermann had not frequented the society of women much, and was usually rather embarrassed in their presence. But on this occasion he thought only of his friend, and found no difficulty in explaining the motive of his visit.

He told her his friend was ill—very ill—dying —and that he had opened the letter addressed to Warren. Ellen did not answer for some time; she seemed not to have understood what she had heard. After a while her eyes filled with tears, and she asked whether she could see Mr Warren. On Hermann answering in the affirmative, she further inquired whether her brother might accompany her.

"Two visitors might fatigue the invalid too much," said Hermann; "your brother may come later."

"Are you not afraid that my visit may tire him?"

"I do not think so; it will make him very happy."

Ellen only took a few minutes to put on her hat and cloak, and they started. The short journey was accomplished in silence. When they reached the house, Hermann went in first to see how the dying man was. He was lying in his bed in the delirium of fever, muttering incoherent sentences. Nevertheless he recognised Hermann, and asked for something to drink. After having allayed his thirst, he closed his eyes, as if to sleep.

"I have brought you a friend," said Hermann; "will you see him?"

"Hermann? He is always welcome."

"No; it is a friend from America."

"From America? . . . I lived there many years. . . . How desolate and monotonous were the shores I visited! . . ."

"Will you see your friend?"

"I am carried away by the current of the river. In the distance I see dark and shadowy forms; there are hills full of shade and coolness, . . . but I will never rest there."

Hermann retired noiselessly, and returned almost immediately with Ellen.

Warren, who had taken no notice of him, continued to follow the course of his wandering thoughts.

"The river is drawing near to the sea. Already I can hear the roar of the waves. . . . The banks are beginning to be clothed with verdure. . . . The hills are drawing nearer. . . . It is dark now. Here are the big trees beneath which I have dreamed so often. A radiant apparition shines through their foliage. . . . It comes towards me. . . . Ellen!"

She was standing beside the bed. The dying

man saw her, and without showing the least surprise, said with a smile, "Thank God! you have come in time. I knew you were coming."

He murmured a few unintelligible words, and then remained silent for a long while. His eyes were wide open. Suddenly he cried, "Hermann!"

Hermann came and stood beside Ellen.

"The pendulum. . . . You know what I mean?" A frank childish smile—the smile of his student days—lighted up his pallid face. He raised his right hand, and tracing in the air with his forefinger a wide semicircle, to imitate the oscillation of a pendulum, he said, "Then." He then figured in the same manner a more limited and slower movement, and after repeating it several times, said, "Now." Lastly, he pointed straight before him with a motionless and almost menacing finger, and said, with a weak voice, "Soon."

He spoke no more, and closed his eyes. The breathing was becoming very difficult.

Ellen bent over him, and called him softly, "Henry, Henry!" He opened his eyes. She brought her mouth close to his ear, and said, with a sob, "I have always loved you."

"I knew it from the first," he said, quietly and with confidence.

A gentle expression stole over his countenance, and life seemed to return. Once more he had the confident look of youth. A sad and beautiful smile played on his lips; he took the hand of Ellen in his, and kissed it gently.

"How do you feel now?" inquired Hermann.

The old answer, "Very well."

His hands were plucking at the bed-clothes, as if he strove to cover his face with them. Then his arms stiffened and the fingers remained motionless.

"Very well," he repeated.

He appeared to fall into deep thought. There was a long pause. At last he turned a dying look, fraught with tender pity and sadness, towards Ellen, and in a low voice, which was scarcely audible, he said these two words, with a slight emphasis on the first — "*Perfectly* well."

GORDON BALDWIN.

I.

George Forbes had spared neither time nor money in furnishing his bachelor apartments as handsomely as possible. He possessed some experience, having seen many countries and many people; he was so rich, that even in New York, from whence he came, men spoke of his "large fortune"; moreover, he had nothing to do but what gave him pleasure. Under these circumstances it is not difficult for a man—particularly if he lives in Paris—to acquire among his friends the reputation of being a man of taste. Forbes had secured the assistance of a talented young artist; he had employed the best Parisian workmen for several months; and, lastly, he had given to his upholsterer an almost unlimited credit. By this somewhat expensive but extremely simple and convenient method, he had succeeded in furnishing his house near the Champs Elysées both elegantly and comfortably.

The paintings by Corot, Rousseau, Diaz, Rosa Bonheur, and others, which adorned his drawing-room, study, and dining-room, ranked among the acknowledged masterpieces of those artists; the large Rubens in his bedroom was undoubtedly genuine; the chandeliers and clocks were models of French art; and nowhere could be found more comfortable easy-chairs and more luxurious sofas than in the cosy rooms of the "Hôtel Forbes" in the Rue Dumont d'Urville.

During one whole week after Forbes had taken possession of his house, he had wandered every morning with renewed delight through the rooms of his new home, with a feeling of pride, as though all the beautiful objects which gave him so much pleasure had been the work of his own hands. He had accepted, with a self-satisfied smile, the compliments which all his visitors paid him on his exquisite taste; but very soon he became as accustomed to his pictures, his china, and his bronzes, as to his comfortable chairs and his good cook; and at the time we make his acquaintance—about four years after he had settled in Paris—all the splendid works of art by which he was surrounded in his own house could no longer attract his attention even for an instant.

George Forbes was now thirty-three, and the life he led was, in spite of much apparent variety, a monotonous one. Seven months of the year he spent in Paris, but, during the summer, he went from one fashionable watering-place to another. He might be seen at Trouville, at Biarritz, or in the Pyrenees; sometimes also he went to Baden-Baden or to Homburg, where, at that time, the gaming-tables were still to be found. Once he had returned to the United States, and had shown his cold, aristocratic, *blasé* face in Newport and Saratoga. In Paris, where he lived during the winter and the spring, remaining till the end of May, he took a ride regularly every morning in the Bois de Boulogne, breakfasted at home, yawned for an hour over the newspapers, his letters, or a novel, and sometimes fell asleep over them; then he paid a few visits, or showed his beautiful horses in the Avenue de l'Impératrice, and at seven o'clock made his appearance at the

Café Anglais or at Bignon's to dine. After that he went to a theatre or to some reception in the American colony. There, he was an object of great interest to the mothers of grown-up daughters, as also to young widows. He frequently met, in this society, with men who, thinking that the young millionaire might prove a serviceable friend, spared no trouble to make themselves agreeable to him. But Forbes was not grateful for the kindness shown to him on all sides, and not one of his numerous acquaintance could boast of being on intimate or confidential terms with him. In fact, he was suspicious. Many times, in former days, he had been deceived—a misfortune which may happen even to poor people in this world; but he had never forgotten nor forgiven it, and he always feared that every one who approached him in a friendly manner wanted his money. Belief in unselfish kindness had never been very strong with him, and such little trustfulness as he had once possessed he had lost long ago. Friendliness, as soon as it went beyond commonplace politeness, seemed to him interested flattery, and made him doubly reserved and cautious. In consequence, young and honourable men, who, under ordinary circumstances, might have been his friends, felt themselves repelled, and gradually withdrew from him; and so it came to pass that, finally, his acquaintance was mainly among men who richly deserved his suspicious contempt for them.

Later in the evening the lonely man invariably went to his club. He played high, and often won considerable sums. He was a cool and cautious player. When the luck was on his side, he was ever ready to stake all his winnings; and he would put, with equal composure, a few louis or a bundle of bank-notes on the table. But when Fortune was not favourable, he would only lose the money he had with him—a few thousand francs at the outside; then he would rise, with a yawn—he had a habit of yawning frequently—go into the reading-room, look over the evening papers, and, at a late hour, drive home. He was a dangerous, careful, unpopular player. You might lose a fortune to him, but you could never win from him more than he happened to have in his pocket. He had never been known to borrow money to go on playing.

One evening in the month of December 186–,

Forbes came to his club, as usual, at about eleven o'clock, and, after exchanging a few words with his friends, took his seat at the green table. He had won largely the night before; and a young man, who had been one of the heaviest losers—Henry Westmore—asked him in a friendly manner to take the bank himself. Forbes did not answer at once; but when Westmore repeated his request, he replied, carelessly, in an undertone, that it was not his habit to consider a new game as the continuation of a former one; he was only beginning to play, and he could not yet say whether it would suit him on this occasion to take the bank or to play against it.

"These are very convenient principles," said Westmore, with a sneer.

Forbes looked at him long and steadfastly; then, after a painful pause, he said: "I can only express my regret if you are vexed because you lost yesterday. I cannot think for a moment that you wish to pick a quarrel with me. You have no right to dictate to me how I am to play, nor do I imagine that you claim that right. But if you believe that I owe you your revenge, pray name the sum for which you wish to play against me, and it will give me great pleasure to place myself at your disposal." Every one present felt for poor Westmore, who, it was known, had borrowed with great difficulty the money to pay his debt that evening, and who, in his heart, was cursing his fortunate and powerful adversary. But Forbes knew he had the right on his side, while Westmore felt that he stood alone, and that the wisest thing he could do was to let the matter drop. He muttered, with a touch of ill-humour, but politely, nevertheless, "You take the thing too seriously; I did not mean it so." Forbes counted his money, played even more cautiously than usual, lost a trifling sum, and went home at about two o'clock. After he had left the club, Westmore began again to complain of him, and this time everybody sided with him.

"One thing comforts me," he said, in conclusion, "and that is, that Forbes never really enjoys his game. I get vexed sometimes when I lose; but then I am all the better pleased when I happen to win. Forbes is always bored; and it serves the odious fellow right."

Forbes, on his way home, knew perfectly well that at that very moment they were abusing him at the club, and that not one of the numerous acquaintances who were in the habit of meeting him with a friendly smile would think of taking his part in his absence.

The next morning, while riding in the Bois de Boulogne, he made some plans for travelling. "I will go for a few weeks to Nice, Florence, and Rome," he said to himself; "perhaps I may amuse myself there a little more than I do here. At any rate, I shall see some new faces, and not always that fellow Westmore and the rest of them. The whole set is insufferable."

When, an hour later, he returned home, his servant handed him two letters, which had just arrived. He put them, without even looking at them, on the table; and it was only after he had dressed, and found that there was still a quarter of an hour left before breakfast-time, that he threw himself into an easy-chair before the fire, and read them. The first was as follows:—

"94 AVENUE FRIEDLAND,
Wednesday.

"DEAR MR FORBES,—It will give us much pleasure if you will dine with us on Friday next, at seven o'clock.—Yours very sincerely,

"MARIE LELAND,
née De Montemars."

"That woman never forgets to remind one that she comes of a noble family, and that she only married old Leland for his money. *Née* Montemars! What do I care? Anyhow, Jane Leland is a handsome clever girl, and I have nothing better to do on Friday; I'll accept the invitation."

The note was carefully replaced in its envelope, and laid aside. The second letter was a longer one. As soon as Forbes had looked at the address and recognised the writing, he opened it with an angry frown, and then read it with great attention:—

"HAKODATE, *Sept.* 2, 186—.

"DEAR GEORGE,—You must do me the justice to admit that I have not troubled you for a long time with news of myself. Nor would I have written now, could I have avoided it. I know my letters give you no pleasure, and, as a natural consequence, I do not care much to write to you. I have, however, nothing unpleasant to say, and I beg you not to throw this letter aside without reading it.

"When I arrived at Hakodate, four years ago, I made the acquaintance of a young Englishman, named Gordon Baldwin. Although I had no claim upon him, he received me into his house with the greatest kindness, and I was his guest during several months. I had been long unaccustomed to kind treatment. Baldwin's goodness made a deep impression upon me, and I felt very grateful towards him. I conceived a great affection for him; and he, seeing this, I suppose, also took a liking for me. I had so long been tossed about like a ship without a rudder, finding neither peace nor safety, that I scarcely dared to hope Fortune had led me at last into a haven of rest. My intention being to leave Hakodate in a few months, I was not as reserved in my conversations with Baldwin as I ought, perhaps, to have been. I meant no harm by being communicative, and I did not think myself bound to spoil the pleasure of our friendly intercourse by a reticence which might have seemed suspicious. I cannot boast of possessing that calm reserve which distinguishes you.

"So I told Baldwin, during the long walks we took together, something of my history. I did not disclose my real name, for I would not break the promise I had given you. I called myself Graham. I told him that I had wealthy relatives, from whom I was for ever separated, through some misfortune which I could not explain. I also spoke of you. You will think this strange; you would certainly never dream of speaking of me. But then, it must be said, we are very different. I said nothing but what was good about you—praising your prudence, your coolness, and your energy. I spoke of the extraordinary success which has attended you through life—a success which you owe mainly to your perspicacity and your determination. I did not allude to the ties which unite us, and I mentioned you merely as a friend of my youth.

"As you see, I did not commit any great indiscretion. It can do you no harm that Baldwin—who is as simple and as trusting as a child—should think that, in times gone by, you once did a good turn to a poor devil called Graham.

"Hakodate lies out of the beaten track. Besides the Japanese, there are only a few English, American, and German merchants living here, and foreign travellers seldom find their way to this place. For many years I saw nothing that could remind me of the past, and I felt as though I were gradually awaking to a new life. I was successful in the first small speculations I attempted. Baldwin procured me credit in Yokohama, Hong-Kong, and Shanghai, and so gave me the means of trying my unhoped-for good luck on a greater scale. All went well, and, at this present time, I possess a moderate, well-earned fortune, and am a respected member of the foreign community of Hakodate. All this I owe to Gordon Baldwin. But for him, I must have gone to ruin; for my means and my courage were equally exhausted when I landed at Yesso.

"A few weeks ago Baldwin told me that, having spent six years in China and Japan, he now thought of taking a trip to Europe. While discussing this plan, he mentioned your name, which he unfortunately remembered, although it had not passed my lips for some time. I had told him formerly that you lived in Paris; and he asked me, without having a notion that it might be unpleasant to me, to give him a letter of introduction to you. I could not well refuse without laying myself open to suspicion. I might, indeed, have invented some excuse, but I did not like to run the risk of your being brought together by chance. I have therefore given him a letter for you. Pray consider all the circumstances of the case, and excuse the liberty I have taken. Remember how much I owe to Baldwin, and receive him kindly. I have given him to understand that it might be painful to you to speak of my past life; and I feel perfectly sure that he will avoid any allusion which might embarrass you.

"You will find my friend the best and noblest of men. He is a few years younger than you are, but his independent life in foreign lands has made him prematurely old. He comes of a good family, but all his near relations are dead, and he stands pretty nearly alone in the world. He is good-looking, well-informed, and well-bred. To complete my sketch, I may add that he has a handsome fortune, and that his business in Hakodate—the management of which he has intrusted to me during his absence—has, for for some years past, brought him in from 20,000 to 25,000 dollars annually.

"And now, my dear George, I must say good-bye.' I do not expect an answer to this letter, and it is not likely that I will soon have occasion to write to you again.—With unchanged affection, yours, THOMAS."

As Forbes finished reading this letter, his servant entered the room to say breakfast was ready. He slowly folded up the letter, put it into the side-pocket of his coat, and with a thoughtful air went into the dining-room.

II.

In one of the most fashionable *cafés* of the Boulevard des Italiens, before a table which was laid for two persons, sat a young man of between twenty-five and twenty-eight years of age. His appearance had already attracted the attention of the waiters, the *dame du comptoir*, and several of the guests; for although one could see at a glance that the stranger was a gentleman, yet in this room, so luxuriously furnished, and among the elegantly dressed ladies and gentlemen who were seated at the tables around him, he did not seem to be quite in his right place. He wore a faded travelling suit, which, like himself, had evidently seen a good deal of rough weather. He had straight light hair, and clear grey eyes, one glance from which caused the inquisitive looks of those who wished to examine him to fall quickly and involuntarily.

His nose and mouth were large but well-shaped; his forehead was high, and, as far as the hat had protected it, remarkably fair. The remainder of the thin, powerful face was much sunburnt, and formed a strange contrast with the ivory-white forehead, the fair hair, and the greyish-blue eyes. A long tawny moustache fell low over the finely cut mouth. The fearless, honest look, the small round head, the broad shoulders, the powerful chest, the large, well-shaped, sinewy hands, and the long legs, presented altogether an appearance which seemed to belong to times long gone by. An iron helmet and a heavy sword would have better suited the figure of the stranger than the black silk hat and the slender cane which the waiter had taken from him on his entering the room.

The young man had looked at his watch several times, and as soon as the clock struck seven he beckoned to the waiter.

"Give me a good dinner," he said.

"Does not monsieur wish to order anything in particular?"

"No, I leave that to you; bring me a good dinner."

"By your order, I laid covers for two."

"Yes, but it seems my friend is not coming. He may, perhaps, be late, and you can serve him when he comes."

The stranger spoke French fluently, but with an unmistakable English accent. The experienced waiter, who during ten years had seen great and noble personages from all parts of the world, at once classed the new guest under this head: "A crazy lord who has been shooting tigers in India, and wants now to beat the Parisian preserves."

The supposed lord had finished his oysters, soup, and patties, and was about to do justice to a more substantial dish which had been set before him, when the door opened, and George Forbes, dressed with faultless elegance, entered the room. He bowed to the lady at the *comptoir*, and went up to the sunburnt stranger, who merely looked up, and, without allowing himself to be disturbed in his dinner, said—

"You are late. But, as you see, I did not let that interfere with me."

"One must be punctual with you, it seems," replied Forbes, with a smile.

"No, I don't care about that, so long as I am not expected to wait. Take a seat. I have already ascertained that my appetite is better than yours, and if you hurry a little, we may reach dessert together."

Forbes did as he was told, and took up the bill of fare, which he appeared to study carefully.

How was it that Baldwin, whom he had known only five days, took liberties with him which none of his Parisian acquaintances would have attempted? Every one of them would have waited for him at least a quarter of an hour, or, if they had not done so, would, at any rate, have offered some excuse. Baldwin had not granted him one minute's grace, and had never thought of apologising. On the other hand, Forbes, who, as a rule, paid no attention to the feelings of others, and who was spoiled by the attentive courtesy he met with on all sides, not only thought Baldwin's conduct perfectly natural, but even said, in an undertone, "I beg your pardon"; while the other nodded good-humouredly, as much as to say, "Never mind; I forgive you."

Only six days before, Forbes had received the following despatch from Havre: "Graham will have informed you of my arrival. I will call on you to-morrow morning.—Gordon Baldwin."

And, on the following day, Mr Gordon Baldwin, in an old grey travelling suit and a soft felt hat, but with faultless linen, had made his appearance.

He had shaken Forbes's hand heartily, like an old friend, and had begun talking at once in such a quiet, sensible, comfortable way, that Forbes, whose manner at first had been somewhat cold and constrained, had gradually assumed a more friendly attitude, and had become almost sociable.

An hour of pleasant conversation had passed quickly. Baldwin sat in an easy-chair, and talked about Japan, and Graham, and about his business and plans. Now and then he indulged in some humorous but always good-tempered remark, and then his bright eyes laughed so merrily that Forbes listened with a real, and, to him, perfectly novel, sense of pleasure. When breakfast was announced, he invited the stranger to share it with him; and after the meal was over, he asked him to stop at his house during the few days he intended to spend in Paris. Baldwin accepted the invitation with the same easy grace with which he had taken the cigar his host had offered ten minutes before, and which he was then smoking with visible enjoyment.

Since then, Forbes and Baldwin had been together from morning to night, almost without interruption, and an intimacy of a peculiar sort had sprung up between these two men who were so totally unlike. Baldwin saw nothing strange in this, and never gave the matter a second thought, but Forbes was astonished. He could not understand why it was that, when he was with Baldwin, he felt himself to be a different and a better man than his usual self. He could talk and joke unreservedly with the "Wild Man of Yesso," as he called him; and more than once he had caught himself speaking to his new friend quite confidentially.

Baldwin wanted absolutely nothing of Forbes. There lay the secret of the pleasant impression he had made on the suspicious rich man. He desired neither his horses, nor his opera-box, nor his money. He ignored thoroughly and sincerely that his host was the "rich Mr Forbes." He saw nothing in his new acquaintance but a pleasant companion. Forbes was conscious of this. It was a new and refreshing feeling for him to associate with a man who wanted no favours of him—with a man, indeed, on whom he could confer no favours, even if he tried.

"Well, what have you ordered?" inquired Forbes, after he had taken his seat opposite to Baldwin.

"A good dinner."

"I hope you will get it. What is it to be?"

"I do not know yet; but I have an excellent appetite, and I am ready for any agreeable surprise."

"Did you leave it to the waiter's choice?"

"Entirely."

Forbes smiled.

"Can you make out this nonsense?" continued Baldwin, taking up the bill of fare: "*Potage Parmentier, Filet de sole Joinville*—why not Nemours or Montpensier?—*Epigrammes d'agneau, Chaufroid de Volaille*, &c., &c. I really understand the language of the Ainos of Yesso a great deal better than this culinary jargon."

Forbes called the waiter; and in a peremptory tone, but with many detailed instructions, ordered a choice dinner. Baldwin, evidently amused, listened attentively.

"You know everything," he said, with a smile. "You must be my teacher here."

"With pleasure. By the by, have you been to your tailor?"

"Of course."

"When are you to have your things?"

"To-morrow night."

"It is high time."

"Is it really?" said Baldwin, quite unmoved. Then he examined attentively the sleeves of his coat, and added thoughtfully, "It is only a couple of months since this suit cost me a small fortune in San Francisco. True, it has seen a deal of rough weather since then—on the Prairies and on the Atlantic; but it seems to me to be very good still. However, after to-morrow I will appear before you in festive garments only."

At about half-past seven an elderly, gentleman-like man, with an elegantly dressed and handsome young lady, entered the restaurant, and took their seats at a table near our two friends. Forbes, who was seated with his back to the new-comers, did not at first notice them; but the young lady quickly attracted the unobtrusively approving attention of Baldwin.

This circumstance had not been unremarked by her, and the eyes of the young Parisian and the traveller met more than once.

After a while Forbes became aware that something was going on behind his back, and asked carelessly—

"What are you looking at?"

"At a pretty face."

Forbes turned round slowly; then, colouring slightly, he rose, bowed, and went up to the table at which the old gentleman and his young companion were seated. They received him in the most friendly manner.

"I suppose Mrs Leland has not returned to Paris," said Forbes.

"No, we expect her to-morrow," replied the old gentleman; "and you see that we are taking undue advantage of our liberty. For the last four days, we have not dined once at home. Jane wants me to show her the Parisian restaurants; and I, like a well-trained father, make it a point to obey her."

"Is that gentleman your friend of whom you spoke yesterday?" asked the young lady in a whisper.

"Yes," replied Forbes in the same tone; and

smiling with some embarrassment, he added, "You see I have not exaggerated; he comes straight from the wilderness; but in a few days he will have a more civilised appearance, and I will then take the liberty of introducing him to you."

"Your friend will always be welcome," said the old gentleman.

Forbes went back to his place opposite Baldwin, and in that affectedly unconcerned manner which we generally assume when speaking of a person who we know is watching us, he told him that the young lady was Miss Jane Leland, the daughter of Mr Leland, a rich banker of New York.

"Rich or poor," said Baldwin, "she is exceedingly pretty, and pleases me very much."

"You shall make her acquaintance," continued Forbes. "I have already spoken of you, and will introduce you whenever you like."

Jane Leland knew very well that the two young men were speaking of her; but she was accustomed to attract attention, and she managed to look perfectly cool and unconscious. A few minutes later, Baldwin and Forbes rose to leave the restaurant. Forbes stepped up once more to Mr Leland's table to say good-bye, while Baldwin passed on, with one of those awkward half-bows which we sometimes make to people whom we know without having been introduced to them.

III.

A few days after Baldwin had seen Miss Leland for the first time, he was formally presented to the young lady and her parents, and in a very short time he became a frequent and welcome visitor at the house of the American family. In the beginning of March he had gone to London on business; but at the end of a week, and much sooner than he was expected, he had returned: and now he had been in Paris two months, without even alluding to any intention of going away soon.

Forbes was more than satisfied with this state of things—he was truly delighted. His whole mode of life had been most agreeably changed by the presence of that cheerful unassuming guest in his house. Already he began to look forward with uneasiness to the time when this pleasant intercourse must come to an end.

Baldwin had said once, before his journey to England, that towards the end of the year he would return to Hakodate.

"Why do you not remain in Europe?" said Forbes.

"Because my business is in Japan, and my money is invested there."

"Cannot you liquidate your business?" asked Forbes again. "You surely do not intend to spend your whole life among those half-civilised Japanese and those wild Ainos."

"Certainly not; but I must bear it a little longer, till I have earned enough to live in Europe without the help of the income which my Japanese business gives me at present."

"And how long will that take?"

"About four or five years, with good luck?"

"Five years if you are lucky! That is a long time. And now, supposing you have no such luck as you expect, what then?"

"I never have given that a thought. I let the morrow take care of itself."

"And when do you think of going back?"

"There is no hurry about that—probably about the end of the year. If I am in Hakodate by next spring, it will be time enough."

The month of May had come, and Baldwin had not spoken again of going away—nor did he seem to think about it. And, indeed, so it was; the thought of leaving Paris never came to him. The beautiful eyes of Jane Leland had cast a spell upon him. He was madly, hopelessly in love with her. He had been, in the fullest sense of the word, bewitched by the brown-eyed, golden-haired, graceful American girl. All his thoughts, wishes, and hopes were centred in her. This unspoken passion made him as happy, as miserable, as light-hearted, as melancholy, as generous, as cowardly, and as silly as it does most people in the same enviable condition. In one respect only, Baldwin differed from most lovers: he did not talk about his love. He had not made a confidant of Forbes, who, nevertheless, had long been aware of his friend's state of mind. Jane, too—to say nothing of Mr and Mrs Leland—had, without much difficulty, guessed their new friend's secret.

Mrs Leland, *née* De Montemars, was by no means pleased at this discovery, but neither was she made uneasy by it. She reposed the most complete and well-justified confidence in her prudent Jane. Mr Baldwin was not a son-in-law according to her coldly calculating heart. She had long ago selected the wealthy George Forbes as a suitable husband for her daughter.

Old Mr Leland felt very kindly towards the young Englishman, but he was not allowed to have any voice in the matter. His wife, indeed, had very quickly put a stop to his remarks when, one evening, he had somewhat timidly alluded to the amiable qualities of "the young man from Japan."

Jane herself was not particularly proud of her last conquest. She was accustomed to triumph. She certainly did not dislike Baldwin, but the thought of marrying him had never once occurred to her.

She was now three-and-twenty, and during the last four years she had been courted in the most various ways. She numbered, in her collection, sentimental, impassioned, melancholy, witty, and even sensible admirers. Each in turn had amused her for a while, and then had gradually become uninteresting, if not tiresome.

Three of them had made her offers of marriage, which she had declined unconditionally, without a moment's hesitation. She really did not quite know herself what were the qualities her future husband ought to possess in order to please her. A great name, a brilliant position, a large fortune, might have, if not conquered her, at least made her hesitate. None of her suitors had possessed these qualifications. Nor had Baldwin an illustrious name or great riches to command particular favour. The natural simplicity of his manners amused her—that was his sole merit in her eyes.

The only man of her acquaintance who occupied her thoughts was Forbes, and he did not owe this distinction to his wealth. She certainly thought of it sometimes, and pictured to herself how pleasant it would be to surpass all her friends and acquaintances in splendour and extravagance; but what attracted her most was the aristocratic bearing and the indifference of the young millionaire.

Now and then, in America, one meets with descendants of German or English immigrants in whom every trace of their origin has been obliterated, after a few generations, by the influences of climate and of a new mode of life. The ancestral type of features has entirely disappeared. They have small refined features, a peculiarly delicate complexion, large, intelligent, bright eyes, small well-shaped hands and feet, and long slender limbs. Their bearing is bold and dignified; their movements are graceful and self-assured. They look more like the heirs of ancient and noble names than the descendants of square-shouldered thick-set farmers and workmen driven by want and misery from their old homes. One even often learns with surprise that they themselves have, in their youth, carried on some trade or business which in Europe is only followed by the lower and poorer classes.

Forbes was one of these, so to speak, unjustifiably aristocratic-looking men. His grandfather had been a poor farmer; his father had dug a fortune out of the Californian mines; yet the slenderly built George Forbes moved about with remarkable dignity, and thoroughly gentleman-like self-possession. His great wealth threw a sort of artificial halo around him. He rode and drove the best horses; he won and lost large sums at play with perfect equanimity; he never asked a service, nor even the smallest favour, of anybody; he was no respecter of persons or of things; he was polite, and at the same time regardless of others; lastly, he knew how to dress plainly but in perfect good taste.

Jane saw all this, and admired it. In her heart she even overrated the value of the manifold recommendations of her wealthy countryman, while at the same time she was conscious that her beautiful eyes had no great power over him, and that his serenity was not disturbed for one moment by her presence. She felt this more bitterly than any one could imagine—far more bitterly than she liked to own to herself.

"If only he were not so rich," she often thought, "I would show him at least that he pleases me more than the silly, tiresome men who surround me; but I scarcely dare to be friendly with him, lest he should fancy that I am thinking of his money, like those girls that flirt with him and those men that flatter him. If he could only lose a good part of his fortune, then he would find out who are his true friends." She treated Forbes with far greater reserve than any of her other acquaintances; and for Baldwin especially, she had always a pleasant smile and a friendly greeting. Forbes noticed this, and laughed at it inwardly. "She wants to make me jealous of poor Baldwin," he said to himself. The son of the gold-digger did not cherish many illusions; he had no very exalted opinion of mankind in general, or of Jane Leland in particular. He was not so easy to decoy and tame as the "Wild Man of Yesso."

On one occasion, when Forbes came home from his club at one o'clock in the morning, having left Baldwin two hours before in Mrs Leland's drawing-room, he noticed that there was a light still burning in his friend's room. He opened the door, and found Baldwin walking up and down, apparently in deep thought.

"Why, what keeps you up so late?"

"Sit down," said Baldwin; "I want to speak to you."

"My advice is: Don't."

"What?"

"Don't marry!"

Baldwin looked up in surprise.

"Who told you that I wished to marry?" he asked.

"Why, you have told me so yourself," replied Forbes, laughing. "Do you really think it is a secret, for any one who knows you, that you are in love with Miss Leland?"

Baldwin was silent for some time. At last he said, "You spare me the trouble of a preface and a confession, and I am thankful for that.

I will tell you at once what has happened to-night: Soon after you left us, I unexpectedly found an opportunity of speaking to Miss Leland alone. Mr Leland was at the whist-table, his wife was talking to some ladies, and Jane was left alone in the little room where tea had been served. There I joined her. I do not know how it happened that I came to speak of my love; but before I knew it myself, I had told her all I had kept hidden so long in my heart. At the very moment when I was expecting her answer, there was a moving of chairs in the drawing-room; the visitors were preparing to go. Jane rose quickly and went into the next room. The guests took leave, and a few minutes later I found myself alone with Mr and Mrs Leland. Jane had disappeared. My heart was so full of what I had said to her, that I was determined to come to an explanation. I related in a few words what had taken place between Jane and myself, and I begged them to grant me the hand of their daughter. Old Mr Leland looked embarrassed, and said, 'You must settle that with my wife.' He then went to the whist-table and busied himself in putting up the counters and the cards. Mrs Leland, who had remained near the fireplace, and did not ask me to sit down, made a long speech in a low voice to this effect: She had heard from you and from myself that I intended returning to Japan, and she could not give her consent to a marriage which would separate her from her only child. I found nothing to say in reply; the whole affair had assumed suddenly such a totally prosaic aspect. I became embarrassed, and I scarcely remember what I answered. While I was speaking to her, she looked at me in a cold, unsympathetic way; old Leland was still busy with his cards and counters; but I could not, and would not, consider myself beaten. Jane had not accepted my offer, but neither had she refused it. I might still hope for the best. So, at last, I said to Mrs Leland that I could not accept her answer as final; that I entreated her to speak to her daughter; and that I would take the liberty of calling to-morrow afternoon for a reply. I cannot tell you how painful was the hard, business-like tone in which this conversation was carried on. Mrs Leland said, 'I will speak to my daughter. Your visits will always be welcome; but I will never consent to separate from my only child, in order to let her go to a part of the world where she would, in fact, be lost to me.'

"There followed a long pause, during which her eyes remained fixed on me with that same unfriendly expression. I did not fully realise my position. I felt as if I were in a dream. Everything seemed so strange, so entirely unexpected. I had gone to the Lelands that evening, as I had done for weeks past, in the hopes of seeing Jane, but without any positive intention of declaring my love. And now I had spoken, and had not even obtained an answer from Jane! Now I was called upon, in this formal, business-like manner—as if it were a mere everyday question — to resign all the happiness I had hoped for! I felt that I could not collect my thoughts. I had just enough self-possession and judgment left to see that one inconsiderate word might hopelessly ruin all my chances. I took my hat and said once more, 'Speak to your daughter, and allow me to call for your decision to-morrow.' A few seconds later, I found myself in the street, and for the last hour I have been here. You see I am quite cool, and yet I do not know what to do. Help me, Forbes! What ought I to do? If Mrs Leland repeats to-morrow what she has said to-night, what then? Help me, I say!"

Baldwin spoke calmly, but his eyes shone with a feverish light; his look was unsteady and his voice sounded hoarse.

Forbes walked leisurely up to the fireplace, looked at the clock, admired himself in the glass, and smoothed his beautiful curly hair. Baldwin never took his eyes off him.

"Do you think," said Forbes at last, very quietly, "that you have Miss Leland on your side?"

"How can I know?" replied Baldwin, impatiently; "have I not told you that she left me without giving me any answer?"

"Well, my dear fellow, then I really do not know what to advise." He relighted his cigar, which had gone out, and then added slowly, "Wait till to-morrow; let us see what Mamma Leland has to say to you."

"But if she simply repeats what she said this evening?"

"Well, if I were you, I would wait, anyhow."

"Have you nothing else to say to me?"

"I really have not."

"Then I am no wiser than I was."

Forbes made no reply. Baldwin, who was seated, remained staring into vacancy, while he whistled softly to himself. At last he said—

"Very well; I will wait till to-morrow." Then he passed his hand across his forehead and eyes, and said, "I am tired to death."

Forbes wished him good-night and left the the room. A quarter of an hour afterwards he was lying in bed reading the evening papers, as was his habit before going to sleep. After a very little while he dropped the paper on the floor, extinguished the light, and was soon sound asleep.

The next morning, Baldwin, who had passed a sleepless night, was sitting in his room, pale and down-hearted, when the following letter from Mr Leland was brought to him :—

"AVENUE FRIEDLAND,
Monday morning.

"MY DEAR MR BALDWIN,—After you left us last night I had a long conversation with my wife and my daughter, and it is my duty to inform you of the decision we have come to. I regret sincerely that I cannot give you better news. Jane is our only child, and you will readily understand that we do not wish to separate from her. She is very grateful for the offer you have made her, and is much flattered by it, but she will not oppose the express wish of her parents. Under these circumstances it would be painful for yourself, and for us, were you to repeat your offer to-day, as was your intention last night. Our decision is irrevocable. I wish you every happiness, with all my heart. I hope that in after-years we may meet again, and renew, under different circumstances, an acquaintance which has been very agreeable to me. My wife sends her best regards; and I remain, my dear Mr Baldwin, yours very truly,

"FREDERICK LELAND."

Baldwin, after reading this letter, sat for a long while motionless, and apparently petrified. At twelve the servant came to announce breakfast, and to say that Mr Forbes was waiting for him in the dining-room. Baldwin replied that he would come immediately; but he forgot what he had said, and a quarter of an hour later, Forbes himself came to find out what kept him in his room. Baldwin, without saying a word, handed him the letter, on which Forbes bestowed merely a passing glance.

"We will talk about this after breakfast," he said; "come down, it is half-past twelve."

Baldwin followed his host as in a dream, and for half an hour he sat opposite to him at the breakfast-table without speaking. Forbes had taken a long ride in the morning, and was blessed with an excellent appetite. When he had satisfied his hunger, however, he was ready to listen to the love-affairs of his best friend.

"Give me that letter again," he said, when he was seated with Baldwin in the smoking-room; "I want to read it over carefully before I give you my opinion."

He lighted a cigar very leisurely, threw himself into an easy-chair, putting his legs up on another chair, and when he had made himself thoroughly comfortable, and had even examined for a moment, with evident satisfaction, his small, well-made boots, he began to read.

"That letter has been dictated by Mamma Leland," he said, when he had reached the signature. "The old gentleman would never have written it—I know his style; and she has taken pains, too, to make it look awkward and natural.

Her own little notes have a much finer finish. But the letter is not bad of its kind. The '*née* De Montemars' has anticipated any new attack which you might attempt, and has defeated it beforehand."

"Forbes, will you do me a favour?"

"With pleasure."

"Go to Mrs Leland; speak a kind word for me."

"But, my dear fellow, what could I say? Father, mother, and daughter unanimously reject your offer. Follow my advice and let the matter drop."

Baldwin looked at him in astonishment, but did not answer. Forbes felt that in his desire to get rid of the whole affair—which did not interest him very much—he had perhaps acted somewhat awkwardly; so, with some hesitation in his tone and manner—like one who is trying to get out of a difficulty, and hopes to find a way while he is speaking—he said,

"Put yourself in that woman's place. . . . After all, she is not so very much in the wrong. . . . She does not wish to separate from her daughter. . . . If you had an only daughter, would you like her to go and live among the

Ainos? . . . Cannot you make a new offer on a different basis? . . . Cannot you say you would remain in Europe? . . . By that means, perhaps, everything might be pleasantly arranged. But go and plead your cause yourself, and don't take an outsider into the business. That might make an unfavourable impression. *Qui veut, va; qui ne veut pas, envoie.*"

"No, I must return to Japan," replied Baldwin; "my interests would suffer too much were I to remain here now."

"Well, make up your mind to a sacrifice."

"If it were only that!" exclaimed Baldwin. "I would gladly give every penny I have if it would make Mrs Leland change her mind. But, as a poor man, I could not presume to offer myself as a husband for Jane."

He stopped suddenly, and walked up and down the room in deep thought; then, speaking to himself rather than to his companion, he said—

"There is perhaps one way of arranging everything."

"How?"

"If I could find somebody to buy a share of my business, which is really a sound and good one." He stopped again and cast a timid glance at Forbes.

"How could that be done?"

"I cannot see my way quite clearly in the matter at present," replied Baldwin; "I will think it over, and talk to you about it this evening."

"Yes, do," said Forbes, in a careless tone. Then he looked at his watch, and added, "I have a few calls to make. I will dine at seven at the Café Anglais, and you can meet me there if you like. At any rate, I will be here at about nine." And he left the room. "I see what you are after, Master Baldwin," he said to himself as soon as he was outside; "always the same old story!"

Baldwin had no idea of what was passing in Forbes's mind. He worked the whole afternoon to draw up a statement of his financial position. He happened to have some documents with him which enabled him to prove the correctness of his estimates by facts and figures. He could show that he possessed a fortune of nearly 150,000 dollars. In order to arrive at this figure, he had, however, thought himself justified in putting down at a fair sum his flourishing business in Japan. He stated that any one who would take a share in the concern, bringing with him 50,000 dollars, would make a safe and profitable investment, and that on these conditions, he was ready to take his friend Graham of Hakodate into partnership. Of Graham's consent he felt sure beforehand. The 50,000 dollars with which Graham would enter the firm would enable them to extend the business, and found a branch establishment in Europe. The management of this European branch Baldwin would undertake himself.

These were the heads of his statement. In an accompanying letter, Baldwin asked Forbes to lend these 50,000 dollars to his friend Graham. As an additional guarantee, he proposed to mortgage his own and Graham's landed property in Hakodate, to secure Forbes. Thus the risk to be incurred in granting the loan would be reduced to a minimum.

Baldwin worked hard for several hours to finish his calculations and his letter. He had been much excited; but as he read over his work when it was done, he felt satisfied with it, and that calmed him a little. He had written with perfect honesty. He had not tried to represent his circumstances as better than they were. A stranger, indeed, might perhaps raise objections—but then Forbes was no stranger. . . .

Baldwin knew that Forbes possessed a large fortune, and he took it for granted that he would be ready to do this thing to oblige, not only him, but also Graham, who had been the friend of his youth.

He looked at his watch and saw that it was too late to go to the Café Anglais. So he took a hasty dinner at a restaurant in the Champs Elysées and rushed home immediately afterwards.

Forbes was not punctual; it was nearly ten when he made his appearance. He said something by way of excuse, to which his friend paid no attention. He was evidently in a bad humour when he followed Baldwin into his room.

"Here," said Baldwin, handing him the long, carefully written statement, "read this first."

Forbes had not taken off his hat, and altogether looked like a man who has not much time to spare. He turned over quickly the closely written pages, and soon came to the end of the memorandum which had cost poor Baldwin so many hours of conscientious labour.

"I do not see yet what is the drift of this," he said, without lifting his eyes off the manuscript, "but I can point out at once one great mistake which may fatally weaken your whole argument. . . . I, too, am a man of business," he added, somewhat pettishly, as if in answer to some implied remark from Baldwin, who had not said a word, and who stood looking at him in anxious suspense.

"You estimate your fortune at 150,000 dollars. That cannot be correct, to begin with, since you are willing to sell one-half for 50,000 dollars. By your own showing, therefore, you are only worth 100,000 dollars. But even from that sum, Leland, who is a cautious man, would deduct one-half, as your money is invested in a business which may be good to-day and bad to-morrow. Again, you are ready, you say, to become joint security with Graham for the 50,000 dollars you wish to raise; but should you be unfortunate in your business—a contingency which must certainly be taken into account—you might be utterly ruined. This alone will cause old Leland to consider your statement as resting upon a very weak foundation, and consequently to reject it."

He had assumed, while speaking, a certain look of superiority, as though he had discovered something very pleasant, and he repeated slowly, "Yes, reject it." After a short pause he continued—

"But, even supposing that Leland were to accept your calculations—which, I am convinced, he will not—your statement will by no means satisfy him. I see you reckon upon a certain income of 12,000 dollars. You mention that sum as a mininum. Leland will not suppose for a moment that you have undervalued your property, and he will set down that sum as a maximum. But, my dear fellow, what are 12,000 dollars a-year for a spoilt child like Jane Leland? In her father's house more than double that sum is spent, and they do not think themselves rich enough. With 12,000 dollars, or about £2500 a-year, one cannot do much in Paris. For instance, you could not think of keeping your own carriage and horses; and just imagine Jane Leland in a cab! Impossible! . . . Believe me, my dear Baldwin, it won't do; better give it up."

"Here, read this," replied Baldwin, gloomily, and he handed Forbes the letter in which he was asked to advance the 50,000 dollars to Graham. Forbes looked at it for a moment.

"You think me richer than I am," he said. "I cannot dispose of 50,000 dollars as easily as you fancy. But even if I could, what would be the use? I repeat, Leland is far too practical a man to accept your offer. Believe me, Baldwin, the best thing you can do is to give up the whole thing."

"Then you will not help me?"

"I will help you with pleasure, if it is possible. I will see what I can do. But I can make no positive promise; and I repeat again, I do not think my help would do you any good."

"What am I to do, then?"

"Well, how can I know?"

"May I tell Leland that I think I can make arrangements to remain in Europe, if on that condition he will give me his daughter?"

"Certainly, tell him so; that can do no harm; but . . . but . . . as I said before, I do not know yet whether I can get that money for you. I would have to borrow it. 50,000 dollars is a large sum—a quarter of a million of francs—a very large sum. . . . If you only knew how many claims are made on me — from all sides. . . ."

Baldwin looked at Forbes with an expression so peculiar, so bitter, and at the same time so pitying, that the poor millionaire was suddenly silenced.

"Let us say no more about it," said Baldwin, gently; "I have been mistaken."

A feeling of shame and anger took possession of Forbes. He felt that Baldwin was looking down upon him, as from some lofty eminence. But had he a right to do so? What did it all amount to? Always the same old story. He, Forbes, was to give money. Was he good for nothing else in this world than to pay, in order to get other people, strangers, out of their difficulties? Who had ever helped him? Nobody. He wanted nothing of Baldwin; what right had Baldwin to ask a favour of him? He had taken a liking to the stranger, because he seemed unselfish and disinterested. But after all, Baldwin was just like the other people with whom he had come in contact. Baldwin, like the rest, wanted to get something out of him. "I will not always let everybody make use of me, and get the better of me," he said to himself. "The friendship of that man is not worth 50,000 dollars. Not a penny will I give for it, if I have to pay for it. It was only of value so long as it was not venal."

"You judge me unfairly," he said aloud; "but it would be of no use to try and clear up this misunderstanding. . . . Good night, Baldwin."

"Good night."

A few minutes later, Baldwin heard the roll of the carriage which took Forbes to his club. There he played as usual, but, if possible, with even less interest than was his wont. His reason furnished him with a hundred arguments to justify his conduct towards Baldwin; but his heart, cold as it was, told him that he had acted meanly and ungenerously. No: Baldwin was no common schemer who wanted to take advantage of him. And by his side there stood another man, whose image Forbes could not drive away—a man with a prematurely aged face, with a sad look, and a sorrowful smile on his lips—Thomas! Baldwin, a perfect stranger, had shown him kindness. "I owe it to Baldwin that I have not gone quite to ruin," Thomas had written to Forbes. This thought gnawed at the heart of the rich man, and his conscience smote him.

"He shall have the money," he said to himself, suddenly, and a genial feeling of warmth, which he had not known for years, filled his heart.

"*Va banque!*" he said aloud, and pushed a heap of gold pieces and bank-notes into the middle of the table. He lost. It took a long time to count the money. He waited impatiently, and had to pay a considerable sum. Then he rose and drove home.

He looked up at Baldwin's windows, and saw no light in them. "He is gone to bed," thought Forbes. He went into his own room, but he was excited, and it was long before he fell asleep. At a late hour the next morning, his servant brought him a letter. He recognised Baldwin's handwriting, and, tearing open the envelope, he read—

"DEAR FORBES,—Accept my best thanks for the kindness with which you have received me. I have made up my mind to go to London. Your servant tells me that you are still asleep, and I do not wish to disturb you.—Very faithfully yours, GORDON BALDWIN."

IV.

Four years had gone by quickly. Baldwin was now thirty-two, and Forbes was not far from forty. Mrs Leland was dead, and had not seen the fulfilment of the great wish of her heart,—the union of her daughter Jane with George Forbes.

Jane was still young and beautiful, but she was discontented and bitter at heart. This was shown by the thin compressed lips of her firmly set mouth, by the sharp look of her dark eyes, and by the almost stern expression of her countenance. Life, with her, had not kept its fair promise. The years of her first fresh youth had gone by. Her friends and companions—many of them less beautiful and less wealthy than herself—had married, and now held a position in society from which they seemed to look down upon Jane, whose superiority they had formerly acknowledged without difficulty. There had been numerous suitors for her hand during all these years, but she had rejected them all. She knew why she had done so. The only man who could make her heart beat faster and whose homage would have flattered her, George Forbes, seemed not to care for her. Quite imperceptibly, the circle of her admirers had dwindled. She felt lonely since the death of her mother. She still was to be seen in the American colony of Paris, where her great beauty and wealth gave her a prominent position, but she seemed isolated there. The young unmarried girls were afraid of her sharp tongue; and the young men felt embarrassed when they were subjected to the cold looks of Jane Leland.

Sometimes George Forbes would sit down by her side. Then her eyes would brighten with a tender reproachful expression, which remained unnoticed by the millionaire. He sat there perfectly cool and indifferent; and while Jane was looking at him to impress the image of the loved face deeper and deeper into her heart, he would criticise with impertinent coolness the dresses of the ladies, or make some sneering remark about the "young people." He treated Jane like a contemporary—an old friend of many years' standing. Towards midnight, when every one was bright and cheerful, when the youthful faces were flushed with pleasure and excitement, he would rise with a scarcely suppressed yawn to go to his club and gamble there for an hour or two.—He was little changed since the last four years. There was still the same slight graceful figure, the same handsome face which was so familiar to the *habitués* of the Boulevards, the Bois de Boulogne, and the *premières représentations.*

Forbes had felt the loss of Baldwin very much for a short time, and had even gone to London in the hopes of finding him. He had also written to him, but had received no answer. Then he had forgotten him. He had to think of so many other things,—of himself, for instance. From time to time, at intervals which grew more and more distant, the remembrance of the "wild man" rose up in his heart. Then he would feel ashamed and humbled, and would pass his hand impatiently across his brow, as if to drive away a painful vision. Sometimes he would try and justify himself in his own eyes, and stifle the sense of mortification. "Well, I have at any rate saved fifty thousand dollars!" he would say to himself; but he knew well enough that he did not believe it. He knew that the money Baldwin had asked him to lend, would not have been lost, and that he had missed an opportunity, which might never occur again in his monotonous useless life, to do a good deed to a good man. Of Thomas Graham, he had heard nothing more. "He may be dead for aught I know," Forbes said to himself. A gloomy feeling came over him when he remembered that the last request that Thomas had made had not been granted, and that the kindness shown to him by Baldwin had not been repaid, as he had begged.

Baldwin had spent those four years in Japan. Fortune had smiled upon him and he had become a rich man. Graham, his true and faithful friend, had been his partner for the last three years. Baldwin had proposed that he should go to Europe and give himself a good long holiday; but the quiet melancholy man had refused very gently but with great determination. "Here in Hakodate, I have at last found peace," he said, "and here I will stay. I want nothing, I desire nothing more than what I have. Go to Europe yourself. I wish you, from my heart, all the happiness you can find at home. I hope all your wishes will be realised. As for me, I expect nothing more from the world out there, and I shall stay here."

Baldwin had told Graham what had taken

place in Paris, and he had also mentioned, but without any bitterness, the mean behaviour of Forbes. Graham had turned pale when he had heard it. "George is cold-hearted and suspicious," he had said, "but I do not think him bad. I am sorry that his distrust has misled him. I would have forgiven him everything—all that I think I have to reproach him with—if he had rendered you a great service."

Baldwin had noticed that any allusion to Forbes was painful to his friend; the recollections of Paris were sad also for himself. The two, by tacit agreement, never spoke again of Baldwin's unfortunate journey to Europe.

In time, the remembrance of Jane grew fainter in Baldwin's heart. His love for her became calmer, colder, and so disappeared gradually. His anger towards Forbes cooled down in like manner. The small-minded man, whom he had at first heartily despised, became an object of indifference. He thought of him seldom and without bitterness. Time destroys everything.

In the last days of the year 186– Baldwin once more said good-bye to Graham, to make a new trip to Europe. Nothing had been definitely settled about his return to Japan.

"Remain at home as long as you like," Graham had said; "I am happy to think that you are going to enjoy yourself. You are too young to bury yourself out here, as I have done. If you care to remain in England or in France, let no thought of me prevent you. I am content to stay some years longer in Japan. If at any time I should wish to get away from here—which is not likely—I shall know it in time to ask you to take my place for a while, or I will be able to settle our business so that it may be carried on without either your presence or mine. Do not trouble yourself about me. I can get on very well alone. Enjoy yourself, and good-bye."

And now Baldwin was once more in Europe—a quiet, serious man, older in heart and in looks than in years; but full of confidence, and inspiring confidence in others, as before. He had arrived at Marseilles two or three days before, in a steamer of the Messageries Impériales, and had been in Paris a few hours. He had gone to an hotel in the Rue de la Paix, where he intended to remain a week before he went on to London. It was the month of March.

As soon as he had landed on French soil, Baldwin had felt a great wish to see Paris once more. He could not have explained what attracted him. He did not hope to see Jane again, he did not even wish it. He had never inquired after her, and thought she must have married long ago. For him she was lost—dead. But he wished to revisit the place where his warm young heart had dreamed a brief and beautiful dream. He thought longingly of the place as one thinks of a spot where a beloved friend lies buried. A sorrowful memory of his younger days drew him towards Paris.

He slowly changed his dress and went to the *café* where he had dined years ago on his first arrival. The Boulevards appeared strangely familiar. It was like the meeting of old friends. He recognised in the shop-windows the same photographs which he had noticed four years before. It seemed to him that he had been absent only a few days. Everything was in the old place; nothing seemed changed—but himself. He had grown so different—so much older, so much poorer in hope, so much sadder!

He sat down at the same table where he used to sit with Forbes, and lo! the same waiter, with apparently the same white apron, the same white neck-tie, and the same patent-leather shoes, came up to him and inquired, in the well-known indifferent tones, what "Monsieur" would like to have for dinner?

"Give me a good dinner," said Baldwin.

The waiter started slightly, and looked more closely at the sunburnt stranger with the white forehead. A faint ray of recollection passed over his sleek pallid face and glistened in his dark cunning eyes. He went to order the dinner, and then returned and remained standing near Baldwin. And suddenly he went close up to him, and leaning over the table with polite familiarity, he asked, "Does Monsieur expect Mr Forbes?"

Baldwin looked up with a smile and said, "You have a good memory."

"I never forget my customers," replied the man, evidently flattered.

He went again to the kitchen, and when he came back he said to Baldwin, "I have changed the bill of fare a little. I remember that Monsieur likes highly seasoned dishes, and I have ordered a curried fowl."

A few minutes later, Forbes entered the room.

The waiter went up to him and said, "Monsieur is expected." Forbes looked towards the table which the waiter had pointed out, and a sudden deep flush covered his face. He hesitated for a second, and then walked up to Baldwin. Baldwin rose from his seat, and for one short moment, the two men stood face to face in great embarrassment. Baldwin was the first to hold out his hand, which Forbes seized eagerly and pressed with earnest warmth.

"I am truly delighted to see you again," he said. "I had no idea that you were in Paris. When did you arrive?"

"A few hours ago."

"And where have you put up?"

Baldwin gave the name of his hotel.

The waiter had taken Forbes's hat and overcoat, and was waiting for further orders. "Give me the same dinner as Mr Baldwin," Forbes said, to get rid of the man. Then he sat down, arranged his cover and unfolded his napkin to fill up a short pause. At last he bent forward, and with greater warmth than was usual with him, he said—

"There has been a misunderstanding between us, Baldwin, and I am sorry for it. I tried to find you after you left me so suddenly, but I did not succeed. I also wrote you a letter, addressed to the care of your banker in London, but I received no answer."

"Let bygones be bygones," said Baldwin. "All that was forgotten long ago."

"No; I must beg to be allowed to give an explanation. I give you my word that on that same evening when I saw you last, I had made up my mind to place the sum which you wanted at your disposal."

"You came a little too late with your friendly intentions."

"Yes, indeed; and I have often regretted it. I regret it to this day. Believe me, I would like to have been of service to you."

"I believe you." It was the same quiet deep voice which Forbes had liked to listen to years ago, and which had inspired him with confidence and affection; but the faithful honest eyes that were now looking at him, and whose steady light he could not endure, were no longer bright and full of life as of yore; they had a serious, almost sad, expression now. A feeling of shame and remorse he had never experienced before filled the heart of the rich man.

He would have liked to beg Baldwin's forgiveness. He would willingly have given a far larger sum than that which he had refused to lend four years ago, if he could thereby have effaced his mistake.

"I regretted your sudden departure very much," he repeated.

"I believe you. Let the matter rest. Tell me what you are doing."

Forbes told him that the last four years had gone by in a dull monotonous way, devoid of any interesting incident. Suddenly he interrupted the story of his own life to inquire after Graham.

"He has become my partner," replied Baldwin. "He is quite well. He is a good honest man; and I have a great affection for him. I only regret that nothing seems to give him pleasure. He is always the same: quiet, friendly, kind-hearted, and sad."

"When you write to him," said Forbes, after a pause, "say that I inquired after him, and that I am glad to hear good news of him."

"Why don't you write to him yourself? I am sure a letter from you would give him pleasure."

Forbes made no reply, and changing the conversation, he asked abruptly, "What did you say to Mrs Leland's death?"

"I did not know she was dead," replied Baldwin with surprise. "And how is Mr Leland?" he continued with some embarrassment—— "and Miss Jane?"

The old pain awoke in him with the recollection of the old time. But it was pain without bitterness. Jane, in his mind, belonged to a far-distant time which, with all its beautiful hopes, had gone by long ago.

"Mr Leland is just the same," said Forbes. "Indeed I think that his wife's death has made him grow younger. He is once more his own master—which had not been the case with him for the last thirty years. The death of that uncomfortable woman was no great loss to anybody. As for Miss Leland, you will find her but little changed. Well, she is no longer a child; she must be about twenty-seven now, and the first bloom of youth is certainly gone. Girls grow old faster than married women. But Miss Leland is still remarkably handsome—the handsomest girl of the whole American colony, which can boast of many a lovely face. It is strange she is not married. There has been no lack of suitors, but she has refused them all."

Baldwin was struck dumb. A thousand thoughts rushed through his brain. Jane was still free! How was that? After all, he had never received a refusal from herself. Her parents alone had spoken. Was it possible that she loved him? Was it too late to ask her for a definite answer? Should he try once more and seek his happiness where, years ago, he had hoped to find it? What if she loved him? . . . His heart throbbed fast at the very thought. . . . And if she did not love him? Well, that would be no loss. The wound he had received four years ago was healed. He was able to look forward with equanimity to meeting Jane. He hoped indeed little; but he had nothing to fear. His feeling towards her could hardly be called love; it was rather a peculiar and intense curiosity. How would she behave when she saw him again? Would she be astonished, or joyfully moved, or indifferent? He wanted to be sure about it.

Forbes perhaps guessed what was going on in Baldwin's mind, for he asked, "Are you going to call on the Lelands?"

"I don't know yet," replied Baldwin; "but I think I would like to see them again."

"You may have that pleasure this very evening. Come with me to the opera; you will find Mr and Miss Leland in my box."

Baldwin hesitated. "Shall I call for you?" urged Forbes, who was anxious to make himself agreeable to his former friend. "I will be at your hotel in half an hour, just in time for the opera. It is nearly eight now."

Baldwin consented, and they left the restaurant. When they entered Forbes's box an hour later, it was empty; but very soon Mr Leland and Jane made their appearance. Jane recognised Baldwin at once, and started back with a little exclamation of surprise. But in an instant, and without any apparent effort, she recovered her self-possession. She had never cared for Baldwin. She had not thought of him for years. He was an acquaintance of former days, an old lover whom she had rejected—nothing more. He had gone down in the stream of Time, and had been forgotten without being even regretted. What was it to her that he had turned up again? She gave him calmly her small gloved hand, nodded to him with a friendly smile, and passed on to take her seat in the front of the box.

Baldwin had to be introduced again to Mr Leland; but no sooner did the old gentleman recollect the "young man from Japan" than he showed genuine pleasure at meeting him again. He inquired after his health and his circumstances, and testified his satisfaction at the prosperity of an old friend, by exclaiming half-a-dozen times, "Delighted! delighted!" He insisted on making Baldwin sit in front, next to his daughter, while he remained standing at the back of the box with Forbes, who had to tell him everything he knew about his newly found friend.

As to Baldwin, he was almost choked with emotion. He had wellnigh forgotten Jane during the last four years, but now the blissful confusion which he had always felt in her presence took hold of him again. Jane appeared to him more beautiful than ever. She was dressed plainly, like a young girl, but to Baldwin's eyes she shone forth like a queen in her simple toilet. She looked carelessly round the house to see if she recognised any acquaintances, and Baldwin was thus able to admire her without meeting her eyes. The outline of her features had become more sharply defined than before, and this gave still greater refinement to her beauty; her complexion, too, was paler; and it seemed to Baldwin that her countenance wore an expression of gentle sadness, instead of the former proud consciousness of victory. For one short moment her eyes met his. He felt himself turn pale. Those eyes had lost the triumphant look of pride which once beamed from them; they were wearied, regretful, almost appealing for help. Jane certainly was more beautiful than ever.

The curtain fell, and put an end to Baldwin's mute admiring contemplation. And now she turned towards him and asked him kindly how he had been, and when he had left Japan, and whether he intended to remain in Europe.

Baldwin completely forgot that an hour before he had only been curious to see what impression their meeting would produce on Jane. Now his inexperienced large heart yearned towards her with all its might. A delightful pain, made up of mingled hope and sorrow, filled his breast. It was with great difficulty he could retain his self-command. And Jane saw it all, as with an enchanting smile, and a kind trustful expression, she looked up at him.

Baldwin went back with Forbes to his hotel after the theatre, silent and abstracted.

"You do not seem to hear what I am saying to you," remarked Forbes, with a smile.

"I beg your pardon; I am a little tired from my journey. You asked me where we should dine to-morrow. It is all the same to me—wherever you like."

"At our old restaurant, then, at seven. Afterwards I go to the Sands's for an hour. Shall I introduce you? You may find some old friends there; at any rate you will meet the Lelands. Mrs Sands is an old friend of mine, and I can introduce you without ceremony."

Baldwin accepted the offer, and the two separated for the night. On his way home, Forbes debated with himself whether he would ask Baldwin to stay again at his house. But he feared a refusal, and without settling the question in his own mind, he went to bed and was soon fast asleep. Jane dreamed that night that Forbes had, at last, declared his love. Baldwin's fatigue had entirely disappeared, and for a long time he walked up and down his room in great excitement. And once more, as it had been four years ago, all his thoughts were with Jane Leland.

V.

Baldwin met many old acquaintances at Mrs Sands's. They all invited him, and he accepted their invitations; and thus it came to pass that very soon after his arrival in Paris, he went out to parties every evening and almost invariably met Jane. He had now been four weeks in Paris. He delayed his departure from day to day, and easily found pretexts for remaining where he could see her.

Baldwin was a quiet man, full of sound common-sense. Life in foreign lands had given him a self-reliance and a determination of character which people who remain at home, surrounded by relatives and friends, seldom acquire in the same degree. But his heart, which for a long time had fed upon his first love in Paris, —the heart of the "wild man," as Forbes had called him,—had never been touched since, and was still young and inexperienced as a child's. He loved with the strength of a man and with the ingenousness of a boy—with all his heart and with all his soul. And Jane was no longer quite indifferent to the passion she inspired.—She resented bitterly the loneliness in which she had lived latterly; and she missed the circle of admirers who used to surround her. She had exercised mercilessly the privilege of refusing all offers, and she did not regret that she had done so; but she noticed with mortification that nobody now seemed to seek her favour, and that she had, apparently, lost that power over the hearts of men which she had used with so little pity. At times she felt really sad—almost sentimental. Even cold heartless people can pity themselves sometimes very sincerely. Could she not reach the goal which so many of her companions had attained? Was she not more beautiful, richer, more intelligent than any of them? If she chose to employ the arts and the manœuvres that they had resorted to, she might triumph even now. But she would not. Her pride rebelled at the thought that she, the beautiful Jane Leland, should ask for love. If she had cared to do that, she might have conquered the heart of George Forbes years ago. She had always been proud and reserved, even to him.

Nobody could know, and nobody should ever know, what was passing in her breast,—George Forbes least of all. She wanted to be loved, and then, by her own free will, to give her virgin heart as a priceless boon to him whom she could love in return.—But now no one seemed to care for the precious gift. And here was Baldwin! She well knew how superior he was to the affected young dandies who surrounded him. How noble and fearless was the glance of those large clear eyes! All other eyes quailed before them. How true and honest was the ring of that deep voice! How serious, calm, and earnest was his speech! But the proud look softened when it met hers; his voice sank to a tender whisper when he spoke to her; and his words, which scarcely dared to hint at what filled his heart, told her with touching bashful simplicity that he loved her as she had never been loved before.

Yes; Gordon Baldwin was a man upon whom she could rely. Every drop of his life's blood belonged to her if she required it. She need not beg for his love as for that of the cold suspicious Forbes. No; in Baldwin's eyes her love was an invaluable treasure.

One evening when Baldwin met Jane at the house of a mutual friend, he told her that he could not stay in Paris much longer, and that he would go to London in a few days.

"I hope you will soon return to Paris," she said.

"Perhaps," he replied; and after a pause he added, in a low voice, "Will you let me see you to-morrow to say good-bye?"

"Certainly, with pleasure," she answered, smilingly.

"Miss Leland . . ." began Baldwin. Then he stopped. She looked at him with some surprise, but kindly and encouragingly. "To-morrow, then," he added, "I will have the pleasure of calling on you at five."

The next day, a few minutes before the appointed time, Baldwin entered the same room where, four years before, he had been a suitor for Jane Leland's hand. Mr Leland had gone out, and Jane was alone. Miss Leland was an independent young lady, who, even during her mother's lifetime, had enjoyed a great deal of liberty, and who, having now been for more than a year quite uncontrolled by her father, could receive anybody she wished to see alone.

On his way from his hotel to the Avenue Friedland, Baldwin had tried to think of what he should say to Jane. He would once more declare his love—that was his settled purpose; but he could not determine in his own mind how to do it. He dared not picture to himself all that might happen. What if Jane were to refuse him, as her mother had refused him years ago in her name?—How would he thank her if she accepted him?—He shook his head as if to drive away the confused thoughts which tormented him. He closed his eyes, so to speak, to all the possibilities of his case, and half hopeful, half despairing, he went to meet his fate. It was a leap in the dark, and he would take it.

Jane was reading in the drawing-room when Baldwin entered. She took a few steps forward to meet him, and offered him her small, slender hand. He kept it in his own and looked anxiously round the large room, like one who seeks for help or is in fear of danger. She sought gently to withdraw her hand, but he detained it firmly, and said—

"Miss Leland, years ago I stood before you, as at this moment, to ask a question which you have never answered. . . . Jane . . . trust yourself to me . . . Jane . . ."

He looked at her imploringly, unable to utter another word. Infinite sadness, love, devotion, were in his eyes. Her heart beat faster. Why should she reject the great love which was now offered to her?—Forbes?—The image of the man she loved appeared for one short moment before her—the scornful mouth, the cold criticising eyes, the proud wearied face. The vision vanished and she saw Baldwin—honest, earnest Baldwin — with his truthful face in which everything spoke of love for her. She did not withdraw her hand. Her eyes fell; she did not lean towards him, but he drew her gently to his heart, and she resisted no longer. Before she was aware of it, her head rested on his breast. She wept softly,—over the great love which she inspired; over the happiness she hoped for confusedly but yet sincerely; and over the sudden but now irrevocable loss of all the cherished dreams of her heart. He kissed her pure brow and said tremulously, "My whole life will bless you for the happiness which you give me." He led her to the window, where, half unconscious, she sank into a seat. He was once more master of himself, and though deeply moved, he was able to speak to her quietly. "Would she tell her father what had taken place, or should he do so?" She did not answer. "Did she think her father would object to their marriage?" "Oh no," she said, in a scarcely audible whisper.

"Well, then, we have nothing more to fear: all will be well."

"Yes, all will be well."

But she could not look into his eyes. Only yesterday she had been the mistress whose smile or whose frown could make Baldwin happy or miserable; now she felt weak and disarmed. She had shot her last arrow; she had made her choice; she had sealed her fate. It was very different from what she had hoped. She looked at Baldwin stealthily, as if she saw him for the first time. Could she be proud of him? He had nothing of that peculiarly aristocratic bearing which had attracted her in Forbes, but he was a noble-looking man nevertheless. She need not fear that the world would laugh at him or at her. Her friends would be astonished at her choice;—after all, she had not won a great prize. Had she been so fastidious, and so exacting, to give, at last, her hand to a man who had neither a great name nor a large fortune? If she had married George Forbes, everybody would have thought her conduct natural. She would have waited long, but she would have won a great prize. But who was Gordon Baldwin? A man whom nobody knew, for whom nobody cared. A sigh escaped her. She heard indistinctly, as in a dream, what Baldwin told her. He spoke of his life in Japan since he had left her;—how unhappy he had been; how he had thought he could kill his sorrow by hard work; and how, at last, he had found rest, but no happiness. He spoke of the longing which had drawn him back to Paris, although he had come there without hope; of the surprise, mingled with fear, with which he had learned from Forbes that all was not yet lost; of their meeting at the opera, where she had appeared to him so sad and so beautiful; of the revival of his love, which had never been really dead; and now of the indescribable happiness of knowing himself beloved.

She smiled sadly. Her heart was ready to burst. He could not know that it was full of despair for the loss of her once hoped-for happiness. The tear that fell on her pale marble cheek, the sigh which made her bosom heave, the smile which glorified the beloved countenance, only seemed to tell him that she loved him.

The large clock struck loudly and slowly—seven. Baldwin looked up in astonishment. Two hours had gone by like a few minutes. She felt wearied and wretched, like a beaten soldier fleeing from the enemy, and longing for darkness and solitude. He rose; she gave him her hand, but remained seated. He bent down and kissed her once more on her forehead.

"Good-bye, till we meet again this evening, my own, my beloved."

"Until we meet again," she repeated, mechanically. And now, at last, she was alone. She remained motionless in the same attitude for a few minutes, staring straight before her. Then she rose, and slowly, noiselessly, as in a dream, she went up to her own room.

This, then, was the end of her ambition! She was to live and die Mrs Gordon Baldwin! She did not repent of what she had done. No! she felt a bitter scornful joy as she thought of it. "Now Mr Forbes will see at last that I did not care for his miserable money." Her greatest wish at that moment was that he should feel this, and that it should give him pain. "Will he, now that I am lost to him, regret that he never sought my love?" She shook her head in despair, "I have never been anything to him." Oh, how bitter, how very bitter was that thought! Should she try her chance once more? Her cheek flushed, her eyes shone at the thought. Should she write to Baldwin and say that she had been mistaken, that she had deceived him, that she begged his forgiveness, and wanted to take back her promise? Baldwin would do anything for her, she was quite sure of that. She rose and went slowly to her writing-table. But there she sank into a chair, and covering her face with her hands, burst into tears. Of what use would her freedom be to her? She had been free all these years, and Forbes had never looked at her with love. No, thank God! she had not fallen so low as to beg for his love. She hated him—she was not going to mourn all her life for his sake. She would not give him the satisfaction of seeing her grow old in solitude. He had once said to her, "Baldwin is the best man I know." He should see that the best of men was happy to devote himself entirely to her. She bathed her face in cold water to efface the trace of her tears. She had suddenly grown calm. The icy coldness of those who have lost all that was dearest to them, and who have conquered that loss, had taken possession of her. In a few minutes she had grown much older. She had done with all the hopes and all the dreams of youth. She went up to the glass to arrange her hair: a pale face, with burning eyes, met her gaze. She nodded to the vision with a gloomy smile,—"Good-bye, Jane Leland," she said. Then she went down to the drawing-room, where her father had been waiting for her to go to dinner.

The relations between Mr Leland and his daughter were not of a kind to make Jane feel any embarrassment in telling him of what had taken place during the afternoon. She did it after dinner in a calm unconcerned manner.

"How do you like Mr Baldwin?" she asked, after she had poured out coffee for her father, who was enjoying a cigar—a liberty he would never have taken in the drawing-room during the lifetime of Mrs Leland, *née* De Montemars.

"A charming man—a very charming young man."

"Would he suit you as a son-in-law?"

"What? What do you say?"

Jane repeated the question. Mr Leland nearly dropped the cup he was holding; he put it quickly on the table, and with a trembling hand laid down his cigar; then he bent over to his daughter and looked at her in mute astonishment.

"Mr Baldwin has asked me this afternoon to be his wife."

"Well?"

"He will ask you for your consent this evening."

"And I will give it him with all my heart. I would never have refused it. . . . My darling child! I am so happy! . . . I am an old man, and I may die any day. The thought that I would have to leave you alone has embittered these last years of my life. Now I can live and die in peace. Baldwin is a noble-hearted and good man. I have always liked him, and I have often regretted that your dear mother refused his offer. My dear Jane! my only child! my own dear daughter!"

He embraced her tenderly, and was much more affected than she was—so much more that her coldness did not strike him. He begged her to tell him how it had all happened; and she had already begun to do so in a very business-like way when the door opened and Mr Baldwin was announced.

Mr Leland, beaming with joy, went forward to meet him. He pressed his hand and could only say, "Welcome, my dear son;" then he sat down trembling and was quite unable to utter another word.

Baldwin was as much moved as the old man. Jane observed them almost contemptuously. She had fought her battle; she was tired and longing for rest. Why all this excitement? She listened with indifference to the plans which her father and her lover made for the future. She nodded, or said "Yes" when a look or a word seemed to ask for her consent. She cared for nothing. Sometimes it seemed to her as though she were not concerned in what was going on before her. It was like a dream. Everything appeared dark and confused. Was it really her own future life they were discussing? Could those two men dispose of *her?* Was she no longer free? Was Forbes lost to her for ever? Once more the desperate resolution which had tempted her in her own room recurred to her. Should she rise and call out, "Stop! you are mistaken! I have deceived you—I love another!" But then Forbes appeared before her, smiling scornfully. No; anything was better than to be sneered at by that man,—perhaps to be pitied by him! And Baldwin was a good noble-hearted man. She would learn to love him. All might yet be well.

It was settled that the more intimate acquaintances should be informed of the engagement on the morrow, and that in two months' time—in July—the wedding should take place.

"Where shall we live—in Paris or in London?" said Baldwin.

"Wherever you like," was Jane's reply.

"In Paris, of course," exclaimed old Leland. "Nowhere in the world can a young married couple live as pleasantly as in Paris. Besides, I am accustomed to this life, and I would find it difficult at my age to adopt any other. Then you have so many good old friends here,—the Lingards, the Kellys, the Sandses, Forbes, and many others. . . ."

'Very well, let it be Paris then," said Jane, —and this ended the conversation.

VI.

Miss Leland's engagement to Gordon Baldwin was for many days the principal topic of conversation among the American residents in Paris. The girls and the young married women talked about it very much in the spirit which Jane had foreseen. They were in no way jealous of her conquest, and there was a touch of sarcasm in their remarks. The young men were indifferent. They had no claims on Jane, and were inclined to consider the stranger from Yesso a bold man. They expressed the hope that he would have energy enough to tame the proud spirit of his bride. Some predicted that he would follow in the footsteps of his father-in-law, who had been the pattern of obedient husbands. Others remarked that he did not look like a man who would consent to be led by any one—not even by an adored wife. As for the old ladies and gentlemen who had long given up all idea of Jane or Baldwin for their unmarried sons or daughters, they were perfectly satisfied with the arrangement.

Forbes alone, though he had long been aware of the affection of his former friend for Jane

Leland, was astonished when he heard of the marriage. He had never made up his mind to ask her to become his wife; he did not love her; but he could see that in beauty and in intellect she far surpassed all the other American girls of his acquaintance. Nor had Jane's preference for himself escaped his notice, though she always treated him with great reserve. Men are as quick-sighted as women in this respect, and have a great liking for those whom they please. Forbes had said to himself more than once that if ever he *did* marry, he would take Jane Leland. He thought of her as he would have thought of a precious work of art for his house, which he could acquire at great cost, but which would give him proportionate pleasure. "She would look well," he said to himself, "as the mistress of my house, at a large dinner-party, or at a ball, or, again, by my side in an open carriage." The thought had never struck him that he might not be able to secure this "precious thing" when he wanted it, just as he never doubted that he could buy a beautiful picture which he liked. The only question was to pay the price. Up to the present time he had thought Jane Leland a little too expensive for him. She was not worth—just yet—the sacrifice of all the enjoyments of a free bachelor life. But he had never quite given her up. In his mind she was "marked"—as it were in a sale catalogue—as a desideratum, and he was only waiting for an opportunity, or for a favourable frame of mind, to conclude the bargain.

He had never thought it possible that Jane could escape him; he had never really feared any of her numerous suitors, and Baldwin even less than two or three of those that the proud beauty had refused. The "wild man" was a good honest fellow, but that would be no great recommendation in the eyes of his practical countrywoman. He possessed a fair fortune; but according to Forbes's ideas, he could not even be called rich. Why should Jane treat him differently and better than her other admirers? And yet so it was: Gordon Baldwin was the affianced husband, and she was lost to Forbes.

At first he did not feel much grieved; he only felt a peculiar unpleasant restlessness. He knew that henceforward something would be wanting in his life. Many things he had not thought of for a long time now came to mind suddenly with painful distinctness. He noticed that he was no longer young, and that his acquaintances began to treat him like an old bachelor. When he went to parties, the lady of the house no longer asked him whether he would dance, but the host inquired in a friendly whisper whether he would take a hand at whist. He remembered that all his wealth had not purchased for him a single friend, and that this lonely life — which had never oppressed him before—was, after all, very unsatisfactory. The remembrance of Thomas Graham, to whom, for a long while, he had not given a thought, came back to him. If they had been together he would not now feel so lonely. But between Thomas and him there was a great gulf—they could never meet again. He thought over all the marriageable girls of his acquaintance, but among them there was not one who could fill Jane Leland's place. He felt angry with her. It seemed to him that she had treated him badly, unfairly. For years there had existed a peculiar kind of intimacy between them; she ought to have "given warning" when she meant to break off. He had thought better of her than to suppose that she would throw herself away on the first stranger she met! But it was now too late to complain; he had to make the best of it. He went to Baldwin's hotel, and congratulated him with, apparently, genuine pleasure; from thence he went to the Avenue Friedland, where he left his card, upon which he had written in pencil, "My best wishes." Then he went home and tried to persuade himself that nothing particular had happened. He yawned more than usual over the papers; found his dinner abominable, and declared to the waiter that he would not come again if he were not better served; thought that the piece played by the best actors of the Palais Royal was uncommonly tedious and silly, and remained only a short time at his club. Contrary to his habit, he walked home to enjoy the fresh air on the quay, and to tire himself by exercise.

The broad beautiful walk along the Seine from the Pont-Royal to the Pont de l'Alma is at a late hour almost deserted. Forbes could indulge in his thoughts undisturbed, and for more than an hour he walked up and down. He was pleased with the loneliness of the place, and from that day he often found his way to it. A great change must have taken place when he, who had never been inclined to reverie, found pleasure in this quiet walk. Now he too had his dreams, just like other less cold-hearted people. He had found out at last that his life might have been better than it promised to be, and that one cannot despise unselfish affection without suffering for it. For Thomas Graham, for Gordon Baldwin, for Jane Leland he had been something more than merely "the rich George Forbes"; yet in them, too, he had suspected selfish motives. And it was now too late to correct his mistake. Too late! Again and again he repeated the bitter words. He well knew that Baldwin had never met him again with the old friendly confidence of former days, and that Jane could never be to him what she had once been. "After all," he said to himself, "I possess very little in this world though I am a rich man."

Summer was come. Most of the friends of the Leland family had either left, or were preparing to leave Paris, to go to some watering-place or other. Forbes, like the rest, had made his plans for the summer, and would have been away already if he had had the courage to refuse Baldwin's invitation to the wedding. He generally found no difficulty in giving a refusal; but on this occasion he accepted, less to please Baldwin than to avoid the appearance of being in any way vexed at the marriage.

Both Forbes and Jane acted their parts before the world so as to deceive everybody except themselves. Forbes affected a friendly desire to make himself useful, and offered many little services to promote the future comfort of the young people. Jane never seemed more satisfied with her fate than when Forbes was present. But sometimes when their eyes met, they exchanged a bitter reproachful glance. The young bride-elect would often think of it at night in her own room, and enjoy the painful triumph of knowing that Forbes, now it was too late, repented of what he had done, or rather of what he had left undone. And when Forbes, with his hands thrust in his pockets and his head bowed in deep thought, walked up and down the solitary quay, he repeated to himself with regretful pride that, had it been his pleasure, he might for years past have occupied that place by Jane's side for which Baldwin had to fight so hard.

Baldwin and old Mr Leland were the best of

friends and perfectly happy. Not a shadow of suspicion crossed their contented minds. Jane had accepted Baldwin's offer: for these two simple-minded men that was a convincing proof that she loved him. They did not know how to solve psychological problems, and suspected no secret. Jane, in her intercourse with Baldwin, certainly did not show that devotion and confidence which, in theory, he might have expected from his betrothed; but he thought that her coldness was only the result of maidenly reserve, and he admired her all the more for it. Old Leland was not naturally very clear-sighted, and his wife had certainly not spoiled him by great demonstrations of affection. Jane's behaviour to her future husband seemed to him perfectly natural and becoming.

The interval of two months between the engagement and the wedding had quickly gone by, and at last the eventful day came and passed like other days. The marriage was celebrated with great splendour. Many of Jane's friends came up to Paris on purpose to see "the beautiful Miss Leland" on her wedding-day. She was indeed very lovely on that occasion. It was noticed that she was very pale, and that her eyes remained so obstinately fixed on the ground during the ceremony, that not one of the wedding-guests could obtain a look.

Only a few intimate friends were invited to the breakfast—among these was George Forbes. His eyes sought again and again those of the bride, but not once did they meet. She would see nothing, and she saw nothing, of all that went on around her.

After the breakfast, the newly married couple disappeared in that mysterious manner which fashion prescribes, and were not seen again for some months.

Forbes shortly after the wedding went to America, where, he said, important business required his presence. Old Leland went to Trouville, where he found many of his friends, to whom he confided—at intervals varying from eight to ten days—that he had the very best news from the young couple, who were making a wedding-tour in Norway and Sweden, and were as happy as two newly married lovers could be.

VII.

Mr and Mrs Gordon Baldwin returned to Paris after their wedding-tour, and established themselves in their new residence in the Avenue de l'Impératrice. They led a very retired life, and, with the exception of Forbes, received only a few of their former acquaintances. Nobody was surprised at this, for the young couple were in deep mourning. A few days before their return to Paris, they had received news of the sudden illness, and almost immediately after, of the death of Mr Leland. He had been a weak, kind-hearted gentleman, and his loss was sincerely mourned by all who knew him.

Mrs Gordon Baldwin, his only child, inherited the greater part of his large fortune; but several distant relatives, as well as a few friends and acquaintances, had been remembered in his will. The old banker had to the last carefully kept the management of his wealth in his own hands, and had expressed his wishes respecting the disposal of it after his death in a clear and business-like manner. His son-in-law, Mr Gordon Baldwin, and Mr George Forbes of New York, now resident in Paris, son of his late friend Richard Forbes, were appointed executors.

One passage in the will had particularly struck Baldwin, and had been listened to by Forbes with evident embarrassment:—

". . . Further, I bequeath the sum of ten thousand dollars to Mr Thomas Lansdale, half-brother to Mr George Forbes, my executor, and son of Major Thomas Lansdale of Baltimore, and of Mary Lansdale his wife, who, after his death, married Richard Forbes of San Francisco and New York. This sum of ten thousand dollars is to be handed over to Mr Thomas Lansdale, with the assurance that, under all circumstances, I have remained his true and faithful friend."

While this passage was being read, Baldwin looked inquiringly at Forbes; but the latter kept his eyes steadily cast down.

Half an hour later, when they were driving home together from the American Consulate, where the will had been read, Baldwin said, "I did not know that you had a brother."

"We will talk about that some other time," said Forbes; "my brother's story is a long and not a particularly pleasant one. I do not feel inclined to tell it to-day."

On the whole, since his return from America, Forbes seemed little inclined to be communicative. He had always been very reticent; and since Jane's marriage he had become still more so. The voyage to America, which he had undertaken immediately after the wedding, had not made him more cheerful. His countrymen struck him as uncultivated; many of them as ill-bred. He thought the men conceited and full of unjustifiable pride; he was shocked at the bold and noisy manner of the women in their intercourse with the other sex. Formerly, he had found it a pleasant pastime to laugh and flirt with his pretty countrywomen; now, he thought their behaviour forward, almost vulgar. He remained only one month in the United States and then returned to Europe.

It seemed to him as though the ten days' passage from New York to Liverpool would never come to an end. He longed for a storm, merely for the sake of a change; but the sky remained clear and blue all through the day, the nights were wonderfully bright, and the ocean, with its overwhelming immense monotony, lay before him like a colossal mirror. He liked to sit alone at the furthest end of the deck, away from the rest of the passengers, and to watch the white dancing furrows of foam which marked the track of the vessel. He had no distinctly sorrowful thoughts, and he was not continually grieving that the only friends he had had in the world were now lost to him. It was only dimly that the vision of Thomas, of Gordon, of Jane, passed before him. But a peculiar gloomy uneasiness, like a presentiment of approaching misfortune, oppressed him. "What is the matter with me?" he asked himself angrily. "Do I not possess everything to make me happy? I am rich; I am still young. Have I not the means of enjoying life? What ails me?" He could find no answer to his questions, but his heart was heavy, and the dark dismal thoughts could not be banished. There was the fruitless past and the barren future;—a joyless life, and a hopeless one.

The summer was not quite over when Forbes landed in England. London and Paris, where he remained a few days only, seemed to him deserted and insupportably dull. In Paris he prolonged his stay for two days longer than he had intended, for the special purpose of carefully examining and finally buying a large picture which had attracted his attention in the shop of a dealer. It was brought to his house, and hung up in the place of the beautiful Rubens, which for years had been the ornament of his bedroom.

It was an ugly picture, on which his eyes now fed morning and evening. It represented Seneca entering the bath dripping with blood, and uttering with his dying breath words of wisdom, which a weeping disciple was writing down. Beneath this ghastly image was written —"*Tædet tamdiu eadem fecisse.*" Forbes had caused this sentence to be translated to him; and when he understood its meaning, his eyes lighted up, and he said approvingly, "That is a good picture and a good sentiment;" and without another word, he paid the high price which the dealer asked for the wretched daub.

Forbes went from Paris to several watering-places. He found everywhere the same well-dressed men, the same elegant women, the same carriages and boats, the same lackeys, waiters, drivers, and boatmen. It seemed to him that everything which he had hoped to leave behind in one place followed him wherever he went. At the railway stations he met the same well-known officious porters; at the hotels he was received by the stereotyped head-waiter, with the stereotyped bow; and when recognised—thanks to his luggage and servants—as a rich visitor, he was conducted into the well-known showy room with its pretentious mahogany furniture, and its velvet chairs and curtains. In the reading-room there was the same ragged-looking number of 'Figaro,' the same copy of the 'Times,' with its stains of tea and coffee, which he had seen at the last watering-place. "It is tedious always to see, to hear, and to do the same thing," he said to himself.

He returned to Paris in October, but he mixed in society much less than he used to do. He neglected his club altogether, and every night between ten and twelve o'clock he might be seen on the solitary quay beside the Seine, where he slowly walked up and down, with his head bowed down, and his hands behind his back.

One night, shortly after the reading of old Leland's will, Forbes was overtaken by Baldwin in his lonely walk.

"What are you doing here at this hour?" said Baldwin.

Forbes replied that this walk by the riverside had almost become a necessity to him before going to bed. "In all Paris," he said, "there is no quieter place than this after eleven o'clock. One is as much alone here as if one were a hundred miles away from the noisy city; and yet he need only walk a few steps to be again in the midst of bright teeming life. I like the contrast. It prepares me, in a way, for the solitude which awaits me on my return to my bachelor home. But this is no place for a young husband. What are you doing here this stormy evening?"

Baldwin made an evasive reply, and rather to turn the conversation than to gratify a feeling of curiosity, he said—

"You still owe me an answer to my question about your brother. Do you feel inclined to speak about him to-night? I do not wish to be importunate, but you must, at any rate, give me his address, as I have to inform him that my father-in-law has left him ten thousand dollars."

"You know Thomas Lansdale's address as well as I do."

"What do you mean?"

"Thomas Lansdale and Thomas Graham are one and the same person."

Baldwin was much surprised, but he remained silent. He could well imagine that something very painful must have occurred to induce his partner in Hakodate to assume a feigned name, and to keep secret his relationship to Forbes. But Baldwin felt no anxiety to have the mystery explained. Whatever might have taken place between the two brothers, he felt sure that Graham, whom he had now known eight years, was worthy of his confidence.

"It is a sad story," continued Forbes, after a pause. He stopped again, and then, with an assumed tone of indifference, he proceeded: "My brother and my father could never agree. My father was very severe. Thomas, when I knew him, was wild and reckless. There were frequently violent scenes between them. During my mother's lifetime she acted as peacemaker; but soon after her death Thomas was obliged to leave the house. He ran into debt, not so much for himself, as to assist a set of low sharpers who had got about him. And that was not the worst. He married, without my father's knowledge, a woman who deceived him, and whom the credulous fool took for a saint. She did much mischief. She died, many years ago, in poverty and wretchedness. The less said about her the better. When my father heard of the marriage he became frantic with rage. He was a violent man, and was not master of himself when he was angry. He went to Chicago, where my brother was living, to force him to give up his wife. Thomas worshipped the unworthy creature. My father's threats exasperated him. . . . It is a fearful story. . . ."

Forbes paused for a moment to collect his thoughts. He had completely lost the composure with which he had begun his narative. His tremulous voice betrayed deep emotion.

"You must bear in mind that there was no actual relationship between Thomas and his stepfather. . . . He was a strong man. . . . He had kept, from his old Californian life, the habit of going about armed. . . . In those days at Chicago there was hardly a man who had not always his revolver ready to hand. . . . My father had been stung to the quick by Thomas. . . . He had shown him the door, he had laid hands on him. . . . Well! My brother was wounded—not dangerously, God be praised!—but still he was wounded. The unfortunate affair was hushed up, and only a few intimate friends—old Leland among the number—knew of it. Thomas Lansdale recovered; but he went from bad to worse; his wife dragged him lower and lower down. Yet he would not consent to what we all asked him to do with so much reason: he would not separate from that woman. My father died without having seen him again, and without forgiving him. Then Thomas addressed himself to me. What could I do? I could not declare my father to have been in the wrong. He had done no wrong. . . . Then I heard nothing more of Thomas Lansdale for a long time—till you, five years ago brought me news of him. . . . That is my brother's story."

Baldwin had not once interrupted Forbes, and remained silent now.

"You think I have done wrong," said the suspicious man; "you consider that I have acted harshly?"

"I do not think that I could have been angry with a brother so long," replied Baldwin, with great earnestness. "Thomas Graham is a good man; every one who knows him loves him."

"He was not always as quiet and good as you have known him. He was wild and disorderly. My father paid his debts over and over again."

"He was your brother."

They had arrived at a part of the quay where their way lay in different directions. Baldwin wished his companion "good-night," and turned off quickly.

Forbes went home slowly. His magnificent rooms appeared to him unutterably sad and lonely. He went into his study, and from among a heap of papers and documents which he kept locked up in a box, he took a large envelope on which was written in his own hand, "Letters from T. L.; to be burned unread after my death." He read the letters through, very carefully. The stern features of his cold face relaxed, as he read, into a gentler and sadder expression. How had he been able to resist these touching complaints and supplications which now so painfully moved his heart? He put down the papers with a heavy sigh, and remained for a long time motionless and in deep thought.

"He was my brother," he said at last, unconsciously repeating Baldwin's last reproachful words. "He was my brother, and strangers have saved him from ruin." And now the past rose up before him.—He remembered, as if it were yesterday, the evening when Thomas had said good-bye to him in his bedroom, before leaving the house after their mother's death. He saw him, as he stood before him then, with his pale face, his long fair hair, his large blue eyes, with their startled timid look—the eyes of their dead mother! "George," he had said, "you must not tell your father that I have come to you. He forbade me to do so. But I wanted to say good-bye to you, as to my brother, and he would not have allowed it. Good-bye, George; think of me kindly." And then he had embraced him, and Forbes had felt his hot tears upon his cheek; and Thomas had noiselessly stolen away.

"He was my brother; he was my brother," repeated Forbes.

He had seen him again, many years after, in a street of New York. He looked wretched and poor then. It was a cold wet night. He wore thin shabby clothes and seemed to be shivering in them. "For the last three days I have been waiting here every evening for you," he said. "Oh, George, listen to me! save me! I am lost!" And he, Forbes, had had the courage to repel him. "Have you separated from your wife?"—"She is ill, George, help me!"—"Will you promise me to separate from your wife?"—"George! help me! help me!" Those words now, after long years, cut deep into his heart. "He was my brother!" The remembrance of that meeting weighed on him like a hideous nightmare. A hopeless sadness enveloped him as in the folds of a dark shroud.—He might have had a brother, a friend, a loving wife: Thomas, Baldwin, Jane. And now he had lost all, lost for ever! What remained? A large fortune! And what could he do with it? Always the same thing—always! "*Tædet tamdiu eadem fecisse.*"

VIII.

When Forbes had alluded to his married life, Baldwin had quickly turned the conversation. It was a subject he did not care to talk about.

His was not, strictly speaking, an unhappy marriage; but the felicity of which he had dreamed, he had certainly not found. Jane, as a wife, remained as cold and as unimpassioned as she had appeared before marriage. She showed no ill-humour or petulance, and gave her husband no cause for complaint; but she never smiled, and she went about quietly and silently, as if some secret sorrow oppressed her. Baldwin felt this bitterly. He had endeavoured, by perfect candour, by watchful tenderness, and by entire devotion, to win her confidence; but all his efforts had been unavailing. After a time his pride rebelled at this state of things—to offer love where he received nothing but dutiful politeness in return. Sometimes his blood would boil with indignation when he longed to clasp this icy creature to his heart, and yet could feel plainly that there was no response to his tenderness; but he mastered those passionate emotions, and only sighed as he released the delicate little hand she had carelessly yielded to him, and which she now as listlessly let drop by her side.

Why was not Jane happy? Baldwin did everything he could to make her so. She did not seem to care for his efforts, or even to notice them. Her face never lighted up with an expression of gratitude; no kindly word passed those firm lips, and her cold eyes looked without interest on all that surrounded her. Baldwin grew uneasy and dispirited.

"What is the matter with you, my dear Jane?" he asked, one evening when they were seated alone before the fire. "Are you ill?"

"Nothing is the matter with me," she answered, wearily.

"You are hiding something from me; what is it? You know that I have only one great wish, and that is to see you happy."

"I want nothing," she repeated. She was staring at the fire with wide-open eyes, and Baldwin could see that in them two big tears were shining, which, after a while, rolled slowly down her pale cheeks.

He went up to her and took her in his arms, and with the tenderness of a mother who is trying to soothe a suffering child, he said, "Speak to me, my beloved—speak!" but she pushed him away gently, and only said—

"I am a little tired. I do not know what is the matter with me. Let me alone."

He looked anxiously at her. "I will send for a doctor; you are ill."

She only shook her head in silence. Her tears came faster, but not a word escaped her lips.

"Will you not answer me?" he asked once more, tenderly and softly.

"What can I answer?" she exclaimed, passionately. "Have you anything to reproach me with? Do I not readily obey every wish of yours? What more do you want? Do not torment me!"

He looked at her in astonishment, and said gently, "I am very unhappy." He then rose and left her to go to his own room, which was at the further end of their apartment, but he could not bear to remain there. He took up his hat and left the house to quiet his excited nerves in the fresh open air.

Baldwin was a sensible practical man, who, in his life, had encountered many difficulties, and who had learned that one cannot overcome them by sitting down quietly and letting events take their course. A threatening danger, a great misfortune, only strengthened his moral faculties. He could clearly discern and carefully examine every way out of a perilous position; but against the grief which now filled his heart, he knew no remedy. He walked helplessly up and down in the dimly lighted avenue, asking himself again and again how he could improve the unsatisfactory relations existing between his wife and himself.

Jane had remained seated in the same place. She had wiped the tears from her cheeks, and continued to stare into the blazing fire.

For a little while, immediately after her marriage, she had done her best to love Baldwin. She had not succeeded at once, and had quickly abandoned the attempt. And now she disliked her husband. She thought him ill-mannered and uncultivated. His heavy step in the room made her nervous; his voice was too loud; his tender attentions, which she did not dare to reject, were irksome to her. "Why will he not leave me alone?" she said to herself, angrily; "why does he torment me with his love?" During her whole life she had never thought of anything but her own comfort and happiness; and even when she had made that feeble attempt to love Baldwin, she had only considered her own interest. She knew that it would be more pleasant to live with a man whom she could love than with one for whom she did not care. For the welfare of others—of strangers—she felt very little concern. Baldwin was a stranger to her. He was her husband—more was the pity! She cursed the hour when, in a fit of irritation and of weak despondency, she had permitted him to clasp her in his arms. He had been short-sighted enough, when she was weeping on his shoulder, to believe in her love. Her love! He had no idea *how* she could love. He became every day more displeasing in her eyes. She had to close her lips tightly to refrain from an expression of anger when he noisily opened the door and she heard his step in the room. She shrank when he threw himself heavily into a chair. She felt weak, tired, miserable; he was strong and healthy. She felt irritated even at this. "Forbes gave him his right name," she said to herself; "he is a wild man, and he ought to have married a savage." What a difference between him and Forbes! As to Forbes, she wished to hate him! He was the cause of all her misery. She would have liked to give him some magic potion in which he would have imbibed that same dumb, heavy wretchedness which crushed her heart. And yet she recognised his light step as soon as he approached her, and his soft soothing voice sounded like music in her ears. She reproached herself bitterly, not because in her heart she was faithless to her husband, but because her pride could not cure her of her love. "I wish he were dead, and I too, and then all would be over," she said to herself.

A ring at the door roused her from her gloomy reverie. It was nine o'clock. Who could come at that hour? She had heard Baldwin go out, but she knew that he always had the key of the house with him.—"George Forbes!" she murmured. He was the only one of their acquaintances who, since her father's death, paid them evening visits; but she had never been alone with him, and she did not wish to be alone with him now. She hastily rose to leave the room. At the same moment, the servant opened the door and announced Mr Forbes.

On a table in the centre of the large drawing-room a lamp was burning, whose light, subdued by a shade, was thrown exclusively on the table. Beyond that narrow illumined circle, a soft twilight reigned in the room.

Forbes approached Jane with apparent composure and sat down in a chair by her side. He inquired after Baldwin. She answered that he had just gone out. Then the conversation dropped. The pause became painful, and Jane tried in vain to find something to say. At last Forbes spoke: there was a peculiar hoarse sound in his voice.

"I am glad at last to have an opportunity of speaking to you alone and undisturbed, as in old times. I have to ask you for an explanation."

She made no answer, but continued to look fixedly before her.

"Mrs Baldwin," continued Forbes, gently and deliberately, "may I ask by what fault of mine I have incurred your displeasure?" She looked at him stealthily without raising her head or moving. He could not see her face, which remained in shadow. After a few seconds, as she made no reply, he went on—

"We have been good friends for many years—at least I always thought so. What have I done to forfeit your friendship? Since your marriage, you have treated me like a stranger—nay, worse than a stranger. I have tried my best to retain your good opinion, or to win it back, and I know too well that I have failed. It has grieved me very much, I can assure you. My acquaintances generally, I am aware, consider me cold and heartless. I owe this reputation to the circumstance that I do not allow everybody to get the better of me. It is not easy, I admit, to win my confidence. I am not in the habit of opening my heart to others. This is the first time in my life that I speak about myself, and I do so because I wish you to know me. As a rule, I do not approve of confidential communications, and I generally mistrust those who want to tell me their secrets. Experience has taught me that those who have taken me into their confidence, have usually wanted to borrow money immediately afterwards. People know that I have grown suspicious in this respect, and very few now attempt to approach me. But precisely because I have so few friends, I set a great value on the good opinion of those who favour me with their friendship. I used to reckon you among those few. Have I been mistaken? That would be a greater misfortune than you can imagine—greater than I dare to tell you."

His voice had become subdued, gentle, tender

—as Jane had never heard it before. Her blood was rushing like fire through her veins. Her heart was almost bursting. How did that man dare to speak to her like that? He had neglected her when she was free, and when she would willingly have given herself to him if he had asked her to be his. *He* had been the cause of all her misery; *he* had driven her to despair. What did he mean now? Was he laughing at her? or did he despise her, and did he wish to take advantage of her nameless misery, to degrade her into an object of contempt to herself and to him?

She did not answer. She could only preserve an appearance of self-control by remaining silent.

"Will you not speak to me, Mrs Baldwin? . . . Jane . . ." He bent forward; she felt his breath upon her cheek, he was going to take her hand.

She sprang to her feet, pale as death; she raised her hand, and with outstretched arm and a gesture full of majesty, without saying a word, she pointed to the door. He rose in utter confusion and attempted to speak. "Mrs Baldwin . . ." he began; her glowing eyes looked at him with such an expression of passionate wrath and contempt that he dared not proceed. Unspeakably humiliated, he moved towards the door slowly. She remained like a marble statue in the same haughty, menacing attitude, and it was only after the door had closed behind him that she sank fainting into a chair.

Forbes rushed down the avenue like a madman. Not far from Baldwin's house he was met by a tall man, who, having recognised him by the light of a street lamp, turned round to look after him in astonishment, and then slowly went on his way.

. . . . . .

"Has Forbes been here?" inquired Baldwin when, a few minutes later, he entered his own drawing-room.

Jane, who was sitting in front of the fire with her back towards him, did not answer. He went up to her. She had fallen back in her chair, with half-opened eyes and white lips like a corpse. He took her up in his arms as if she had been a child, and carried her into another room, where he laid her on a bed. He had often seen sick and dying people, and he did not for a moment lose his presence of mind. He saw at once that Jane had fainted, and by the help of a few simple restoratives she soon recovered. She slowly opened her eyes and looked strangely at him. "The wretch!" she murmured.

"What has happened?" inquired Baldwin, anxiously.

She recognised her husband, closed her eyes, and turned her head away, as if she wanted to sleep.

Baldwin remained for a short time at the bedside without speaking; then he asked again what had happened. She answered, scarcely audibly, "I am tired—I cannot speak—let me rest." Against this weakness, real or feigned, he felt himself powerless. He called his wife's maid, gave her some instructions, and went into his own room. But he only remained there a few minutes. Anger, suspicion, and jealousy tormented him.—He had seen Forbes rush past him in the street in a wild, excited manner, and immediately afterwards he had found his wife in a fainting state. — What had taken place between those two?—He must know it, and at once. His wife could not, or would not, give him an explanation; Forbes, at any rate, should give him an answer.

It was a mild evening in March. The street door was open, and the *concierge* was standing a few yards off, talking with a neighbour. Baldwin left the house unperceived. He walked quickly to Forbes's house, and from the outside examined carefully the windows of the room where Forbes usually sat when he was at home in the evening. When he saw that all was dark he turned away. A few minutes later he was on the quay. The place seemed even more deserted than usual. Not a step was to be heard. The dark, turbid waters of the river, swollen by the spring rains, rushed gloomily along on his right. Countless lights from the opposite shore and from the bridges were reflected in long tremulous lines in the water. On his left were the old trees of the *Cours la Reine*, casting a dark shadow around. In the distance was heard the heavy unceasing roll of carriages.

When Baldwin had reached about half-way between the bridge of the Alma and the bridge of the Invalides, he noticed, at a short distance in front of him, the figure of a man, who had been hidden, up to that time, by the surrounding darkness. He was leaning over the low stone parapet of the quay, and seemed to be looking down into the gloomy river. Baldwin recognised the man he was seeking.—Forbes, hearing the quick, heavy step, looked up, and in a moment the two men stood face to face. A street lamp near them gave sufficient light to enable them to distinguish each other's features clearly. Forbes was very pale; Baldwin, excited by his quick walk and the tempest of passion which was raging within his breast, stood before him with burning cheeks and flashing eyes.

"What have you been doing in my house?" he said. He spoke with an ominous tremor in his voice.

Forbes looked at him in confusion, without answering.

"What have you done in my house?" repeated Baldwin, in a louder tone.—A short pause.—"Will you not answer, Forbes? Do you hear me? Will you answer?"

"You are too excited," replied Forbes, regaining some composure; "come home with me. Be quiet, I can explain everything."

"I will not cross the threshold of your house again. You shall answer me now—here—at once!"

Forbes stepped back involuntarily. Baldwin caught hold of him by the shoulder.

"You shall not escape me.—Answer! answer!"

Baldwin was a powerful man, and his passion gave him the strength of a giant. He shook Forbes like a light lifeless body. "Answer!" he cried again, with blind fury.

For the space of the tenth part of a second he saw before him a ghastly pale face, out of which a pair of large black eyes stared at him in wild terror; then he saw Forbes, whom he had pushed violently away, fall backwards against the sharp edge of the low wall; he heard his head, with a dull heavy thud, strike against the stones;—a fearful groan;—then all was still. Forbes was lying on the pavement, close to the wall, and Baldwin was leaning over him, looking anxiously into the convulsed face.

"Forbes!"

No answer.

The eyes of the dying man opened once more in his last agony—a horrible rattling sound in his throat—a short convulsive writhing of his body—and then suddenly complete repose—the repose of death.

Baldwin looked wildly around. For a few seconds he stood irresolute; then that cool self-possession which always came to his aid in the hour of danger, awoke him. He recognised his perilous position with perfect lucidity. He heard the roll of a heavy carriage, and saw to his right, only some hundred paces off, the red light of an omnibus. With a few strides he crossed over to the other side of the quay, and was hidden beneath the shadow of the trees of the *Cours la Reine.*

The omnibus went by without stopping; but from the Invalides two men were coming towards him. The night was so still that Baldwin could distinctly hear what they said.

"What's this?" exclaimed one, as they came up to the body.

"A drunken man."

They both stooped down.

"Call a policeman; I'll stop here; this man is dead!"

One of the two men ran towards the Place de la Concorde. Baldwin took the opposite direction, and, hurrying as much as he could without attracting the attention of those he overtook in his way, he reached his own house. Scarcely half an hour had elapsed since he had left it. The *concierge* was smoking a pipe, and walking up and down before the open door. Baldwin recognised him from afar, and managed to enter the house without being seen by him. He walked noiselessly up-stairs, and reached his own room unnoticed. He quickly took off his overcoat, and threw himself into a chair by the fire.—Then, and only then, when he had effaced every trace of his deed, when he had escaped the most pressing and immediate danger, did he begin to reflect on what had taken place.

A thousand thoughts pressed upon him, but not in wild confusion. Things passed before him in logical sequence, and he could calmly consider and weigh every circumstance: Forbes had insulted his wife; she had alluded to him, and to no other, in that exclamation, "Wretch!" He was fully justified in demanding an explanation of what had taken place. Jane would not give it; he had gone to Forbes for it. Forbes, too, had refused to answer. He had wanted to force him to speak, and had grown angry; but even in his wrath he had never intended to kill Forbes. Without knowing what he was doing, he had pushed him violently. But Forbes was dead; and who could now stand up and bear witness to Baldwin's innocence? If he gave himself up as the author of this involuntary crime, he would have to submit to strange suspicious judges, who would consider his truthful testimony as mere lying and perjury, and who would treat and perhaps condemn him—an innocent man—like a common malefactor. Nothing obliged him to expose himself to such a risk. His conscience reproached him with nothing; he had meant no harm.—Should he accuse himself? Should he stand forward and say, "That man died by my hand"? Should he deliver over his good name to malicious comments and suspicions? No! he would not do that. He would, on the contrary, do everything in his power to avert such an undeserved misfortune.

He called to mind every circumstance which had immediately preceded or followed the accident. Nobody had seen him go out; nobody had seen him return home; he had been absent only a short time. It was impossible that any suspicion should attach to him.—"Nobody knows what I have done," he said to himself, as he weighed every point over and over again; "and nobody shall know it."

At this moment he heard a violent ring at the door-bell, followed by loud talking in the ante-room. His quick ear caught repeatedly the name of Forbes. He placed the lamp, which was covered with a shade, on a low table, so that his face might remain in darkness, and waited a few seconds in intense anxiety. The door of his room was thrown open violently, and Forbes's old servant entered. Baldwin's servant followed, but remained standing at the door.

"Well! what is it?"

"They have brought home my master dead! He has been murdered."

With easily feigned surprise, Baldwin sprang to his feet to follow the messenger of woe. He addressed several questions to the servant, as he would have done if he had had no knowledge of all that had happened, and in a few minutes they reached Forbes's house. The door stood wide open, and was guarded by two policemen. Baldwin and his companion were, however, at once admitted, and entered the bedroom without being questioned.

There, on a bed, lay the half-undressed body

of the dead man. Three persons were in the room, who in a few words introduced themselves as the doctor, the chief police officer of the district, and his assistant. The officer, at whose request Baldwin had been sent for as a friend of the deceased, told him all he knew of the case. About three-quarters of an hour before, two gentlemen, accompanied by a *sergent de ville,* had come to the police station and had given information that they had found the dead body of a man on the quay, between the bridge of the Alma and the bridge of the Invalides. The identity of the deceased had soon been ascertained, as a pocket-book with his address and a large sum of money had been found on his person. The officer wished now to know if Mr Baldwin, whom the servant had designated as an intimate friend of the deceased, could give any information likely to throw light on the tragic end of the unfortunate gentleman.

No; he knew nothing.

"When did you see Mr Forbes for the last time?" inquired the officer.

"A few hours ago. I came home at about nine o'clock, and I met him close to my house where he had called to see me."

"What did he say to you?"

"He did not speak to me. He did not recognise me in the darkness, and walked quickly past me. I had seen him during the day, and had nothing particular to say to him. I did not stop him."

"Did he leave any message for you with your servant?"

"No; if he had, I would have received it."

"With whom did he speak in your house?"

"With my wife."

"What did he say to her?"

"I do not know. My wife was not very well when I got home, and in attending to her I forgot to ask about Forbes. He was a frequent visitor at my house, and there was nothing strange in his calling."

The conversation assumed the shape of a regular examination. Baldwin noticed this, and began to be careful. He determined to answer every question truthfully, and to conceal only what nobody but himself could know, and what nobody else was ever to know. Not once did he contradict himself; the officer was far from suspecting him, and finally closed the conversation by saying that Mr and Mrs Baldwin, as well as the servant who had opened the door for Mr Forbes, would probably be examined on the morrow by a police magistrate. Baldwin merely bowed assent, and turned to the doctor to ask him what had been the immediate cause of death. He listened attentively to the learned explanation of the physician, and was able to look on the corpse without any outward sign of emotion. All his energies were directed to the one object of not betraying himself by word, look, or deed. All else was of secondary importance for the time being. When he would be alone he would reflect upon it all. Now, there was no time for reflection. The first thing was, that he should not be suspected by that intelligent, shrewd police officer. He felt vaguely that he could not yet realise all the consequences of his deed; that misfortune was threatening him as the natural result of such an event; that blood calls for blood. All these thoughts rushed through his brain indistinctly, but he managed to keep them under control. For the present, all he had to do was to secure his retreat. While he was thinking of this he heard the officer say to his assistant that two policemen would keep watch in the house until everything had been officially sealed. Then he asked Baldwin if he knew where the deceased was in the habit of keeping his money and papers of value. Baldwin pointed out a box in which Forbes usually kept his cash and any important papers. This box was opened with a key which had been found in the dead man's pocket, and a considerable sum in gold and bank-notes was discovered. While the police officer was busy counting the money in the presence of witnesses, Baldwin noticed in the strong-box a carefully sealed envelope. He took it out and read the address:—

"GORDON BALDWIN, Esq.
(of Hakodate),
PARIS.

"To be opened after my death."

"This may contain some useful information," he said to the police officer. "Do you not think it would be well to open it at once?"

The officer assented, but added that the letter must be communicated to the magistrate. Baldwin offered no objection. He opened the letter and began to read, while all present observed him with curiosity.

PARIS, *February 26th.*

MY DEAR BALDWIN,—I have made up my mind to put an end to my life, and when you receive this, I will have carried out my intention."

Baldwin uttered an exclamation of surprise, and read these first lines aloud.

"That is very strange," remarked the officer. "From the doctor's report I would have thought it impossible that your friend had committed suicide."

Baldwin continued :—

"I tell you this in order to prevent all erroneous conjectures and inquiries as to the cause of my death. I have always disliked sensational excitement, and it is my last wish to leave this world as quietly and as noiselessly as possible. I have made arrangements to facilitate, as far as I can, the fulfilment of my wish.

"My will has been deposited at the American Consulate, and has been drawn up by an experienced lawyer in such a manner that it cannot possibly be disputed after my death.

"The reason why I kill myself is a very simple one : I am weary of life. A Frenchman would say it in fewer words: *Je m'ennuie.* In your opinion, this can hardly be called a misfortune. You cannot conceive how insupportable *ennui* may become with time — *Tædet tamdiu eadem fecisse.* This is the only Latin sentence I know, but this one I understand better than any scholar: it is tedious to have always the same things to do; to know that as long as we live we always will have to do the same things, and to feel that those things are wearisome and unprofitable.

"I have often regretted that I did not render you the service which you asked of me years ago. I beg you to forgive me. Use your influence with Thomas to make him forgive me likewise. I have never knowingly done your wife any wrong. I hope she will sometimes think of me kindly.

"When I have said farewell to you, to your wife, and to my brother, I will have done with the world. How poor I have been—I, the rich man! You, Baldwin, were my best friend, and how little were you my friend! Thomas was my only brother, and for years he has been dead and lost to me! Jane Leland is your wife.—A woman who is another man's wife, a brother who is lost, a friend who is indifferent—that is all I possessed.—It was not enough.

"At this moment I am neither excited nor cast down. A feeling of profound rest, such as I have not felt for a long time, fills my breast. The thought that I can lay down the burden of life whenever I please gives me new courage. Only a quarter of an hour ago, when I began to write to you, it was my intention to kill myself to-night. Now that I know to a certainty that I shall kill myself, now that I have made every preparation for the last act of my life, and am assured of being able to carry out my intention whenever I please, I feel courage to try the experiment of living a few days longer. Perhaps something new may happen to me. I can wait quietly. I have nothing more to lose, nothing to fear. Satiated, even to nausea, I stand on the boundary of life; when you read this I will have overstepped it. GEORGE FORBES."

While Baldwin was reading this letter, the officer had sealed up the money and other valuables. He then carefully drew on his gloves, remarked that it was late, gave his assistant some further directions, and left the house with Baldwin. He bade him good-night at the door, requesting him to come again early the next morning. Then he pulled up his coat-collar, put his hands into his pockets, and trotted briskly home. Baldwin walked slowly down the avenue. He remained a few minutes lost in thought in front of his own house; then he rang the bell and was admitted.

IX.

The last wish which Forbes had expressed in his letter to Baldwin was fulfilled. He was buried very quietly. Parisian papers only alluded discreetly to the tragic affair. All the inquiries of the police proved fruitless. The evidence of the doctors showed, it is true, that the hypothesis of suicide could not be admitted; but, on the other hand, it was difficult to believe in a murder, as a large sum of money had been found on the person of the deceased, and as Forbes was not known to have a single enemy.

Baldwin's servant deposed that on the fatal evening Mr Forbes had paid a short visit to Mrs Baldwin. He had noticed nothing peculiar in Mr Forbes's manner. — Mrs Baldwin declared that, after she had told Forbes that her husband was not at home, he had not stayed long with her. She, too, had noticed nothing extraordinary in his behaviour, nor had he said anything that could lead her to believe that he was threatened by any danger.

The evidence of the two gentlemen who found the body showed that Forbes had died between ten and half-past ten o'clock. A policeman who was on duty near the bridge of the Alma, said that, about ten o'clock, he had seen an open carriage driven by at a furious rate; he could not say whether it was a private carriage or a cab. The doctors, the chief officer of police, and the police magistrate came unanimously to the conclusion that Forbes must have been in that carriage, and that in his fear when the horses ran away, he had jumped out and so caused his own death. This explanation satisfied everybody, and the fatal event was very soon all but forgotten. Only between Baldwin and his wife it stood like a dark shadow.

Baldwin was conscious that, whenever he was alone with Jane, her eyes followed anxiously and suspiciously all his movements, as if she were afraid of him. Even the sham familiarity which up to that time had existed between them, disappeared. They lived together in gloomy, oppressive silence—each with a secret and a suspicion at heart. Baldwin had never dared to ask his wife again what had taken place between Forbes and herself at that last meeting. The words seemed to choke him whenever he tried to utter, in her presence, the name of the man who had died by his hand. His peace was gone, and he knew that he could never again find it. Henceforward he had to live under a heavy burden, and only death could bring repose. Fear—a feeling which he had never known before—took hold of him. If his secret were discovered? If his dark deed were brought to light? He shuddered at the very thought.—He would leave Paris; he would seek occupation; hard work might drive away those terrible thoughts, might give him peace, would tire him at least and bring back sleep, which had fled since that terrible night. He longed to go back to Yesso, among the simple-minded islanders, who had confidence in him, who knew nothing of what had happened in Paris, who would never know it. He would escape from his wife's searching, hostile looks, which watched and tormented him. He had never in all his life cast down his eyes before any human being, and now he did not dare to look up in presence of his wife. It was unbearable.

Immediately after the death of Forbes, Baldwin had written to Thomas to inform him of his brother's sudden end, and to urge him to take possession of the large fortune which had been left to him. Baldwin now resolved to go to Hakodate and take charge of the business during Graham's absence. He was, in fact, as much afraid of Thomas as of Jane. He pictured to himself a meeting with his old friend. How could he look at him, while he told him the story of his brother's death? He fancied he could see Graham's eyes looking with full trust and affection into his own. Would he be able to dissemble and to lie under the light of those honest eyes? No! he could even better bear Jane's suspicions than Thomas's trustfulness. He would start at once for Hakodate. By that means he was almost sure to avoid seeing his friend, who, in all probability, had sailed for Europe immediately on hearing of his brother's death.

Having carefully weighed every consideration,

he made up his mind one day to speak to Jane without further delay. He only waited till it was dark. He felt ashamed and humbled in his own eyes to take such a precaution, but he was forced to it—he could not help it. When the lamp was brought in, he placed himself with his back to the light. Jane sat opposite to him, pale, silent, and indifferent.

"Thomas Lansdale will have left Hakodate on receipt of my letter," he began; "one of us must be out there to take care of our business. I will return to Japan shortly. Will you go with me, or do you prefer to remain here?"

She did not reply to his question, but said—

"You are going to leave Paris?"

"I am obliged to go."

"I thought so."

He tried to appear surprised, and asked, "What made you think so?"

She merely shrugged her shoulders contemptuously."

"What made you think so?" he repeated. He made an effort, and looked straight into her face as he spoke.

"Do not ask me; you know it."

Her voice had a peculiar threatening accent.

He felt humiliated, but he dared not press for an explanation. He repeated his question, "Will you go with me to Japan?"

"No"—and after a pause she added carelessly, "I expect a letter from my aunt Alice in a few days. I have made up my mind to live with her in future."

It had come to this! She knew that he had no longer any power over her, and that he would not dare to assert his rights. "I do not understand you," he said gently, "but I will not hinder you from doing what you wish. Since I have known you, I have had but one thought, and that was to make you happy."

He said these last words in a voice of indescribable sadness, and he felt the tears rising to his eyes. What had he done to deserve the misery which he had to endure? If any one was answerable for this horrible fate it was Jane, whose coldness had first awakened his suspicions, and whose unconsciously uttered exclamation about Forbes had excited his anger. The thought that some wrong had been done to his wife had maddened him when he laid hands on Forbes. She, above all others, ought to forgive him, and to comfort him—and she alone tormented him! He covered his face with his hands and wept. He had become another man since Forbes's death. All his former energy had forsaken him. Now he was weak and irritable. Jane saw his tears and his sufferings unmoved. She sat there cold and pitiless like a stone image, her distrustful eyes fixed steadily upon him. At last he rose and said, "You are hard and unjust towards me, but I will not complain. The time may come when you will regret that you have rejected my love. When that day comes, call me and I will return to you. Now I will go."

He left the room slowly. She followed him with her eyes; her mute lips moved, and without uttering a sound she breathed the word "Murderer!"

Baldwin felt sure that he had not betrayed himself to his wife. She could know nothing of the dark deed; but he felt sure now that she had guessed it. He knew, however, that his peace was gone, even if Jane had not suspected him. Her undeserved confidence would have been less bearable even than her suspicions. *One* thing only could have reconciled him to his fate. If he could have taken his wife into his confidence, if she had acknowledged his innocence, pitied his misfortune, and shared it with him; —yes, then he would have found comfort and peace in her presence. But Jane's looks sternly forbade any approach, and he must bear alone the heavy burden of his secret.

Baldwin spent the next day in putting his affairs in order. He made every preparation for his departure, without interference on Jane's part, by word or deed. She looked on, as if she were deaf and dumb. Two days after their last conversation, he went into her room to say good-bye. He had dreaded that moment, but it was soon over. His heart was so overwhelmed with grief that he hardly noticed Jane's coldness. She did not offer him her hand, and when he leant forward to kiss her, she drew back in silence.

"Farewell, Jane!" he said; and in a tone of entreaty he added, "Let us meet again." She bowed her head without saying a word. He hesitated for an instant; but when he saw no sign of relenting in that cold face, he turned away.—It would have been better for him to stand before the most severe judge than to face that woman who had never loved him, who saw in him the cause of her unhappiness, and who now hated and dreaded him.—She had heard him on that fatal evening when she was lying ill on her bed; she knew when he had gone out and when he had come back. She knew that he must have been in the street at the very time of Forbes's death. The fact that he had concealed this circumstance had first aroused her suspicions; his gloominess, his confusion, had confirmed her in her belief. Since their last conversation, when that strong man had wept in her presence, she had felt absolutely sure of his guilt. "He is a murderer," she said to herself; but, nevertheless, she would not stand forth as his accuser. She, too, had a secret to keep; and her secret was more safe if she remained silent.

A few days after Baldwin's departure, Jane's aunt, Mademoiselle Alice de Montémars, arrived in Paris. She was a poor and elderly maiden lady, the sister of Jane's mother. Aunt Alice saw at a glance that she might secure a comfortable home for the rest of her days if she made herself agreeable to her wealthy niece. She spared no pains to make herself not only pleasant, but useful and even indispensable; and she succeeded, after a few weeks, in persuading Jane to go with her to her home, and to settle in a cheerful watering-place in the south of France.

X.

Baldwin had accomplished the greater part of his journey, and was in San Francisco awaiting the departure of the Pacific mail-steamer for Japan. He intended to go by that line to Yokohama, where he was sure to find easily an opportunity for Hakodate.

In New York, in Chicago, and in San Francisco, he had inquired after Thomas Lansdale, or Thomas Graham—for he did not know under which name his friend was travelling—but he could learn nothing about him.—"He must have gone by way of China, India, and Egypt," he said to himself. "So much the better! Now I am quite sure not to meet him." His heart ached when he thought that henceforth he would have to avoid those two, whom he loved best in the world—Jane and Thomas. But he strove hard to accustom himself to the idea, and he now felt more able to bear his fate. He had become calmer and stronger since he had left

Jane. He knew that she was well taken care of, and he felt no anxiety on her account. If she had loved him, she would have followed him; but she did not love him, she never had loved him. She had been false from the beginning—when she had given him her hand, when she had promised solemnly to "love and cherish him," and to be his "for better, for worse." His misfortune should not have estranged her from him. *He* had every reason to resent her conduct; *she* had nothing to reproach him with—he had done her no wrong. It was a comfort to feel himself innocent, at any rate, so far as she was concerned. His account with her was closed, and the balance was in his favour. He was her creditor, and he forgave her her debt. But it was different with Thomas. Against Thomas he had sinned, and he dared not face him—at least not now. Perhaps he might be able to do so in years to come. It was well that Thomas had gone by way of India; he need not fear to meet him.

Baldwin left San Francisco on the 1st of July, and, twenty-two days later, he arrived at Yokohama. Those three weeks of peaceful rest on the great Pacific Ocean had acted like a healing balm on his wounded heart. He was still incapable of cheerful thoughts, but the gnawing anxiety which had tormented him in Paris had disappeared. In Yokohama he was welcomed by some old acquaintances. They all asked him, as soon as they saw him, what ailed him, and what had turned his hair so grey. He replied that he had been ill, and then quickly changed the conversation. Here, again, he inquired after Graham. There had been no news from Hakodate for the last two months, he was told, and nobody could say whether Graham had gone to Hong-Kong or Shanghai. The steamer Osakka was to leave in a few days for Hakodate, and would bring back letters from the North.

The captain of the Osakka was willing to take Baldwin as a passenger, and he was thus able to continue his voyage after only a few days' delay at Yokohama. On the 3d of August he arrived at Hakodate.

While the steamer was steering about the harbour to find a suitable anchorage, a number of small boats filled with Chinese and European merchants came alongside to get the letters and news she had brought.

Baldwin soon recognised his own house-boat, carrying a young Englishman named Howell, who for some time had been in his employ as book-keeper. Baldwin went to meet him at the gangway. Howell started with surprise at seeing his chief so unexpectedly. He shook hands warmly, and then inquired immediately, with evident anxiety, whether Mr Baldwin had been ill, and if he were still unwell. Baldwin gave the same answer he had given to his friends at Yokohama, and then asked in his turn when Mr Graham had left for Europe.

"Mr Graham is in Hakodate, and you will see him in a quarter of an hour. A few weeks ago he received a letter from you, and determined to go to Europe; but just before the departure of the steamer he changed his mind. He has written to you twice since then; his letters must have crossed you on the sea, and have reached London about a month ago."

Howell went away to look after his employer's luggage, and this gave Baldwin time to collect his thoughts. The meeting with Graham was now unavoidable—there was no help for it. He could do nothing for the present but wait and see what course matters would take. With assumed composure he got into the boat, and in a few minutes he was landed on the quay. Many of the Japanese, among whom Baldwin had lived for several years, welcomed him back with true heartiness; but all those who knew him well enough to speak to him put the same question, "Have you been ill, Mr Baldwin?"

Graham was seated in his room reading. He jumped up with an exclamation of joyful surprise when the door opened, and Baldwin's well-known voice called out, "How do you do, Thomas?" But no sooner had he looked at his friend than he started back and said anxiously, "Some misfortune has befallen you, Baldwin! For God's sake, tell me what is the matter?"

Baldwin felt something rise in his throat which kept him speechless for a few seconds, then he said, "I have had a hard time of it, Graham; but we will speak about that presently. Tell me first how it is that you are here? I thought you were on your way to Europe, and I have come out here to fill your place."

But Graham could not take his eyes off Baldwin's face, which he scanned with the anxious tenderness of a mother looking at her sick child which has been brought home to her.

"Gordon, what is the matter?" he asked again, with an imploring voice. "I cannot rest till I know all."

He took Baldwin's right hand between his two hands, and looked at him steadily. There was the old confiding look of which Baldwin had been afraid!

"I have been obliged to part from my wife," he said at last, without raising his eyes.

"My poor friend!"

Then followed a long pause. Baldwin covered his face with his hands.

"My poor friend!" repeated Graham.

Suddenly Baldwin became conscious that in order to extricate himself he had inadvertently exposed his wife to suspicion. No! that must not be. His unfortunate deed had cost him all his happiness—he did not complain; blood will have blood—but his honour, his self-respect, must not be sacrificed. He would not, by an act of cowardice, throw the burden upon Jane and injure her fair name. He said, in a low inquiring tone—

"Graham, you are my friend?"

"Yes, indeed I am. I have no one in the wide world but you. You may confide to me all that weighs on your mind, and I will do all in my power to help you." He paused for a moment, and then added solemnly, "So help me God!"

Beneath the window of the room where the two friends were seated lay the broad harbour of Hakodate. Heavy junks with brown square sails, and numberless fishing-boats, glided gently on the white-crested waves of the dark-blue sea. Baldwin kept his eyes fixed on this grand picture; and, without looking once at his friend, in low passionless accents, he told his miserable story. He did not accuse Forbes—he did not even know that he had been guilty—neither did he try to exculpate himself. He had been angry and excited; he had, without knowing what he was doing, pushed away Forbes, who had stumbled and had fallen. . . . "I bent over him, and saw him dying; killed by my hand. I see him at this moment. . . ."

He stopped, and for the first time looked anxiously into his friend's face. Graham, pale as death, kept his eyes bent on the ground.

"Nobody but you knows what has happened," continued Baldwin; "I owed this confession to no one but to you. To you I have given up my secret and myself; you can do with me what you like, I am in your hands. If I am guilty, I am ready to bear any punishment that may be imposed on me; but if I am innocent, then acquit me and release me from the torments which I can bear no longer. See how wretched I am, Thomas! Have pity on me! I have suffered terribly."

There was a long pause.

"I have nobody in the world but you," said Thomas, at last.

In his eyes shone all the old confidence, the old love, and Baldwin could look into them without fear. Now—as with Jane, his debtor—his account was settled with Thomas, his creditor, who had forgiven him, likewise, his trespasses. He drew a long deep breath. Once more he was a free man.

. . . . . .

Jane lives alternately in the south of France and in Paris—a young, rich widow. She has become very pious. Her piety is of that frigid sort which causes those who practise it to be venerated by the public at large, and feared by their friends. Her house is kept with exemplary order. Her servants—though she never scolds them—tremble before her. No beggar ever approaches her doors, but the name of Mrs Gordon Baldwin figures with large sums on the lists of every public charity. Her beneficence is, however, as free from vanity as from compassion. She does not endow schools, hospitals, and asylums, to hear her name quoted and praised, but because she thinks it her duty to be charitable; and she can only fulfil this duty by placing large sums of money in the hands of professional philanthropists. She finds it impossible to take an interest in the sufferings of individuals. She can think only of her own sorrow; and to alleviate that, she gives to suffering humanity. She is not wicked; she has never done anything positively wrong—nor anything unselfishly good. She has never cared much for those about her. Nature has denied her that faculty. She certainly cannot be admired; she can hardly be blamed. Kind people—and there are some in this world—will pity her.

Thomas Lansdale has settled in New York. Hundreds among the poor bless his name. Whoever is in want and can appeal to him leaves his door comforted and relieved. The last misfortune which has befallen him—Baldwin's death—has made the kind, tender-hearted man more charitable than ever. He often gives to the undeserving, but he continues to do good, to the best of his knowledge. His simple heart knows no suspicion. It is better to be deceived by some and to help many, than to mistrust all and to stand alone.

Soon after his return to Hakodate, Gordon Baldwin died the death of a hero. While swimming to carry a rope, in order to save from certain death the crew of a foundering vessel, he was dashed against a rock and frightfully crushed. He lived about six hours—long enough to learn that the crew had been saved, and that his life had not been sacrificed in vain—long enough to know that Forbes's death had been expiated and atoned for. The members of the foreign community surrounded his house during the hours of his agony.—Thomas Lansdale closed his eyes. His loving, faithful look, of which Baldwin had once been afraid, was the last consolation of the dying man.

And so they are all provided for. Forbes and Baldwin are dead, and have found rest. Only two people, Jane and Thomas, think of them, and feel that with them is buried something that belonged to their own life and happiness, and that can never be replaced. Otherwise, it would be as though they had never been.—Thomas has never got over his grief for the loss of his friend; but he is not unhappy. He is deceived by some; honoured and loved by many. He continues to do good, and will continue till the end.—Jane lives retired, lonely and cold, high above all her surroundings, as on some frozen pinnacle amid eternal snows, and is in a fair way of earning the reputation of a saint.

WEARINESS:

A TALE FROM FRANCE.

MONSIEUR CASIMIR VINCENT, the old and very wealthy Lunel banker, had been for more than thirty years the regular and honoured frequenter of the Café de l'Esplanade. There he might be seen twice a-day without fail: in the afternoon about one o'clock, after his breakfast, to take his cup of coffee, glance over the newspapers, and exchange a few words with his old acquaintances; and again towards eight in the evening, after his dinner, to play his game of piquet, which generally lasted till about eleven.

Every one at Lunel knew M. Vincent. He was a small thin man, with marked features, large dark eyes, short thick hair that was turning grey, and a calm indifferent expression of countenance. M. Vincent was of a taciturn nature, and when he spoke it was slowly and thoughtfully. Notwithstanding his unmixed southern blood, he was sober in gesture, and nothing in his movements betrayed the proverbial vivacity of his countrymen. He dressed simply and very carefully, and paid particular attention to his linen, which was always of dazzling whiteness.

M. Vincent's story was as well known to the inhabitants of the town as his appearance or his mode of living. His grandfather, during the first Revolution, had been the founder of the house of Casimir Vincent. There were old men living who still remembered him, and spoke of him as a man who had possessed no common share of intelligence and energy. In a short time he had amassed a large fortune by his banking business, and also as an army contractor. His son had carried on the business under the Empire and the Restoration. In his turn, the Casimir Vincent of our story, who had been brought up in the paternal school, after having spent a few years in Bordeaux, Marseilles, and Paris, settled at Lunel in the year 1840. His steadiness inspired his father with such confidence that he at once admitted him to partnership. The firm was thenceforward styled "Casimir Vincent & Son."

Vincent junior was then about thirty. He was considered a *dandy*, and the young beaux of his little town copied his dress, and asked him for the addresses of his tradesmen.

The wealthy citizens who had marriageable daughters used to get up parties and picnics in his honour.

On two occasions there had been rumours of Monsieur Vincent's marriage. Soon after his return to Lunel he had paid his addresses to Mademoiselle Coulé, and his proposals had been joyfully received by her family. All the gossips of the place were already busy reckoning up the large fortune that the young couple would have, when bright, pretty, joyous Caroline Coulé suddenly fell ill, and almost immediately died. Casimir Vincent wore no mourning for his affianced bride, but her death grieved him deeply. For several years he remained in strict retirement, entirely occupied with his father's business. The old man died in 1844, leaving by his will "all he possessed to his only and well-beloved son Casimir Vincent."

Three years after this event, Vincent came forward as a suitor for the hand of Mdlle. Jeanne d'Arfeuille. He was then thirty-six, but looked much older; his hair was turning grey, and the lonely life he had led since Caroline's death had made him taciturn and gloomy. It was not, therefore, very surprising that a girl of eighteen should look upon him as an old man. Jeanne d'Arfeuille uttered a scream of affright when her mother, all radiant with joy, announced to her that the wealthy banker had done her the honour to make her an offer of marriage. She declared at once that she would rather die or shut herself up in a convent, than marry "that ugly, little, old man."

"He might be my father," added she, bursting into tears. "I shall never love him, and I won't marry him."

At first the mother tried her eloquence to convince her daughter that it was madness to refuse the best match of the department; but as Jeanne persisted in crying, and rejected all idea of yielding, Madame d'Arfeuille at last lost patience, and ended the debate by exclaiming, "I order you to marry him, and marry him you must."

Something, however, occurred on the occasion of M. Vincent's first official visit at Madame d'Arfeuille's that ruined all the plans which that lady had formed. Vincent noticed the red eyelids and downcast air of the girl he was to wed, and, leading her up to the window, spoke to her for a few minutes in whispered tones. Madame d'Arfeuille, who was seated at a little distance, saw with secret anxiety her daughter burst into tears, and heard M. Vincent, to her intense surprise, say in a gentle, serious voice—

"Calm yourself, my dear child—I only wish for your happiness; I was mistaken."

Then going up to the mother with his usual slow, steady step, he said, in a tone which imparted singular dignity to his small stature—

"I must thank you, Madame, for the honour which you have done me; and it is with sincere regret that I relinquish the hand of your daughter."

So saying, he bowed low to the mother and daughter and went away, leaving them both in amazement at what had happened.

Madame d'Arfeuille, as was her custom when she found herself in an awkward position, began by fainting; then, coming to herself, she got into a violent passion with Jeanne. When at last she recovered her composure, she hastened to the banker's, and vowed that there was in all this merely a deplorable misunderstanding, and that her daughter would be proud and happy to become Madame Vincent. But the little man had some peculiar notions of his own, especially on the subject of matrimony. He let Madame d'Arfeuille speak as long as she liked without interrupting her, though he caused her no little embarrassment by looking at her steadfastly all the time. When at last she came to a stop, after stammering out for the tenth time, "What a deplorable misunderstanding!" Vincent merely repeated the words he had uttered an hour before—

"I have to thank you, Madame, for the honour you intended me; and it is with sincere regret that I relinquish the hand of your daughter."

Madame d'Arfeuille could not believe her ears; for one moment she had a mind to faint again, but the icy deportment of the banker deterred her from that bit of acting. She displayed great cleverness in trying to alter M. Vincent's resolve; she even stooped to entreaty.

But it was of no avail; M. Vincent remained unmoved, and looked more gloomy than ever. Then Madame d'Arfeuille flew simply and frankly into a rage; she accused the banker of having caused the misery of a poor innocent girl, and of striving to bring shame on her mother. Vincent remained as insensible to her fury as he had been to her prayers; till at last, at the end of half an hour, thoroughly worn out and defeated, she retreated from the field where she had thought herself sure to achieve victory.

A few months later, pretty Jeanne d'Arfeuille married a young country gentleman of a neighbouring department, who was both well-born and wealthy. Her mother was delighted at a marriage which realised all her fondest wishes; but she retained a bitter resentment against the banker who had offended her, and never forgave him. Her southern imagination enabled her to fabricate, in respect of this affair, a whole story, which she repeated so often to her friends that she ended by believing it herself. According to this version, M. Vincent, whom she styled "a vulgar, forward *parvenu* and money-lender," had had the "audacity" to aspire to the hand of an Arfeuille. "Fortunately," she would add with magnificent dignity, "my daughter had been too well brought up not to know how to teach a fellow like that his proper place. Then he came to supplicate me to intercede with Jeanne on his behalf, and I really thought I would never be able to shake him off."

This strange story was repeated on all sides by Madame d'Arfeuille's family and friends, and came at last to M. Vincent's ears. He took no trouble to contradict it, and merely shrugged his shoulders. Some one, more curious than the rest, ventured to ask him point-blank whether there was any truth in it. He answered quietly, "You are at liberty to believe this story, if you like; as for me, I have something better to do than to trouble myself about gossip."

After Mdlle. d'Arfeuille's marriage, Vincent appeared to have given up all thoughts of seeking a wife. Some proposals were made to him, for there was no lack in Lunel of good and prudent mothers who would willingly have given their daughters to the rich banker. But he avoided rather than sought opportunities of associating with unmarried women. When his friends expressed their regret, he would say, "I am no longer young; I have nothing to offer to a young woman but my fortune, and I would not care for a wife who took me for that. If ever I become foolish enough to imagine that I may be loved for my own sake, you may perhaps see me come forward in the character of a suitor. In the meantime, I hold myself satisfied with the two failures I have experienced, and I mean to try and get accustomed to the life of an old bachelor."

Many years went by; Vincent became an old man, and it entered nobody's head to think of him as a marriageable man.

M. Vincent's mode of life was simple and unvaried. He rose very early, shaved and dressed at once, and started in his *cabriolet* for a small estate in the neighbourhood of the town, which he had inherited from his father. He was no agriculturist, and did not affect to be one: his visits to the *Mas de Vincent*—so his property was called—had no practical object; but he had taken so thoroughly the habit of this daily excursion, that, summer or winter, in rain or in sunshine, he never failed to make it. His coachman, old Guerre, who sat beside him in the *cabriolet*, was a morose man, who never opened his lips except to answer laconically his master's questions. Such a companion was no restraint on the banker, who could indulge in his own thoughts during the whole journey. These must have been of a serious kind, for the countenance of the old bachelor always preserved the same cold expression of reserve.

On arriving at the *Mas*, he would unbend a little. The manager of the estate came out to meet him, asked news of his health in a few words—always the same,—and then conducted him to the place where the work was going on. *Païre* Dufour[1] was a clever fellow, who knew how to interest his master by telling him something new every day. On this hillside the vines were prospering; on that other they were attacked by disease. The silk-worms were thriving, while those of the neighbours were merely vegetating. Sheep had been sold at Béziers; and it had been found necessary to purchase mules at the fair of Sommières. To all this Vincent listened attentively, and made no objections. As a rule, the *païre* did exactly what he liked; and all his equals and fellow-managers round about considered him the most

[1] In the south of France, *païre* is the name given to the foremost workman on a farm, and often to the manager himself.

independent and fortunate man of the whole district.

M. Vincent returned to Lunel about eleven o'clock. He went into his office, where an old clerk handed him the letters which had come by that day's post, and took his orders concerning the answers. It was not a long business, for the firm of Vincent & Son had been established on solid foundations, and all went on with perfect regularity. The business of the bank was chiefly with the wealthy landowners and farmers of the neighbourhood of Lunel, who, from father to son, had had dealings with the firm for the last half-century. They used the agency of the bank to discount the bills they drew on the manufacturers and merchants of Cette, Marseilles, Lyons, and St Etienne, in exchange for their oil, wines, or cocoons. These bills were always "duly honoured"; or if, by a very rare mischance, they were "protested," the drawers always took them back without difficulty. Legal proceedings and lawyers' strife were things unknown, or only known by name, to the firm of Vincent & Son. As the head of this respected house, M. Casimir Vincent had large profits and little trouble. In the space of one hour, between eleven and twelve, he generally found time to do all his business. He then breakfasted — almost always alone; and, after that simple repast, went to the Café de l'Esplanade.

That establishment was the rendezvous of the best Lunel society. It was situated on the promenade and occupied the ground-floor and first storey of a rather large house. Jacques Itier, the master of the *café*, lived on the second floor with his wife Mariette and his numerous family. Jacques Itier was a very sharp fellow. He had not been the proprietor of the *café* very long before he perceived that he could extend the custom of his establishment considerably by dividing it into two distinct portions. So he induced his more "eminent" customers to form a *cercle*, or club, by placing the whole first floor at their disposal. Admittance to the club was not absolutely forbidden to strangers; but a chance intruder would not be likely to remain there long, so unmistakably would the demeanour of the habitual guests show him that he was not in his proper place.

On the other hand, the wealthy citizens and merchants of the town, and the principal landowners of the environs, felt themselves quite at home at the "Cercle de l'Esplanade." Every one had his accustomed corner, chair, table, and newspaper. For smokers, there was a little grated closet, with lock and key, from whence every man could extract his own particular pipe on arriving; the billiard-players had their particular cues marked, and it was a settled and acknowledged thing that at certain hours the table belonged to a particular set. One would often hear exclamations like this: "Make haste! It is nine o'clock, and M. Vidal and M. Coulé are waiting to play their game." The waiter who attended on the first floor was called by his Christian name of "François"; and he did not confine himself to merely answering, "Yes, Monsieur," but would say, "Yes, M. Vidal; Yes, M. Vincent," &c., according as the notary, the banker, or any other personage called to him.

The members of the club were mostly middle-aged or old men, and three or four young men only had managed to obtain admittance. These were the sons of deceased members, and they did not seem out of place in this exclusive society. Among these young men, the foremost was René Sabatier, whose father had been a goldsmith. René was a good honest fellow of four-and-twenty, very talkative and very familiar, who used to treat the old gentlemen of the "club" as if they had been his comrades. Nobody took offence, for he was a general favourite. He owed this kind of popularity to his conduct during the war, when he had joined the army as a volunteer, and done his duty bravely. He was considered as the chief of the young Legitimist party in Lunel; and all the members of the "Cercle de l'Esplanade" were fierce Royalists.

On the ground-floor, where the real public *café* was, republicanism prevailed. The young men of the town met there, and strangers often dropped in. The two waiters who rushed from table to table were merely *garçons* for the customers, and no man cared to inquire what their Christian names were. Madame Itier, who presided at the bar, exercised the strictest control, in order to preserve the reputation of respectability enjoyed by her establishment: now such vigilance, if displayed on the first floor, would have been utterly purposeless.

Jacques Itier was to be seen alternately in

the upper and in the lower rooms. On the first floor, he went respectfully from table to table inquiring, in an obsequious tone, whether "the gentlemen" had all they required; the gentlemen, on their part, treated him somewhat haughtily and allowed of no familiarity. On the ground-floor it was the reverse, and there the master of the *café* was almost a personage. He was on the best terms with many of his customers: would play his game of piquet with one or another; order refreshments for his own consumption, and strip off his coat for a game of billiards. The political opinions of Jacques Itier took the colour of the place where he was. On the first floor he adored the Comte de Chambord; below, he swore by Gambetta. He was a man without political prejudices. The Bonapartists of Lunel congregated at another *café;* had they come to his establishment he would no doubt have found something pleasant to say about the Prince Imperial. Casimir Vincent had frequented and patronised the Café de l'Esplanade for many years. He was already considered as an old *habitué* when the establishment passed into Jacques Itier's hands. That was fifteen years ago; and since then, scarcely a day had gone by in which the little man had not been there both in the afternoon and in the evening. Vincent clung to his habits; his visits to the *café* were as much a part of his existence as his morning excursions to the *Mas de Vincent.* Every day he met the same faces at the club:—old Coulé, who had remained his friend ever since Caroline's death; M. Vidal, the notary, in whose office were the deeds of half the property in the town; René Sabatier, who was bold enough to apostrophise the banker as "*Papa Vincent*"; Bardou, the corn-merchant; Coste, the doctor; Count de Rochebrune and the Baron de Villaray, large landowners, &c. By all those Vincent was highly considered: he was known to be a rich man, a Legitimist, and the descendant of an old family of the town. All these things entitled him to honour.

Yet no one could boast of intimacy with the old bachelor. Vincent's habitual reserve kept curiosity at a distance, and he neither encouraged nor bestowed confidence. He never spoke of himself or his concerns, and wore on all occasions a serious countenance, with a tinge of sadness even. Some people asserted that he had never recovered the death of his fair Caroline, and that solitude weighed on his heart. They quoted expressions which he had let drop from time to time, in which he alluded to a monotonous life "without either sorrow or joy."

As soon as M. Vincent entered the club after breakfast, François, the waiter, hastened to bring him his *demi-tasse*, and a tumbler of water; while Itier presented the 'Gazette de France,' and the 'Messager du Midi.' Vincent would acknowledge these civilities silently by a nod, sip his coffee and slowly smoke a cigar. He would read the Parisian newspaper all through, cast a look on the quotations of the Bourse as given in the 'Messager,' and then take his seat on the divan which ran all round the billiard-room to hear the small news of the day from some obliging neighbour. He himself scarcely ever spoke. When his cigar was finished, he walked back slowly to his office, where he worked till five o'clock. Then, in obedience to a habit he had contracted during his travels, he dressed for dinner and took his solitary repast. Now and then he invited a few friends. On those occasions the old family plate shone on the table; and the best wines, the most delicate dishes, delighted the palates of the provincial epicures. But when Vincent dined alone, the fare was of the most simple description. An old woman waited on him; he read during his dinner, and scarcely noticed what was set before him.

After dinner, Vincent went to the *café*, as we have said, for the second time. In a few minutes he never failed to find a partner for a game of piquet. At the neighbouring tables the other members of the club played cards likewise. The play was not high, but was nevertheless carried on with the greatest ardour. Conversation went on in low tones,—such was the custom. Any stranger whom chance or curiosity led into the club-room soon felt awkward and intrusive amid this company of old men, all busy shuffling cards, marking points, or exchanging the whispered remarks which the course of the game called forth. The members of the "Cercle de l'Esplanade" were accounted first-rate players in all Lunel. At half-past ten the games had generally come to an end, and by eleven o'clock the great room was empty. Casimir Vincent would then go home.

When the weather was fine, he took two or

three turns on the Esplanade, and by half-past eleven was in his sitting-room. A large lamp with a shade burned on the table; the evening papers and the letters of the last delivery were laid out beside it. Vincent read for about half an hour, and then passed into his bedroom. In summer, before undressing, it was his custom to stand for a while at the window, from whence he could see a park which lay behind the house. The rustling murmur of the trees seemed to have a peculiar charm for him. He would stay listening to it attentively for a long time, though his countenance betrayed no emotion, and remained calm and serious as ever. But he would often heave a deep sigh as he turned away from the window. In the winter time he would spend that last half-hour in front of the fire, his eyes fixed on the dying embers, while his features preserved that same look of thoughtful contemplation with which he listened in summer to the last hushed sounds of nature. Advancing years had made Casimir Vincent a singularly thoughtful, serious, and taciturn man.

When the war with Germany broke out, M. Vincent shared the fever of patriotism which took possession of all France. From morning to night he read the papers; drew up plans for the campaign, and discussed the conditions which should be imposed on the vanquished enemy. He had recovered the enthusiasm of his youth, and took the liveliest interest in all the burning questions of the day.

The first defeats produced a sort of stupefaction, though they did not shake his confidence.

"We will take our revenge," he said; "and woe to the northern invaders who have dared to pollute the sacred soil of France!"

But after the disasters of Forbach and Reichshoffen, after the bloody battles of Mars-la-Tour and Gravelotte, came the fearful news of the catastrophe of Sedan; and then, one following another, resounded the terrible blows under which France was crushed by the fortune of war — Strasbourg, Metz, Paris, fell into the power of the enemy. Whole armies were annihilated or led into captivity; new armies were raised, and were overtaken by the same fate; the northern and eastern provinces of France were like a vast cemetery, drenched with the noblest blood of the country. In the south, in the neighbourhood of Lunel, there was fury or despair, and in some cases a still more harrowing feeling of resignation. Casimir Vincent went about his business with the air of a ghost, and his dumb, pent-up sorrow was pitiable to witness. Still, just as before the war, he never failed to go every morning to the *Mas*, and to show himself twice a-day at the club.

After peace had been concluded, everything resumed its accustomed aspect in the little town, which was far removed from the seat of military events. Vincent, who had sustained no loss of fortune or of position, appeared almost to have forgotten the misfortunes which had befallen his country. He scarcely ever spoke of the war, and never joined in the general clamour for revenge which arose on all sides. But he grew daily more gloomy, more sad, more taciturn, till his best friends admitted that "old Vincent had become quite impracticable."

Vincent, however, continued to follow the political questions of the day: he subscribed to some of the leadiug Paris newspapers, and spent the better part of the day in reading them.

In October 1873, when the news spread that the Comte de Chambord was going to ascend the throne of his ancestors, the old Legitimist had a last burst of enthusiasm.

"I would die happy," he said, "if it were given to me to see Henry V. at the head of the country."

The letter by which the Comte de Chambord annihilated the hopes of the so-called "fusionists" caused the banker a great shock.

"The king is right," he said; "he always is right: but what can be said of a country where the foremost citizens dare to propose to their legitimate sovereign to attain, by devious and crooked paths, the throne which God Himself gave him? Poor France!"

René Sabatier, who had always been a favourite with the banker, and who, in his turn, felt a real affection for him, became anxious at last, seeing him so completely dispirited. One night he accompanied him home, and took advantage of the opportunity to question his old friend on his sadness.

"You are not well; you seem tired. What is the matter? Why do you not consult the doctor?"

"The doctor can do nothing for me," replied Vincent. "I am bored, that's all."

"Travel; try a change."

"I am as well at Lunel as I should be anywhere else. Here, at least, I am surrounded by well-known faces, and I have my regular occupations, which make the days seem less insupportably long."

"Go to Paris. It is my dream to go there. Ah! if I were rich and free like you, I would start this very night."

"Paris! Thanks for the advice. No! anywhere rather than there! Paris is the ruin of France! Paris is the birthplace of the evils of which we are all dying! The Revolution, the Empire, the war, the Commune, all came from Paris! Paris has killed France! Curse it!"

"Softly, softly, *Papa* Vincent," replied Sabatier; "do not fly into such a passion. Whatever you may say, Paris is the finest town in the world. Paris has its vices, I admit; but its brilliant qualities make it the capital of civilisation."

"Pray, spare me your Victor Hugo phrases! Yes, Paris is verily the most civilised town in the world, if by civilisation you mean the reverse of all that is natural and true. Shall I tell you what you, a provincial stranger, will find in Paris? The first tailors and the first shoemakers in the world; the best hairdressers and fencing-masters; the greatest coquettes and the most profligate women; the most cheating hotel-keepers, the most selfish politicians, and the most wonderful actors. That is all that you, as a stranger, will see; as to the Paris of work and self-denial, it will be hidden from you. The honest folks of Paris—and, thank Heaven! there are some left—do not frequent the places where you go to seek excitement and see sights. Busy with their work, and ashamed of the enervating pleasures that strangers rush to so greedily, they know how to respect their mourning country. Their houses would be closed to you, nor would they be thrown open to me. No, no, I will not go to Paris. Lunel is a dull town, I confess; I am weary of the life I lead here; it weighs me down, and I long to have done with it: still, I prefer it to life in Paris."

He paused for a minute and bent his head as if he were absorbed in painful reflections, then he resumed slowly in a low voice, as though he were speaking to himself, "Ay, indeed, life in Lunel is dull and colourless, . . . life in Paris is repugnant to me. . . . Life is unbearable everywhere in France. . . . Formerly it was not so, and life then had an object; men lived, men died at least for something. But what can I do now? Fold my arms, and impotently witness the ruin of my country. . . . All is going, perishing, falling to pieces, . . . and I am but a weak old man."

A long silence followed, which Sabatier dared not break till the two friends reached the banker's door.

"Monsieur Vincent," Sabatier then said, in a respectful tone, "I wish you good-night; try and sleep well."

"Good-night, my dear René," said the old man. He was holding the door still ajar, when he suddenly turned round and said abruptly to the young man—

"How old are you?"

"I am four-and-twenty."

"Well, follow the advice of an old bachelor: marry. A life full of cares is better than a life which is utterly void. Woe to the man who is alone in the world! . . . Take a wife. . . . Man was not made to live alone. . . . Solitude begets unwholesome thoughts. . . . Good-night, Sabatier!"

The next day Vincent appeared at the usual hour at the *café* of the Esplanade, and in a few minutes he was seated opposite to Sabatier, apparently absorbed in the intricacies of a game of piquet.

"You have just thrown away ninety," remarked Sabatier.

"Have I?" said Vincent. He took up the cards he had discarded, looked at them, and said quietly, "You are right; here's my knave of clubs."

There was another deal.

"Why, what is the matter with you to-day?" cried Sabatier. "You have not reckoned your quint."

"You are right again, young man," said the banker; "I had forgotten it. I do not know what I am thinking of." So saying, he pushed away the cards.

"Go and play with Coulé," he added; "it amuses me no longer."

He got up and placed himself near another table, where two other men were playing. Old Vidal came up and proposed a game of bezique. Vincent assented willingly, and they seated themselves at a vacant table. Vincent won the game.

"Bezique is child's play," he said; "I prefer piquet." He got up and apologised for not going on. "I will give you your revenge to-morrow," he said. He remained half an hour longer in the club-room, going from one group to another, and exchanging a few brief sentences with his friends; but he went home somewhat earlier than usual. No sooner had he left the room than every one began to talk about him.

"Old Vincent looks very ill. What is the matter with him?"

"He did not know his cards, and threw out his best. I never saw him like that."

"How are his affairs? Are they all right?"

"That they are. He bought largely into the funds only last week."

"Then, what ails him?"

"Nothing—he is bored."

"Has he ever been anything else for the last thirty years?"

"No. But apparently he has found out at last that it is not amusing to be bored."

While remarks were being exchanged at the club, Vincent was walking slowly homewards. More than once he stopped on his way, and stood plunged in deep thought, stroking his chin the while as was his wont. Once he took off his hat, brushed his hair back with a slow and regular movement, and then pressed his hand on his temple as though he had felt a sharp and sudden pain. His cravat seemed to choke him; once or twice he passed his finger between his throat and his shirt-collar, and breathed hard like a man who has been making some violent effort.

On entering his apartment he found everything in its accustomed place; there was the lamp, and beside it the papers and a few letters. He glanced at these; and recognising the writing on the addresses, laid them aside without opening them. Even the papers had not the power to interest him; he opened one, and after looking through the leading article he crumpled it up in his hand and threw it on the ground.

"Always the same twaddle!" he exclaimed. The clock of a neighbouring church struck eleven. Vincent took up a candlestick and went into his bedroom. As he stood before the chimney his eyes fell on the large mirror. He remained motionless and gazed long at his own image; it was that of an old man, bent under the weight of years, with a yellow, shrivelled-up face, dim eyes, and a despondent countenance.

"I never would have believed," he said, speaking very slowly, "that a life as long as mine could have been so joyless. To eat, to drink, to sleep, to read letters and newspapers, to shuffle and deal out cards, to be of no use for anything or to anybody, . . . to care for nothing, to care for nobody, . . . and to be bored."

He walked up to the open window and looked out into the night—a soft balmy night of spring. Above were the cloudless, starry heavens—below, the old plane-trees seemed to slumber; a solemn silence reigned all around.

"What fearful silence!" he said; "a death-like silence, . . . without and within myself." He shuddered and closed the window.

The next morning he went as usual to the *Mas de Vincent.* The *païre* came out to meet him at the gate.

"A fine morning, Monsieur Vincent. I hope I see you well. See how everything is getting on; one could not wish for better. If Providence only sends us a little rain, and we have no frost or hail, this year's crop will be splendid."

"We have no reason to complain," replied Vincent; "the *Mas* has always made a capital return."

"Ah, you are a fortunate man, sir. All you touch seems to turn to gold. The *Mas* is worth double what it was in your father's time. One may indeed call you a fortunate man."

When, half an hour later, Vincent was driving back in his *cabriolet*, he more than once repeated to himself, "Yes, yes, I am a fortunate man." But his countenance was not that of a fortunate man.

He scarcely tasted his breakfast; at dinner, he ate little or nothing. His old servant, Martha, became anxious, and inquired if her master was ill.

"No, I am not ill, but I have no appetite. To-morrow I will be better."

At the club he refused to play. As on the preceding evening, he wandered from one table to the other, looking on and stroking his chin without saying a word.

"Why don't you play?" inquired Sabatier.

"I have played piquet thirty years long. Is it very surprising that I should be weary of the game?"

"Play bezique."

"Bezique is child's play."

"Whist, then?"

"I don't know whist."

"You will learn."

"I am too old."

"Oh, *Papa* Vincent, you are hard to please to-night."

"Very hard to please, verily. It is of course unconscionable to expect from life something more than the pleasure of playing cards for halfpenny points."

Sabatier did not reply, and at the end of an hour Vincent left the club without having exchanged another word.

When he reached his own door, he stood irresolute, and looked right and left as though he expected somebody. He whistled softly, and, as on the previous day, took off his hat to press his hand upon his forehead. At that moment a poor beggar-woman, with a child in her arms, went by.

"For God's sake, my good gentleman," she

said, in a supplicating tone, "give me something for this poor child!"

Vincent drew out his purse, and looked into it for an instant, as though he were searching for small coin. Finding none, he took a five-franc piece and gave it to the woman.

"Mercy!" she exclaimed, almost in a tone of fear. "How can I thank you, sir? May God preserve you and yours, and return to you in blessings what you have done for me!"

She moved on, and Vincent's eyes followed her. "Holloa! here, woman!" he called out, abruptly.

The beggar-woman looked round and hesitated. She feared to turn back lest the banker should have made a mistake and wish to take back his alms.

"Come back, I say," repeated Vincent. "No one wants to harm you; on the contrary. But make haste; I have no time to lose."

The poor woman came up.

"Here," said Vincent, "take all," and he poured the contents of his purse into her hand. The woman was struck dumb with surprise for a few seconds. When she recovered her speech, and began to stammer forth her thanks, Vincent had disappeared.

. . . . . .

Guerre, the coachman, had been waiting more than an hour. At last he grew impatient.

"Martha!" he cried, "is not Monsieur up? It is nearly eight."

The servant went to the kitchen door and glanced up at the bedroom windows. The curtains were still drawn.

"This is very strange," she said, "for Monsieur always gets up at six. I'll go up and see what has happened."

In a few minutes she came down again, scared, pale, and trembling.

"Guerre," she said, in a hoarse whisper, "come quick. Our master——" She could say no more, but the old coachman understood that some misfortune had happened. He came into the house and ran up-stairs as fast as his old legs would carry him. Martha followed. The two servants stopped at the entrance of the sitting-room, and Martha pointed silently to the bedroom door. Guerre went in with faltering steps.

The bright sunshine lighted up the room in

spite of the curtains and the blinds. On the table stood two candlesticks, in which the lights had burned down to the sockets. Between them, placed so as to catch the eye at once, Guerre saw a paper, on which a few lines were written; and in front of the hearth, lying in a pool of blood, the corpse of Casimir Vincent. Guerre picked up an open razor, smeared with blood, and placed it, with a shudder, on the table. He then took up the paper which he had noticed on entering the room, and read as follows :—

"Weary of life, I have sought death. My affairs are in good order. My will is in the hands of M. Vidal, the notary.

"CASIMIR VINCENT."

The funeral took place quietly the next day. All the members of the "Cercle de l'Esplanade" attended.

A portion of the banker's wealth went to distant relatives. René Sabatier, however, had a large legacy, and a still more considerable sum was bequeathed to the town of Lunel for the foundation of a charitable institution. The clergy offered no opposition to the burial of the suicide in consecrated ground; and René Sabatier, remembering the last remarks of his unhappy friend, caused a stone to be placed on his grave, with the following inscription :—

"A MAN, WEARY OF LIFE,
HAS SOUGHT REPOSE HERE:
PRAY FOR HIM!"

THE SEER:

A TALE.

I.

The fast train from London to Paris, *viâ* Folkestone and Boulogne, stops for a few minutes at Verton—an unimportant station where passengers are rarely set down or taken up. In general, the engine merely renews its supply of water, and the train proceeds on its way.

We were seven in the same carriage one fiercely hot day in July, and we had been grumbling, ever since we left Boulogne, at the parsimony of the company which, in order to avoid adding a carriage, had thus crowded us, when suddenly, at Verton, just as the train was moving off, the door of our carriage was hastily opened, and an eighth—and most unwelcome — fellow - traveller made his appearance.

I occupied a corner near the door by which he entered. On my right an Englishman was sleeping soundly; and in front of him was the only vacant seat. It was filled with rugs, umbrellas, and other articles which we had all thrown there. Next to this unoccupied place, and opposite to me, sat a young man of about twenty-five, as to whose nationality I had entertained some doubts, until he drew from his pocket a cigarette-case in solid silver, filled with Russian *papyros.* He selected one of these, squeezed it gently between his fingers, and lighted it by means of a long match attached to the case. He then inhaled the smoke with a deep breath, and afterwards exhaled it, with a peculiar look of enjoyment, through his fine and well-cut nostrils.

This young Russian, who wore a fashionable travelling suit, seemed out of health. His manners were those of a gentleman. He was very tall and thin, and, from the olive hue of his complexion, he might have been mistaken for a Spaniard or a Brazilian. The long, slender fingers of his well-shaped hand seemed endowed with strange flexibility, and were constantly stroking the long moustache which covered his upper lip. His small, regular, well-set teeth were of dazzling whiteness. His dark-brown hair was short and very thick; it grew low down upon the forehead and upon the back of the neck, covering the narrow, elongated cranium, as with a dark fur cap. The youthful mouth, with its full ruddy lips, betrayed a nervous temperament, a kind, weak, and irresolute nature, and served to render attractive a countenance which otherwise might have appeared uninteresting, and even, to a certain degree, repellent. But the most striking feature in the face of my *vis-à-vis* was his eyes, which were round, black, set wide apart, and of exceeding brightness. They were restless to an almost wearying degree—wandering from one subject to another, though from time to time they would be riveted on one or other of his fellow-travellers with curious pertinacity. I had, in my turn, been subjected to this strange examination, and had been disagreeably impressed by it. It was a suspicious, disquieting, inquisitorial look, and one felt strongly tempted to reply to it by a direct question: "Do you know me? Why do you look at me thus? What are you seeking to discover?"—This uncomfortable stare of the young Russian seemed the more strange from its being in complete contradiction with his otherwise polite and even courteous manners. It was a searching look, taking no account of those on whom it rested—a bold look, which I am tempted to compare to that of a police detective who, being in quest of a malefactor, is inclined to suspect that every newcomer is the man he wants.

The other end of the carriage was occupied by four Frenchmen who seemed to know each other, and who discussed the topics of the day.

All—with the exception of the Englishman, who continued to sleep imperturbably—glanced reproachfully at the intruder; but he seemed to take little heed of our ill-humour. "If you please," he said sharply, pointing to the heap of things which encumbered the vacant seat; upon which, each of us, with more or less good grace, hastened to select the articles which belonged to him, and stowed them away, either in the net or under the seat. One railway rug, however, remained—its owner, the Englishman, being fast asleep. The new-comer waited an instant; then he unceremoniously bundled it up and kicked it under the seat. I could not help wondering at the free-and-easy way in which he treated another man's property. The train started at once, and then I examined attentively our new fellow-traveller.

His appearance was coarse and repulsive—the appearance of a rough, low-lived man in his Sunday clothes. His linen was rumpled and soiled with perspiration; his clothes and boots were ill-made and covered with dust. His age may have been about thirty, and he showed every sign of great bodily strength. He was short and thick-set; bull-throated, with round, massive shoulders, thick red hands, swollen with the heat, and flat hard nails; muscular wrists, and short, clumsy legs. A man with straw-coloured hair, cut short and brushed forward on the temples, bushy whiskers, and no moustache; the sunburnt complexion of one who has led an outdoor life; a low forehead, a thick nose, a wide mouth, with thin tight lips, and a prominent jaw; bright, sharp, wicked eyes, which glanced stealthily and yet defiantly around. Such was the new-comer.

He was no sooner seated than he took a rapid survey of his fellow-travellers. It was apparently satisfactory, for he pulled out of his pocket a large coloured check handkerchief, and breathing loudly, he wiped the moisture from his brow. I then noticed that the first and second fingers of his right hand were bound up with fine cambric — apparently a woman's pocket-handkerchief. In the palm of the hand there was a large stain of clotted blood. Those two fingers had evidently received a wound. After a few minutes he loosened his long black neck-tie, and drew a deep breath, like one who has gone through some violent bodily exercise, and is about to seek repose. Throwing off his round black hat with a jerk, he stretched out his legs, placed his two hands on his thighs, and, with his head bent forward and his eyes staring straight before him, remained apparently plunged in deep thought.

The young Russian had not failed to bestow on the new arrival that scrutinising look with which, a short time before, he had examined me. This man seemed to interest him in a peculiar degree ; for, whereas a single glance had sufficed for me, he now turned round towards his left-hand neighbour, and looked at him with strange fixedness, as though he sought to engrave those vulgar and repulsive features on his memory.

The man who was the object of this persistent scrutiny was not aware of it for some time; he was too absorbed in his own reflections to notice what was going on around him. But suddenly, as the train slackened speed on nearing Abbeville, he raised his head to look out, and his eyes met those of the Russian. This latter seemed painfully embarrassed, while the new-comer, with an angry frown, and an inflamed countenance, turned upon him, and said roughly—

"Why are you looking at me? Do you know me? What do you want with me?"

I could not but consider these questions as quite justifiable; for I had been on the point, a short time before, of putting them to my opposite neighbour. The tone in which he replied, however, impressed me favourably.

"I beg your pardon," he said, in a gentle and deprecating voice. "Believe me, I had no intention of annoying you."

The man from Verton muttered something

between his teeth. He then got up, and with a scarcely audible "By your leave," leaned forward between the Russian and myself to look out towards the station we were rapidly approaching. After a moment he sat down again; but the train had scarcely stopped when he jumped out of the carriage, and, with his right hand thrust into the side-pocket of his coat, where he seemed to be holding something, he looked impatiently right and left. The platform was empty. Besides a few railway officials, there was only one gendarme, who walked slowly and unconcernedly along the train, looking into each carriage as he passed it. It chanced that he lingered a little in front of ours, and I then distinctly saw our fellow-traveller's hand take a tighter hold of the unseen article in his pocket. The gendarme passed on. When the train started again, the man got in; but he stood for some time between the Russian and myself, and only resumed his seat when we had left the station behind us, and were going at full speed.

The Russian had opened a book, and tried to assume the appearance of an unobservant reader; but his thoughts were not with his book—and now and again I saw him steal a glance at his neighbour. His countenance betrayed great perplexity, as though he were seeking the solution of some difficult problem. Once our eyes met. His look seemed to ask assistance from me, and to say, "Help me, if you can, to understand." I was beginning to feel rather puzzled at what was going on around me; so, at Amiens, finding myself near the Russian at the buffet, I asked him whether he thought he recognised the traveller from Verton, as he watched him so perseveringly.

"No, I do not know him," he answered politely, and in a tone which seemed to encourage further conversation; "but the man has something about him which attracts me."

"Well, really," I answered, smiling, "I was not prepared for that answer. For my part, I must confess that his face has no attractions for me. It strikes me as peculiarly repulsive. The man looks like an escaped convict."

"An ugly face, truly,—a repulsive face,—quite a strange face."

The Russian, as he spoke, shuddered nervously.

"Will you excuse my giving you a piece of advice?" I added.

"Pray do."

"Well, then, I think you would do wisely not to pay further attention to your neighbour. Without wishing it, you might get embroiled in a quarrel. He seems a rough customer, and, at any rate, is a very ill bred man. You must have noticed the rude, free-and-easy manner in which he thrust himself between you and me to look out of the carriage-window: he did it at Amiens, as well as at Abbeville. I felt angry, but held my tongue from prudence. With a man like that, I fancy, there would be little space between a word and a blow,—and the idea of coming to fisticuffs with him does not tempt me."

From Amiens to Creil we continued to converse. I found him a well-bred, agreeable companion, and we soon discovered that we had some acquaintances in common, both in Paris and in St Petersburg. He handed me his card, and, in my turn, I told him who I was. His name was Count Boris Stachowitch, and he lived in Paris, Avenue Friedland.

"How small the world is!" said my new friend. "Have you noticed that no man of a certain age, if he has seen something of the world, can ever meet any one with whom he is not connected by some anterior link? Half an hour ago you were a perfect stranger to me. The few words we have exchanged have shown me that one of my cousins is a friend of yours, and that I was at school with one of your relations. That does not surprise me; it is always so. I would wager that if I talked to your neighbour there who is snoring so sweetly, I would find out that he and I have something in common. Oh, what a little world it is! I have often wondered how anybody can manage to hide in it. I had, not long ago, a very interesting conversation on that very subject with one of the heads of the Secret Police. He was a man of wide experience, who could reckon by hundreds the thieves and murderers he had helped to capture. Among other things, he told me: 'Many crimes are never discovered at all, and those who have committed them of course elude justice; but scarcely one criminal out of a thousand, when once known, can long escape the grasp of the law. Sooner or later, whatever disguise he may have assumed, in whatever hole he may have taken refuge, we find him out. The trace of blood is never effaced. Once on the track we are pretty sure never to lose it. The world is——' "

Here our conversation was interrupted suddenly. Stachowitch had been speaking loud enough for every word of his to be overheard by his neighbour, the man from Verton. This latter got up hastily, and, as at Abbeville and at Amiens, pushed forward between us to look out. All at once, before we could offer any opposition, he opened the door rapidly and stepped down on the narrow ledge which runs along the carriages.

We looked at each other in mute surprise. The next instant the man had leaped out on the line. I leant forward and saw him rebound forwards, and then, with outstretched arms, fall flat upon his face. In a few seconds he was hidden from view by the wall of a garden which skirted the line.

The Russian had turned very pale. The four Frenchmen ceased their talking, and looked anxiously towards us. The Englishman was awake at last, and was looking for the railway rug the Verton man had thrust under the seat.

"What does it all mean?" said Stachowitch.

I could only shrug my shoulders, for I could

not make it out myself. We were soon to be enlightened.

We were drawing near to Paris and the train was beginning to slacken its speed. About a hundred yards from the terminus it came to a stand-still. Two railway officials, who had been waiting for us on either side of the line, jumped on to the train, and passing along the carriages, said in a loud voice, while the engine began to move on, "Keep your places, gentlemen, if you please."

A minute later we entered the station. The place was empty. Then from the superintendent's office there came out two gentlemen, followed by one of the higher officials of the railway—one of them wore the ribbon of the Legion of Honour. They walked quickly up to the train, and stopped for a few seconds before each carriage. At last they came to ours. The gentleman with the red ribbon looked in, and cast a scrutinising glance on each of us in turn.

"Has any one left this carriage since Verton station?" he asked.

He spoke to me as being the nearest to him; but one of the Frenchmen cut in before me, and related rapidly all he knew about the eighth traveller—namely, that he had joined us at Verton, and had jumped from the train before it reached St Denis. "This gentleman," he added, pointing to me, "can, no doubt, indicate the precise spot, for it was on his side that the man—a villanous-looking fellow—escaped."

The police agent—as we had rightly judged him to be—requested me then to describe the missing passenger. I was able to answer accurately, for I had examined the man closely.

While I spoke the agent nodded repeatedly, as in assent.

"No doubt," he said, when I had concluded my description, "that is the man. Please, sir, to follow me."

I gathered up my wraps and got down. Stachowitch followed. The railway guards shouted, "Paris," and while the platform was filling with passengers and porters, Stachowitch and I entered the office of the Special Commissary of Police. The order was given for an engine to be placed at our disposal, and a few minutes later I found myself seated in a luggage-van, in company with the police agent, his attendant—a vigorous and apparently agile man of about thirty—two gendarmes, and lastly, the young Russian, who had obtained leave to come with us, after he had related to the agent the altercation which had taken place between the Verton stranger and himself. I had already described the spot where the man had jumped out, and had added that I felt confident of being able to point it out exactly.

On the way I learned from the police agent that the Baronne de Massieux, who lived with her daughter on a property near Boulogne-sur-Mer, had been murdered on the previous night, and that her coachman, Bèchouard, was strongly suspected of being the author of the crime.

"The description of the man was telegraphed to us barely an hour ago," he added, "and we would have been in time to arrest him on the arrival of the train, if he had not thought fit to make off, before reaching Paris. But that won't avail him much. He can't be far, and we will soon overtake him. A murderer can no more be lost in the world, than a needle in a bundle of hay. All that's wanted, in either case, is patience to look for them."

Stachowitch nodded to me, as much as to say, "You see, I was right; the world is too small to hide in." But there was no time for further conversation. We had passed St Denis, and we were now moving on slowly, in order to give me time to point out the spot.

"I know that house again," I said; "and this is the garden wall. Here is the place; but see! the man is there still—he has not moved.—He is dead!"

We all got down. And there, just beyond the rails, flat on his face, lay the poor wretch we were seeking. His left arm was doubled beneath his chest, but the right arm was stretched out forwards, and was covered with earth. The cambric handkerchief had come undone in the violence of the fall, and from the reopened wound it had concealed a few drops of blood had trickled. The body lay motionless.

The police agent's assistant, who had been the first to jump out, sprang upon the prostrate form with the eagerness of a blood-hound on the track. He stooped down, and taking hold of a shoulder and a leg, with a dexterity which betrayed professional practice, he turned the body slowly over. Sure enough! the man was dead. The face was uninjured. At the corners of the mouth there was a slight foam of a reddish tint, and a few drops of blood which had gushed from the nostrils stood clotted on the upper lip. The wide-open eyes, of which only the whites were visible, were horrible to see. Stachowitch, who had leant over my shoulder to look at the corpse, uttered a loud cry, and fell senseless to the ground.

II.

The murder of the Baronne de Massieux was soon forgotten by the general public. The judicial inquiry had established that the crime had been committed by Béchouard alone: he had not long eluded punishment, and was dead. Human justice had obtained satisfaction: the case offered no particular interest, and people ceased to talk about it. Two persons only thought of it often,—Madame de Massieux's young daughter Marie, who mourned the loss of a beloved mother, and Boris Stachowitch, whose life appeared to have been deeply influenced by that tragic event.

It was December, and six months had gone by since I had made the young Russian's acquaintance on the railway. We saw a good deal of each other. We lived in the same part of the town, had many common intimates, dined at the same restaurant, and rarely spent a day without meeting. My new friend interested me. Stachowitch, on many subjects had original, and even wildly eccentric, ideas; but it was evident that with him there was no affectation either in speech or thought. I soon discovered many excellent qualities both of heart and mind in the young Russian; he was truthful, charitable, generous, and singularly gentle; he was eager for information, and, considering his age and position, had read and learned much. He was, in the true sense of the word, amiable. I should add, that I felt pity for him. Stachowitch, it was evident, was unhappy, but I found it impossible to discover the cause of his secret sorrow. He never complained, and when I ventured to question him discreetly, his answers were so evasive, and his embarrassment so evident, that, for fear of offending, I soon desisted from any inquiry as to the cause of his constant and gloomy preoccupation. His apartments were splendid; he had carriages and horses, and was reckless of expense: evidently it was no want of money that troubled him. Nor could his health give him cause for anxiety. True, he always seemed languid and depressed; but he enjoyed an excellent appetite: and during an excursion we had made together, I had had opportunities of ascertaining that he was not only an indefatigable walker and a bold rider, but also that he could indulge in the most violent bodily exercise without any apparent effort.

He was a capital fencer, and was known as such in all the fencing-schools of Paris. He was considered eccentric, but he was a general favourite, and people were disposed to be indulgent to his peculiarities. For instance, there were men belonging to the club with whom he positively declined to fence, without giving any reason for his refusal. It was certainly no fear of defeat or loss of reputation for dexterity which actuated him, for he bore being beaten with very good grace; and, moreover, some of those with whom he refused to measure himself were notoriously less expert than he was.

Apparently, in the choice of his adversaries he followed his caprice, for which he always offered some polite excuse, but no frank or sufficient reason.

I was present on one occasion when this peculiarity of his was shown in a very characteristic way.

"I say, Stachowitch," said the young Vicomte de Drieux to him one day, "take your foil; I want to try my strength with you."

"Excuse me, my good fellow," replied Stachowitch; "you know very well that I will not fence with you."

"But why not? Do be rational. You don't fear, I suppose, that I will run you through?"

"Not a bit; only I would rather not have you for an adversary."

Drieux placed himself in front of Stachowitch, and said with mock gravity—

"There must be an end of this, Count Stachowitch. I must know why you hold my doughty sword in such respect. I am resolved to fight you; and if you refuse me satisfaction here, in the fencing-school, I insist that you do me the honour of killing me on other ground."

"Pray, do not make those jokes, my dear Drieux. You do not know what pain you give me."

Drieux and I looked at each other in mute astonishment: Stachowitch had turned pale.

"What a queer fellow you are!" said Drieux,

laughingly; but noticing the gloomy expression of the Russian's countenance, he added, more seriously, "I value your friendship too much, Stachowitch, not to yield in this matter. So that is settled: I never will ask you again to fence with me. But on your part, pray satisfy my curiosity, and tell me what is your objection."

"Do not be angry," replied Stachowitch, "and believe me when I say this is not mere caprice. I have a presentiment that you would come to grief if you fought against me. Your hand, Drieux. We are friends, are we not?"

"To be sure we are. But that does not prevent your being the queerest and most incomprehensible of men."

Stachowitch, who seemed to have a strong liking for me, and was disposed to be confidential on most subjects, never referred again to this incident when we were alone. For some time past, it must be added, we had matters of greater importance to discuss. I had fathomed with no great difficulty the cause of the strong affection the young Russian had conceived for me; and I had easily found out why, in spite of the difference in our ages, I was, of all his friends, the one with whom he liked best to talk. The fact was that I was the only person with whom he could speak of Marie de Massieux.

His theory of the "smallness" of the world had received new and striking confirmation. Very soon after the death of Madame de Massieux he had learned that his sister, the Countess de Villiers, married to a Frenchman, had known the murdered lady; and, moreover, that his friend Drieux, whom he met daily at his club and elsewhere, was related to the Massieux. Since she had become an orphan, Marie de Massieux had lived with her aunt, Madame de Baudy, in the Faubourg St Honoré, in the very same house as Madame de Villiers.

Stachowitch was delighted when he made these discoveries; for several days he recurred to the subject continually, talking to me incessantly of the "small, small world."

"Just ride out daily for a fortnight," he said, "and you will know every horseman and horsewoman of Paris: only follow a course of concerts for a month, and you will know every amateur of music in the town. And you call that a great capital! About the size of a playhouse, my good fellow. Well, maybe a little larger, but not much. If you would only take the trouble, in a month you might know all who live in it; and when you did, you would find out that hardly ten in the whole number are complete strangers to you. One has written a book that you have read; another has said something that you have heard; this one you know from meeting him every day at the same hour on the boulevard; that other is in love with some woman you know. Indeed, you may notice that there is general and instinctive distrust felt of any one who has no link with something or somebody that is known. The world is very, very small, I tell you. One can discover nothing in it that was quite unknown before."

Stachowitch, who frequently went to see his sister, had one day met at her house Madame de Baudy and Marie de Massieux. He had been introduced, and Marie had from the first felt a painful interest in him, having heard that he was the last person to whom her mother's murderer had spoken.

"What induced you to notice that man so particularly?" she asked one day, when he had told her that he had been very near having a quarrel with Béchouard. "Had you any notion that he was a murderer?"

"I neither knew nor guessed anything about him, but his face was strange and horrible. Curiosity and fear attracted me towards him. He had upturned eyes—the eyes of a dead man, —white eyes. And Stachowitch shuddered as he spoke.

"White eyes!" repeated Marie with surprise. "What do you mean? I knew the man; he had wicked grey eyes—I think I see them now."

Stachowitch made no reply, and turned the conversation into another channel. In a few minutes Vicomte de Drieux was announced. He cast a not very friendly look towards the Russian, said a few words to his cousin, and then sat down near Madame de Baudy, at whose house for the last few months he had been in the habit of meeting Stachowitch almost daily. This latter, for whom time passed quickly whenever he could talk with Marie, became suddenly aware that he had paid an unconscionably long visit, and took his leave at once. From Madame de Baudy's he came straight to my house, and I had to listen for the hundredth time to the recital of the first chapters of his love for Marie. If I did not always lend a very attentive ear, at any rate I heard him with friendly sympathy. And thus it was that I became his dearest friend, from whom he was constantly seeking advice and encouragement.

"Take heart," I said, "all is going on well. You are timid,—that's all. You seem to expect that the girl is to declare her feelings of her own accord. It is asking too much. I cannot understand your hesitation. From what your sister has told you, you have reason to feel sure that Madame de Baudy does not object to your paying your addresses to her niece. Indeed, any looker-on can see as much as that. If she did, would she allow you to see Mademoiselle de Massieux every day, and talk to her as much as you please? The aunt is on your side. That of itself is a capital card in your hand. Your rival, Drieux, inspires me with no apprehension. He is a charming fellow, I admit; but he does not realise the ideal which the poetical heart of your beloved has doubtless formed for itself. I have noticed that she is always joking with M. de Drieux, and that, with him, she never launches into one of those grand philosophical subjects which, strangely and comically enough, form the favourite theme of conversation between true and virtuous lovers.

Drieux tells his pretty cousin many amusing stories, and I have no doubt that she finds time pass very pleasantly in his company. She learns from him what plays are being acted, who are the best dressed women in Paris, and the name of the favourite for the 'Grand Prix de Paris.' All this is very useful knowledge for a young lady who hopes to be at the head of a *salon* of her own before many winters have gone by; but it is the subject that interests her and not the teller. If her aunt would but allow her to read the 'Figaro,' she would find in it ample compensation for the loss of her cousin's conversation. Drieux succeeds in making Mademoiselle de Massieux laugh very often. That's an excellent sign for you, for a man who makes a young girl laugh is not a dangerous rival. He may be successful with older women, but never with a young girl. In very young people love does not manifest itself under a smiling aspect. Love in their case is a sentimental comedy, which must be played very seriously. For the more mature spectator, who has gone through it all, and who, alas! will never go through it again, there is something at once laughable and touching in such seriousness.

Well! you and Mademoiselle de Massieux are both quite perfect in your lover's parts. She tells you of her passion for flowers; she plays Chopin's music for you,—for Drieux she plays waltzes: and lastly, I have heard her describe to you with gentle melancholy her moonlight walks under the old trees of the park at Massieux. All this is as it should be, and the charming girl will, I have no doubt, be some day an excellent mistress of a well-ordered household. You, on your part, recommend good books to her; you read verses to her, and you lead her out on the balcony to make her admire the glorious constellations of the firmament—Orion, Cassiopeia, and Ursa Major. This is as innocent as it is instructive, and it serves to imbue her with profound admiration for your boundless knowledge. You teach her the elements of geology; she does not understand, but she listens with scrupulous attention. You explain to her the beauties of a Murillo, the deep and hidden meaning of Don Quixote; you are ready to initiate her into the music of Wagner or the philosophy of Kant. All this, as I said, is just as it ought to be. Go on, my young friend, you are in the right way. Take heart, and ask for the hand of Mademoiselle de Massieux: you will obtain it, I warrant you."

Poor fellow! He listened to these and similar speeches with every wish to believe what I said, but I could not induce him to follow my advice. Something he would not tell me weighed upon his heart, and prevented his putting an end to the doubts which tormented him.

One evening, after a long silence, Stachowitch asked me suddenly whether, in my opinion, a man who had not long to live was justified in marrying.

The question took me by surprise. I got up, and standing in front of him, examined him attentively. He had grown thin; he looked ill and weary, and there was an unusual brightness in his eyes, which wandered restlessly from one object to another.

"Stachowitch, you grieve me," I said in a fatherly tone. "Come now, man, look me full in the face."

His wild look gave place at once to a serene and friendly expression.

"You look like a kind and venerable grandfather," he said; "it does me good to look at you."

I could not help laughing. "You do me too much honour, and I do not ask as much as that. I am your senior by nearly fifteen years, it is true, but that is no reason for speaking of me as a grandfather. But never mind me; let us speak of yourself. What now? Do you fancy you are going to die? What does it all mean? This is really pushing eccentricity too far. Even your love affords no excuse. And pray, what will it please you to die of?—of heart-disease, or of consumption? Any other illness, I suppose, you would not think sufficiently poetical. What do you complain of?"

"I do not complain."

"Then why did you ask me that absurd question as to whether a man who was soon to die had a right to marry?"

"I am wretched. Nobody knows, nobody can suspect, how much I suffer."

He spoke with sorrowful resignation, staring fixedly at the fire which was burning in the grate. I saw tears gather slowly under his eyelids, and trickle silently down his wan cheeks. I laid my two hands on his shoulders, and this time I spoke seriously:

"You are a *malade imaginaire,* my dear

Stachowitch. Yours is not an exceptional case, and certainly not one that is considered incurable by the faculty. Promise me to see a doctor."

He shook his head.

"Do it to please me," I said.

"What good can a doctor do me?"

"More than you fancy; and I must insist upon your consulting one. You have reposed confidence in me, and I am your friend. This imposes duties upon me which I am ready to fulfil, and gives me privileges which I mean to exercise. To-morrow, at one, I will call for you, and take you to a doctor whose opinion you may trust. You must go with me, or tell me why you refuse to do so."

He turned to me and replied very gently, "I will go with you quite willingly. I am grateful for the interest you take in me; but, believe me, it is of no use. Do not be angry with me, and, above all, do not give me up. I am miserable."

The doctor's opinion was most satifactory. He pronounced my friend to be apparently in good health; heart, lungs, and all essential organs were in good working order. As to the nervous excitement to which I called his attention, he could not be brought to attach much importance to it, as he felt convinced that it would yield to the regimen which he prescribed. He dismissed us, saying to Stachowitch—

"You are constituted to live a hundred years, my dear sir. Above all, do not disquiet yourself about your health."

When we got out into the street, Stachowitch shrugged his shoulders despondingly.

"What?" said I; "are you not satisfied? What do you want? Do you wish to live to a hundred and fifty?"

"I knew beforehand," he replied, "that this visit would be of no use."

And indeed there was no amendment in his sad condition: on the contrary, his melancholy increased daily to a disquieting degree. I had almost made up my mind to return alone to the doctor's and ask for further directions, when an unforeseen occurrence changed the whole position of affairs.

III.

Winter was over, and we were in March. I had been obliged to accept many invitations, and, for the first time since I had made Stachowitch's acquaintance, some days had gone by without our meeting.

One night as I was going home, at about eleven, I chanced to pass before his door. Glancing up at his window and seeing a light, I went up and found him busy writing.

"I am very glad to see you," he said, coming forward to meet me. "I have a favour to ask of you."

He begged me to sit down, and took a chair himself in front of me. I noticed at once that he was labouring under great and painful excitement.

"What has happened?" I asked.

Stachowitch rose and walked up and down the room with a hurried step. Then stopping before me, he said abruptly—

"Do you think me a coward?"

"Decidedly not," I answered. "What do you mean?"

"I have been insulted—grievously insulted,—and I cannot fight the man."

"Hem! it's awkward.—There are men who will not fight from principle. It is a question of conscience—or of taste. There is no discussing it, but——"

"You are mistaken," said Stachowitch, quickly. "I have fought more than one duel in my life, and I may fight again. But it is Drieux who has insulted me——" He appeared to hesitate.

"Well," said I, to encourage him to proceed, "Drieux or another, what does it matter?"

"I cannot fight him."

"Why not?"

"I cannot; I must not." He spoke with great animation.

"My good fellow," I said, rising from my seat, "I am quite at your service; but on one condition: you must give up speaking in riddles, and you must tell me clearly what has occurred."

"Drieux has insulted me."

"You have told me that three times already."

"I am entitled to demand satisfaction."

"We will see about that when you have been good enough to give me all the particulars of this business. Drieux is a man of honour, and he will not refuse you satisfaction if you have a right to demand it."

"But I cannot fight him."

I was beginning to lose patience.

"I will come back to-morrow," I said. "I trust you will be sufficiently calm by that time, to be able to speak intelligibly. Good-night."

"Stop, I beseech you. Do not leave me! Help me!"

"So be it. I remain. Now be calm; give me a light. Thanks! And now, please, light your cigarette.—All right! Are you ready? Well, then, tell me now why you will not fight Drieux."

He looked fixedly at me, and his staring, wide-open eyes assumed an expression of unspeakable horror.

"Because I will not be his murderer," he said at last slowly, emphasising each word.

"You grow more and more mysterious."

"Because I am sure to kill him if we fight."

With an undisguised gesture of impatience, I answered somewhat crossly: "Enough of all this; we can talk about it later. Tell me what has taken place. Until I know, I do not see that my interference can be of any use."

The story Stachowitch told me at last was commonplace enough. The good feeling that had formerly existed between Drieux and himself had for some time past undergone a gradual change. The two young men had become jealous rivals, and had watched each other with distrust whenever they met at Madame de Baudy's. Drieux had proposed to Marie, and had been refused. Since then he had ceased to visit at his aunt's house. His pride had been nearly as much wounded as his affections. He felt sore and angry with every one, but more especially with Stachowitch. When they met, Drieux bowed stiffly, and with an aggrieved air. The Russian, feeling sure that he meant to pick a quarrel, avoided him as much as he could. In the afternoon of that very day they had met again at the fencing-school. There Drieux had asked Stachowitch abruptly whether he would do him the honour of a match with him.

"I refused," continued Stachowitch, "and I feel certain that I did so in the most courteous terms; but Drieux would not be put off, and it became evident that he had an object in view. He insisted in such an aggressive tone, that I might well have considered myself affronted, had I not been resolved to avoid a quarrel by every possible means. Some members of the club who witnessed the painful scene tried to interfere. They pointed out to Drieux how irrational this outburst of anger was ; they reminded him that they had all made up their minds long ago to put up with my apparent caprice in the choice of my adversaries,—that nobody took offence at it, and that Drieux, by acting differently, seemed to be reading them a lesson. Nothing could pacify him : on the contrary, raising his voice still more, he apostrophised me in such an offensive tone, that I was obliged at last to break through my self-imposed restraint, and to request him to explain or to retract his words. He merely laughed, saying that his words were intelligible enough to require no commentary; that he had no reason to retract them, and that it rested with me either to accept them or to demand satisfaction. That is how the matter stands. What do you advise ?"

I replied that the first thing was to try all means of conciliation. "I will see your opponent to-morrow morning. He may have got good advice from his pillow. I will try and make him understand that he is committing himself foolishly by his obstinacy in this matter.

Do not worry yourself unnecessarily. Happen what may, your honour is safe in my hands."

Early next morning I called on Drieux. He evidently expected my visit. At my very first words he stopped me, and giving me the names of two of his friends, begged that I would settle the matter with them. I tried in vain to obtain an explanation from him. He listened politely, and his behaviour was unobjectionable; but to all my remarks he merely replied, that his friends having kindly consented to conduct this business, it was no longer any concern of his, and that he felt quite satisfied that they would do what was right. I took leave of him without having made the slightest impression, and went to see his friends.

Drieux had taken care to select two very young men, who did not belong to our club, and who, being duly impressed with the importance of their functions as seconds, would probably have been disappointed if they had not had to play a part in an "affair of honour." With them, likewise, I was completely unsuccessful.

"But," they argued, "why should we hinder those two gentlemen from fighting if they wish it? A hostile meeting between them is unavoidable, unless your friend gives up demanding satisfaction. The Vicomte de Drieux has declared positively to us that he will make no apology. He has requested us to be his seconds, and we have accepted: nothing remains now but to settle the conditions of their meeting, if Count Stachowitch considers that any reparation is due to him. We admit his claim, and we are at your orders."

I made an appointment with these hot-brained young fellows, and returned to Stachowitch to give an account of my mission, and to inform him that all my attempts at conciliation had failed.

"I knew as much beforehand," he said; "but now my conscience will not reproach me. I have done all I could to avoid this unfortunate duel, and the blood that will be shed will be on the head of the aggressor."

Stachowitch spoke calmly, but in a tone of despondency which few men in his situation would have cared to exhibit.

"You take too tragical a view of the matter," I said. "A man has insulted you; you demand satisfaction, and he agrees to fight with you; this is no very unusual occurrence. You have right on your side, and temper too; that is the essential point."

The duel took place at daybreak the next morning, in the wood of Vincennes. I had felt some apprehension lest Stachowitch should not behave becomingly on the ground, for the day before he had given way to his intense anxiety, quite regardless of my presence. But when the morning came, and we were in the carriage together, he took care to reassure me.

"You seem to fear that I may betray weakness in presence of my adversary. Make yourself easy on that score: I know what I have to do, and will give you no cause to be ashamed of me."

And, indeed, he bore himself excellently. He was serious, dignified, and collected. When he had laid aside his coat and waistcoat, and loosened his neck-tie, and I saw him standing, sword in hand, in front of Drieux, I could not help admiring his noble presence, his supple and vigorous frame.

Drieux attacked him impetuously. At first Stachowitch seemed content to parry the furious thrusts of his adversary; but after a while he warmed to the work, and attacked in his turn.

More than once I fancied that I had seen the point of his sword graze the breast of his adversary, but he never touched him. All at once he lowered his weapon and stepped back. We ran towards him; he had been wounded rather seriously in his right arm. Further fighting was pronounced impossible. Drieux gloomily and slowly prepared to depart, while his seconds eagerly offered their assistance. I declined it with thanks, and they too, bowing low, retired.

I then turned to Stachowitch, whom I had left in the hands of the doctor. I was struck with the expression of his countenance, which was radiant with delight.

"Heaven be praised!" he cried. "It is well over. If you knew what a weight has been lifted from my heart!"

I was rather surprised at this overflowing joy on the part of a wounded man, and I rejoined—

"I would rather Drieux had got that wound, but as you seem so delighted with it, I have no business to complain."

When the doctor had dressed and bandaged the wound he left us, and Stachowitch and I drove back alone to the Avenue Friedland.

On the way the Russian could not restrain

the expression of his joy. At times he appeared absorbed in his own thoughts; but these must have been of a pleasant nature, for his face, which I had always seen so sad and anxious, was lighted up by a smile of intense satisfaction.

"I feel as if I had come out of a bad dream," he said. "Here am I awake, and I now know that all that troubled me was only a chimera. I, too, may hope to be happy. This very day I will go to Madame de Baudy's and make my offer. I feel confident that I will be accepted. I have been miserable so long. My turn to be happy has come at last. Yes, I will succeed. Good-bye! Congratulate me; I'm so happy!"

I could not understand this exultation; but as I did not wish to damp his joy, I took leave of Stachowitch at the door of his own apartment, well pleased at heart that this duel, which I had dreaded, had not had more serious consequences.

IV.

Stachowitch's proposal had been well received by Madame de Baudy and her niece, and my friend was the happiest of men. He was transformed. The unaccountable sadness of former days had given place to a joy so exuberant, that I had some trouble in getting accustomed to it.

After all, I could see nothing very extraordinary in what had happened to Stachowitch. Marie de Massieux was no doubt a charming girl, and to a certain point his satisfaction seemed natural enough: still, with a little clear-sightedness, he might have known beforehand that he would be accepted, and I could not comprehend why he was so strangely surprised at his own good fortune.

"I am the happiest of men," he kept repeating; to which I would reply, "I am delighted to hear it; but really, my good fellow, it is your own fault if you were not as happy as this three months ago."

Upon this, Stachowitch would look at me wistfully, as though he were deliberating with himself whether he would confide something to me or not. But he kept silent, and left his exceeding happiness as unexplained as his former sadness had been.

Drieux had left Paris immediately after the

duel, and I learned by chance that he was travelling in Greece.

"I wish him well, with all my heart," said Stachowitch, when I told him this. "I owe him all the happiness of my life."

"At your riddles again!" I exclaimed. "What possible connection can there be between Drieux and your happiness?"

Stachowitch smiled mysteriously, as if to say, "I alone know, but I am not mistaken."

This conversation ended as many others had ended before; and when Boris Stachowitch left me, I could not help wondering whether there was not something disordered in the state of his mind.

This doubt recurred with greater force some days later, under the following circumstances. One evening, towards ten o'clock, I went to see Stachowitch by appointment. We were to go together to spend the evening with the Countess de Villiers. The servant who opened the door, knowing how intimate I was with his master, let me go in alone. The drawing-room was empty. I crossed it noiselessly, thanks to the thick carpet which covered the floor, and I was on the point of entering the bedroom, when, on the very threshold, my steps were arrested by the strangest sight.

Two lighted candelabra stood on the chimney-piece, and were brilliantly reflected in a large mirror; and in front of that mirror stood Stachowitch, indulging in the most singular grimaces. First he looked at himself with that deep, searching gaze, which reminded me involuntarily of the way in which he had looked at the murderer Béchouard in the railway carriage; then he drew back a few paces, without taking his eyes off his own image in the glass—which naturally at that distance became less distinct. After a while he began to screw up his eyes, draw down the corners of his mouth, wrinkle up his brow, and, in short, try to impart to his face a wearied and dejected expression. When he had performed these tricks for a few seconds, he once more drew near to the mirror, and, to my intense astonishment, I saw him take up a crayon, and, like an actor about to play the part of an old man, trace with it wrinkles on his forehead and round his mouth.

I looked on in mute and painful surprise. Here was I, the unexpected witness of a dismal farce—of an act of madness! I retreated on tiptoe to the door of the drawing-room, and after waiting a minute to recover my composure, I opened the door, closed it again noisily, and from the entrance called out to Stachowitch.

"I will be with you in an instant," he answered, from the inner room, with no apparent emotion in his voice; "read the paper, to take patience."

He closed the door of the bedroom without showing himself, and, after leaving me alone for a few minutes, he appeared, with the smiling, cheerful countenance which he had worn ever since his duel with Drieux.

I was sorely tempted to question him about the strange scene of which I had been an involuntary spectator, but the fear of appearing obtrusive kept me silent.

We went out together. At the corner of Avenue Friedland and of the Faubourg St Honoré we took a cab.

"Here's a good number," I said, glancing at the little ticket which the coachman had given me,—"No. 1107."

"Why should that number be better than another?" inquired Stachowitch.

"Because it can be divided by nine."

Stachowitch looked at me interrogatively.

"I make it a rule," I said, "to read attentively the number of every cab I take, and every house I go to. If the sum total produced by adding up all the figures of which the number is composed can be divided by nine, I call it a good number, and I am pleased. If, on the contrary, the addition of the figures gives me thirteen as a result—as, for instance, in the case of No. 643—I feel uncomfortable. I like to go and see friends whose houses are luckily numbered; whereas I live in dread of quarrelling with people who live at Nos. 49, 67, &c. &c. Fortunately, there are not many such. Now, for example, I like your street, because there is no No. 13 in Avenue Friedland. The houses on the side of the odd numbers follow thus: No. 11, No. 11 *bis*, No. 15. The owner of that No. 11 *bis* is a wise man. I do not know him, but I cannot but respect him."

Stachowitch listened to me with deep attention.

"Seriously, do you believe in such things?" he asked.

As I scarcely knew whether he was in earnest

or only joking, I answered, gravely, "Of course I do."

"Then I suppose you have likewise a fear of Friday, and would not choose that day for setting out on a journey?"

"Oh! oh!" I replied, keeping up the same serious tone, "that would be sheer superstition. To take account of No. 9 and No. 13 is quite another thing. It is a habit one may cultivate and cherish till it develops into a full-blown mania. One may indulge in it, quite harmlessly, twenty times a-day; and, for my part, I find that it adds considerably to the enjoyment of life."

"Take care," exclaimed Stachowitch, sharply; "you are playing a dangerous game. Believe me, I speak as one who knows by sad experience."

"Are you speaking seriously?"

"Quite seriously."

"Then, my good fellow, let me tell you, no less seriously, that you are once more becoming incomprehensible. I would like to know what harm can accrue to me or to any one else from my preference for cab No. 999 over cab No. 13? Or why should I not, when selecting an apartment for friends or for myself, be attracted by No. 27 rather than by No. 85 ?"

"Every mania is dangerous. *Mania, Maniacus* are terrible words, my dear friend. Any one who leaves the path of reason is on his way to madness."

I did not care to continue the conversation, as the serious turn it had taken seemed to me, considering the subject, rather absurd. I therefore merely replied by an "Oh yes! of course; quite true, quite true!" knowing by experience that unconditional assent generally puts an end to all argument. Then we talked of other things. I must add that I felt disinclined to go on with the joke. The remembrance of the scene before the mirror, which I had just witnessed, made me feel uncomfortable when I heard Stachowitch speak of madness.

The painful impression produced by that scene wore away quickly enough. The behaviour of my young Russian friend during the days that followed was, as far as I could see, perfectly rational, and the remembrance of what I had seen was fast being effaced. I tried to think of it as a mere childish freak.

There are many men, and women too, for

whom their own image reflected in a mirror has strange and peculiar fascination. Not only do they find pleasure in looking at themselves constantly—a thing which seems scarcely explicable by any rational motive—but I have known, and still know, not a few who smile and make eyes at themselves, and who, for their sole and private satisfaction—for they are always ashamed when surprised in the act—assume in turn pensive, cheerful, sad, or angry airs. I persuaded myself that Stachowitch had indulged in this innocent foolery. It made him a little ridiculous in my eyes, but did not impair my friendship for him; and I did my best to forget his grimaces before the mirror.

His marriage was fixed for the 8th of June. The last days of May were come. Stachowitch dined almost every day at Madame de Baudy's, returning home about ten. I had formed the habit of going to him at that hour, and we used generally to wind up the evening—those pleasant evenings of the end of May—by sauntering down the Champs Elysées together.

One evening I called at his house at the accustomed hour, and was told that he was out, but that he requested me particularly to wait for him, as he had something important to communicate. I imagined that it was some commission relative to his marriage that he wanted me to execute for him; and having nothing better to do, I settled myself in an arm-chair, and began to read. The evening was beautiful. From the windows I could see the trees of the avenue, and I could hear the roll of the passing carriages. There was nothing in my surroundings likely to produce lugubrious or fantastic ideas.

Suddenly I started up with a cry of terror. Before me, pale as death, with wild and flashing eyes, stood the tall and spectre-like form of Stachowitch.

"Read that! read that!" he cried, in a hoarse voice, without giving me time to speak, and thrusting a crumpled newspaper before my eyes.

Instead of looking at the paper, I surveyed Stachowitch with surprise.

"What is the matter?" I inquired.

"Read, read!" he repeated. "You will see how right I was! Oh my terrible forebodings!"

I took the paper, and read the paragraph to which he pointed with an unsteady finger. It was a despatch of the *Agence Havas* in these words :—

"We learn from Athens that Vicomte de Drieux has been murdered by brigands during an excursion he had undertaken in the neighbourhood of this town. The identity of the victim has been established by the French Consul. M. de Drieux was stabbed in the heart with a dagger. The police are making active search to discover the authors of the crime."

"Poor fellow !" I said. "This is, indeed, sad news, and I am truly sorry."

"I knew, I knew that Drieux would die so !" exclaimed Stachowitch.

This exclamation struck me as strange. It occurred to me suddenly that Stachowitch had shown great reluctance to fight with Drieux because he felt sure that he would kill him. In spite of myself I felt a queer sensation of awe creep over me ; but I did my best to overcome it, saying to myself that, after all, it could only be a strange coincidence, and that my duty was to recall Stachowitch by argument to reality and sober reason, instead of following him in the fanciful theories and imaginings which seemed to have taken hold of him. I therefore urged him strongly to tell me what it was that troubled him.

His excitement was so great that he was thrown off his guard, and he could no longer maintain the reserve he had so long imposed upon himself. After a while he consented to give me an explanation, but even then his agitation did not subside. He walked up and down the room, speaking in a loud voice, and gesticulating vehemently. His speech was so disconnected, and touched on so many points in quick succession, that for some minutes I could scarcely understand what he was saying. Gradually, however, he became more intelligible, and when he had done speaking I was in full possession of his sad story.

I cannot transcribe it here as he told it; but, in substance, this is what has remained engraved on my memory.

V.

The story of my friend Count Boris Stachowitch was as follows: "One day I was seated near a beautiful girl at a large dinner-party. Her figure was faultless. I do not remember to have ever seen such lovely shoulders, or such a perfect hand and arm. Her large, blue, liquid eyes beamed with intelligence; her mouth was fresh and rosy. The line of the eyebrow was exquisite, and the long, thick eyelashes lent inexpressible charm to her enchanting countenance when she looked down. I was literally bewitched by such a combination of beauty; and, so long as the dinner lasted, I was exclusively occupied with my neighbour. She listened with flattering attention when I spoke to her: at times she smiled with good-humoured familiarity, as though we had been old friends; at others she assumed a grave and almost solemn expression, as if all I was saying were worthy of her most serious attention. From time to time she raised her eyes to heaven, and seemed absorbed in a gentle reverie; and then again she would cast them down, and veil them for a few seconds with the magnificent fringe of her eyelashes. The more I looked at her, the more beautiful she appeared to me.

"After dinner our hostess begged her to give us some music. She required no pressing, and executed some difficult pieces of music with the precision and taste of a master. Then she sang.

Her voice was powerful, and wonderfully cultivated. Never in my whole life had I met with so accomplished a being. She was at once surrounded and assailed with compliments, and to every one in turn she replied in a few words of graceful and becoming modesty. My eyes followed her wherever she went. Suddenly I saw her go with timid steps up to a middle-aged lady who had been seated in front of the piano, and whom nobody appeared to have noticed.

"The face of the lady was not quite new to me, and yet I tried in vain to recollect where I had seen it before. I examined her attentively. She was not ugly, and yet there was something in her appearance which was singularly repellent. It was a harsh, cold, and even cruel countenance. She was tall and thin, and wore a plain, dark-coloured dress. Her hands, which were encased in black shiny gloves, were singularly small. Her thin hair, black as jet, was dressed simply and unpretendingly. Her skin, of the colour of wax, was dried up like that of a mummy, and her eyes, which seemed to take heed of all that was passing around, were deep sunk in their sockets. Her lips were thin and colourless.

"'What an odious creature!' I said to myself. 'That woman must have a heart of stone.'

"Just then she raised her eyes to the ceiling.

"'Where have I seen that face before?' I asked myself again.

"Her eyelids drooped slowly, and closed as if in slumber. I felt more and more convinced that she was no stranger to me.

"'Do you know the lady to whom Mademoiselle Olga M. is speaking?' I inquired of an old family friend, who was also very intimate with our host.

"'She is Countess M., the mother of your neighbour at dinner.'

"'What! Can it be possible that so lovely a being has such a mother?'

"The old gentleman smiled.

"'I knew the Countess before her marriage,' he said. 'We used to call her "the fair Nathalie." She was incomparably handsomer than her daughter Olga; and moreover, so clever! so amusing! Every man who approached her was captivated. There was no resisting the witchery. I, too, was madly in love with her; and as to your father, Boris, he nearly died of love for "the fair Nathalie." Ah me! she was a girl who knew how to make the most of her charms. She talked, she laughed, she danced, she sang like a siren. But neither your father nor myself was what she wanted. Her choice had fallen on Count M., a very rich man; and of course she managed to make him marry her. In the course of five years she bore him three daughters, and by the sixth year she had killed him by her cold, cruel wickedness. Two of her daughters are married; the youngest, Olga, is still free. But if you will listen to good advice, my young friend, you will have nothing to do with that dangerous beauty. Olga reminds me of her mother at eighteen. The smile is the same, and she knows how to call up that same soft look her witch of a mother had. Just look at them both raise their eyes and drop them again in the same fashion; they have the same hands and feet, the same forehead and the same mouth. All that is angular and sharp in the Countess is rounded and soft in her daughter; that is the effect of time. Years will transform your fair Olga as they have transformed my fair Nathalie: thirty years hence the one will be the living image of what the other is now. *Experto crede Roberto.* Good-night, Boris.

Do not dream of Olga. Rather, if you needs must dream, let it be of that young girl you see yonder in the pink frock, who is seated quietly and shyly near her mamma, as smiling and as blooming as herself. Just look! she has taken hold of her mother's dress, as if she were afraid of losing her. Olga has no fear of that sort; she knows how to stand alone.'

"I withdrew into a corner of the room to think over what I had heard. I am gifted with good eyesight, and at the distance I was from Olga, I could distinguish every feature as plainly as if I had been at her side. Yes, it was true, she resembled her mother,—not at first sight, but only when you stripped her features of the charm of youth. What cold hard looks those eyes might dart! How forbidding that mouth appeared, when, in fancy, I extinguished the lovely smile that was playing round it! 'This, then, is what Olga will be thirty years hence,' I said to myself, as I looked at her mother. All at once, I felt afraid of the girl who had captivated me an hour before. I cannot say why, my thoughts suddenly reverted to my grandmother and an old great-aunt of mine, both of whom were alive at that time. There was an extraordinary likeness between the two sisters; and yet my father had often told me that his mother, in her youth, had been a beauty; while his aunt, on the contrary, had been a plain girl. A whole train of ideas rushed through my brain concerning the immutable stability of the typical lines in each individual, —lines that external accidents—youth, ease, misfortune, illness, or good health—may dissemble as under a veil for a given time, but which, towards the close of life, stripped of all accidental circumstance or artifice, reveal the original plan, so to speak, upon which the individual was constructed, 'That original structure,' I said, 'is the true man; all else is but a semblance.' Having come to that conclusion, I left my nook and mingled once more with the crowd. Chance brought me again near Olga. Her expressive look spoke a flattering welcome.

"'What a meditative air, Sir Philosopher!' she said. 'What can you be thinking of? Give me your arm and take me out of this furnace. I am suffocated here.'

"I led her into another room; we went up to a window, and, still leaning on my arm, she raised her beautiful eyes to the starry sky. There was an expression of gentle melancholy on her countenance. I could feel the regular beating of her heart, and a deep sigh upheaved her maiden bosom. . . . And I knew—with absolute certainty I knew—that her whole being was a lie: a lie, the dreamy eye; a lie, the smiling mouth and tender words; a lie, each throb of that stony heart! As she stood there, mute and motionless by my side, like a beautiful statue, I saw her, not as she *seemed* to be, but as she *would* be thirty years hence. I could perceive distinctly her real, her *typical* features. They were those of her mother, the woman with the wicked stern eyes and the cruel mouth. I let go her arm and drew away.

"'What is the matter?' she said with surprise. 'You are quite pale.'

"No commonplace excuse was at my command; I was under the spell of truth. 'You are horrible,' I faltered out. She burst into a merry laugh, supposing, doubtless, that some joke was intended; but without heeding her, I fled from the house.

"From that day a new life began for me.

My former light-heartedness was gone for ever. I could not help scrutinising every new face with peculiar attention. Young people especially interested me. Whenever I met them in company of their parents, I could not take my eyes off them until I had succeeded in metamorphosing their young and blooming faces, and had given them the weary, furrowed, care-worn, harsh, resigned, or desponding countenance—as the case might be—of their father or mother. The youthful complexion faded, so to speak, under my gaze; the skin seemed to wither, and either to pucker into wrinkles, or to distend itself in flabby folds over the blurred and bloated outline; the turned-up corners of a smiling mouth were drawn down; the liquid lustre of the eye was extinguished. My passionate desire to discover the real face of the future under the visage actually before me became a real mania. It often got me into trouble, for strangers have more than once asked me what I meant by my inquisitorial looks. I resolved a hundred times to conquer this unfortunate habit, but it soon overmastered my will. At theatres, in concert-rooms, I was constantly seeking problems to solve. I looked out for some unknown youthful face, and then, in fancy, I made it grow old. When this was effected, there was no stratagem to which I would not have recourse to get at the father and the mother of the individual I had studied. At first I was frequently obliged to recognise that I had been mistaken; the parents bore no resemblance to the image my fancy had conjured up. I would then seek the cause of my error, and, generally, I was successful in discovering it. At last I ascertained the true laws, the fixed rules in obedience to which each essential feature was to be transformed in the course of years, so as to return to its typical form; and soon I became proficient in the useless, unprofitable, and painful art to which I had devoted myself. One glance was sufficient for me to discover the future under the present visage.

"The period which I may term my apprenticeship did not last long, as I have said; but no sooner had I perfected myself in the art of observation, and acquired the certainty that I could unmistakably discover the typical face under its temporary disguise, than I was struck with the fact that some faces remained, so to speak, *refractory* under my process. It was in vain that I applied to them all the rules that I had drawn up in order to reduce them to their original type; I found it impossible to make them grow old.

"One of these refractory faces was that of my own brother; another was that of a friend of my sister's, a young girl whom I saw daily at home, and whom I secretly worshipped.

"'Why is it,' I would often ask myself, 'that I am unable to transform those two?' I would then bury my face in my hands and think it over and over again. When I did that, Alexis and Sophie used to appear to me, pale, with closed eyes, but still bearing the stamp of youth upon their features. Soon after I saw their two corpses looking just as they had appeared to my mind's eye. In an excursion on the lake, the boat in which they were together capsized, and both were drowned.

"The deep grief I felt at the loss of my brother and of the girl I loved, to which was added the painful certainty I had now acquired of my power to discern the signs of early death on any countenance, nearly drove me mad. I fell dangerously ill, and for many weeks my life was despaired of. In time I recovered from the malignant fever which had attacked me, but the horrible visions that had haunted me during two years remained.

"I retired to a family estate in Southern Russia, and for a whole year I lived in nearly absolute seclusion. My servants were old,—good and simple people whom I had carefully selected from among my father's peasants. No one else was allowed to approach me.

"One day the mortal *ennui* to which I was a prey begat the unfortunate idea of subjecting my own face to the process which I had been in the habit of applying to others. I discovered that it belonged to the refractory class; it was impossible to make it grow old. I saw myself, pale, with bright eyes and sunken cheeks, but still young—young as I had seen Alexis and Sophie. 'I shall die soon,' I said to myself, and the thought was almost a relief to me. Life had become a burden, and yet I was barely two-and-twenty! When winter came round for the second time, the oppressive solitude to which I had condemned myself became unbearable. I went to Moscow for a few days, and from thence proceeded to Paris. I thought I would try to enjoy the few days I had still to live. Moreover, I wished to see my sister, the Countess de Villiers, once more before I died.

"During my journey I resumed my experiments. It had become impossible for me to see a human face under any other form than that of the future—the *typical* form. I got used to it. I lived, as it were, in company of old people who wore the mask—transparent for me alone—of youth. I easily recognised the real person beneath the disguise. Some pleased me, and I sought to make friends of them; others appeared hideous, and I avoided them. People set me down as eccentric and queer—I let them talk.

"My illness—for that it was an illness I well knew—was soon to make great and fearful progress. I had proof of this, for the first time, during the journey to Paris.

"When the train in which I was had passed the Belgian frontier, and entered French territory, a railway *employé* got into our carriage to examine the tickets. He had a *refractory* face. I was looking with interest and pity at one who I knew was fated to die young, when I suddenly perceived a red line crossing his forehead like the trace of some fearful wound. I could not take my eyes off him as long as he remained near our carriage, and I watched him at every station when the train stopped. Wherever we passed he seemed to find friends, with whom he exchanged greetings. He never appeared in a hurry. He would quietly let the train start, and then, running after it, he would jump on the step of his carriage with an adroitness which denoted long habit, and so get in. At St Quentin he delayed too long. I was watching him out of the carriage-window. It was only by running as fast as he could that he managed to get up to the last carriage. I saw him leap on to the step; I saw his feet touch it; his hand sought a hold and found none; he staggered and fell. . . . I heard a cry which was soon drowned in the shriek of the engine. The guard had noticed the accident and stopped the train. Some of the officials jumped on the line, and ran towards the spot where their comrade lay. When they reappeared they were carrying a corpse. The poor fellow had fallen headforemost on the metals, and had fractured his skull. On the forehead there was a terrible wound.

"Could I still believe that all this was only the creation of a diseased brain? No. That was no longer possible, though my reason rebelled against the notion of admitting the supernatural as positive truth. Could it be chance that had shown me in imagination three living beings under the aspect that they were to wear in reality after death? No. Others might believe it—others might call my second-sight hallucination, and try to explain it by saying that my over-excited brain created images with such vague outlines, that I could fancy I had already seen certain things, which in reality I was perceiving for the first time. But I could not rest satisfied with such explanations. I was constrained to acknowledge, on the contrary, that —fearful and mysterious as it was—I possessed the baleful gift of recognising those who were fated to die young, and of even discerning in certain cases the peculiar marks foreshadowing their mode of death. Thus, I had seen Alexis and Sophie; thus, when he was seated beside me, I had seen the murderer Béchouard with upturned eyes—the eyes of a corpse; and in like manner again, whenever I looked at Drieux, I saw the mark on his heart of a mortal wound.

"After my duel with our poor friend, I felt new life return. I had been possessed by the idea that I would kill him if ever I encountered him, sword in hand. We had met, we had fought, and he it was who had wounded me. I blessed him for it. I persuaded myself that since I had been mistaken once, that was a proof that my second-sight was not infallible. Why should I not be mistaken a hundred times? Why not always? That fatal gift, which I had fancied mine, was not real; it was an offspring of my diseased imagination, — a fearful dream that time and experience were dispelling. Thus I argued, and felt relieved. I was eager for happiness; life once more seemed so attractive! I hoped to be able to enjoy it in peace. Yesterday, this morning — nay, a few hours ago, I hoped still. Now it is all over. . . . I know that Drieux has been murdered; that he died as I had foreseen; that I was not mistaken; that I cannot, alas! be mistaken. . . . And I know, with absolute certainty, that I too must die soon. I have nothing more to hope for in life. All is lost, irrevocably lost!"

. . . .

As he said these last words, Stachowitch sank back in his chair, and, burying his face in his hands, burst into tears. In vain I sought to quiet him. At last, finding all argument useless, I called in his servant. The old man began to talk to him gently in Russian, and at last prevailed upon him to go to bed. I ran to the doctor, who was an old acquaintance of mine. I had some difficulty in gaining admittance to him at that late hour, but at my urgent entreaty he at last consented to return with me to Stachowitch's bedside. This latter lay in a troubled sleep; the doctor discovered all the symptoms of a violent fever, and after prescribing some remedies to be applied immediately, left us, promising to return early the next morning.

I passed the greater part of the night at my friend's bedside. At daybreak, feeling myself overcome by sleep, and seeing, moreover, that Stachowitch was sleeping calmly, I went home, after charging the Russian servant not to leave the room.

It was rather late when I woke the next morning. I dressed hurriedly and hastened to Stachowitch's house. The porter stopped me at the foot of the stairs.

"There is nobody up-stairs," he said; "the Count and his servant left this morning at seven."

"What! Gone! Where are they gone?"

"I cannot say. The Count passed before my

loge without even looking at me; the servant, who carried a small portmanteau, said, 'We are going away for a few days.' That's all I know; not much, as you see; but then, if every lodger——"

I did not wait for more, but went at once to Stachowitch's sister. "Madame la Comtesse is not at home," I was told. There was nothing left for me to do, but to go on to Madame de Baudy's. I was admitted at once, and before I could utter a word, she asked me in an agitated voice, "Have you come to explain what this means?"

At the same time she handed me an open letter which contained only a few hurried lines:—

"I am obliged to forego the happiness of all my life. Do not accuse me; I am innocent. Pity me; I am unhappy. Comfort Marie.

"Boris Stachowitch."

What was the use of explanations? The only excuse I could offer for my poor friend was to confess that I thought him mad. That would have done him no good, nor would it have comforted Madame de Baudy or her niece. I did not care to cut off Stachowitch from all hope. Who could tell? Matters might be arranged perhaps. I merely said, therefore, that he had been seized with violent fever the day before, and had left Paris that same morning. I pointed out that his letter bore evident traces of great excitement, and that too much importance should not be attached to it. Finally, I entreated Madame de Baudy not to condemn her niece's future husband without hearing from him more fully. Having thus discharged my duty as a peace-maker, I took my leave, to avoid further questioning or useless recrimination.

Time passed, and I heard nothing more of Boris Stachowitch. I called several times on the Countess de Villiers, and was invariably informed that she was not at home. I came at last to the conclusion that it was painful to her to speak of her brother's illness, and I ceased my visits; but as I felt a deep interest in the young Russian, I wrote to the Countess to ask news of him. She answered at once, but her letter told me nothing new.

"My brother is ill," she wrote, "and by the advice of his physicians he has gone to reside on one of my father's estates in Southern Russia. He seems to be progressing, if not rapidly at any rate uninterruptedly, towards recovery. It will give me great pleasure to communicate again with you, as soon as I have better news to tell. I hope it may be soon."

Years have gone by since then. Madame de Villiers has not "given herself the pleasure" of communicating with me. Probably she had no good news to write, and thought it needless to communicate bad tidings. I do not know what has been the fate of poor Stachowitch. Had he recovered, he would have written to me. If he is still alive, we may meet again in this "small world" of ours. Perhaps he is dead, and another of his strange forebodings has thus been realised.

Marie de Massieux did not die of grief after the disappearance of her affianced husband. She consoled herself, on the contrary, very quickly—and in my opinion she was quite right. To make up one's mind to an irreparable loss is a proof of courage as well as of good sense, and in all ages the advice to do so has been embodied in words of wisdom. As a rule, and for the majority of human beings, life in this world is a delusion—a long catalogue of unkept promises. Fortunate are those who, having secured a certain amount of happiness and ease, are wise enough to enjoy it without fears for the future or regrets for the past. Marie de Massieux must be numbered among these favoured few. She is married to an honest country gentleman, and her household seems prosperous. I met her, not long ago, in the Champs Elysées, where she was walking with two pretty little children. She looked smiling, proud, and satisfied. It seemed as if nothing could ruffle her placid happiness, and that at eighty she would wear the same expression of goodness and serenity that she had now. Our eyes met, but I saw by her look that she did not recognise me. Devoted to her present duties, she lives forgetful of the past, careless of the future. Hers is true wisdom. I deemed it needless to recall the remembrance of a painful period, and I passed on without even bowing to her.

"FRED:"

A TALE FROM JAPAN.

FRED was a stray dog whose origin and whose name even were shrouded in mystery. In 1861 he had landed in Yokohama from an English tea-clipper, in the company of a melancholy traveller. Nobody, of course, took any notice of the dog at the time, and he, on his part, avoided all familiarity with strangers, having, apparently, eyes and ears only for his master, whom he followed everywhere.

This master, Mr Alexander Young, was a rather mysterious character. Nobody knew whence he came or whither he was bound. The captain of the Georgina had made his acquaintance in Java, and had given him a passage to Japan on very moderate terms. During the voyage, Alexander Young—or Sandy, as he was commonly called—spoke very little, but drank a good deal. The captain, who, when at sea, made it a rule never to take anything stronger than water, was not at all disinclined, when ashore, to indulge in an extra bottle or so. In consequence, he treated the weakness of his companion with compassionate fellow-feeling, and even felt, on that very account, a sort of sympathy for him, which showed itself in many little kindnesses. Sandy was very grateful; and in his sad, dreamy, blue eyes there was a tender and friendly expression whenever they rested on the rugged, weather-beaten features of the captain.

Fred was Sandy's constant companion, and the dog's nose was never many inches distant from his master's heels.

"Fred is a curious name for a dog," said the captain, one evening; "why did you call him so?"

Sandy was silent for fully a minute, and then answered slowly, "Because he was a present from my cousin Louisa."

The captain was much impressed by this unexpected explanation; but as he was himself accustomed to clothe his ideas in most enigmatical language, he made no doubt that Sandy's reply had some deep hidden meaning; and without indulging in indiscreet questions, he made many and fruitless efforts to solve the problem unaided. From that time Sandy rose in his esteem. Neither Sandy nor he ever recurred to the subject; but when, at a later period, the captain was asked why Mr Young's dog was called "Fred," he answered, authoritatively, "Because the dog was a present from his cousin Louisa."

Fred was a thorough-bred bull-terrier, snow-white, with one black round spot over his left eye. His fore-legs were bowed, his chest was broad and powerful, his head wide and flat as a frog's. His jaws were armed with a set of short, uneven, sharp teeth, which seemed strong enough to crunch a bar of iron. His eyes were set obliquely in his head, Chinese fashion; nevertheless there was an honest and trustworthy expression in them. One could see that Fred, though he was a dangerous was not a savage or a wicked beast.

Fred could smile in his grim way, if his master showed him a bone and said, "Smile!" But, as a rule, he was as grave and serious as

Young himself. He was no bully or street-fighter. Confident in his own strength, he looked with contempt on the small curs who barked and yelped at him. But if a large dog, a worthy adversary, attacked him, he fought with mute, merciless fury. He neither barked nor growled on such occasions, but the quick deep breathing under which his broad chest heaved, betrayed his inward fury. His green eyes shone like emeralds, and he fastened his fangs into his enemy with such mad violence that it was a matter of great difficulty to make him loose his hold.

During six months Sandy and Fred led a quiet life at Yokohama. Sandy was known, it is true, to consume in private an incredible amount of spirits; but in public, his behaviour was unexceptionable, and no one had ever seen him intoxicated. A few days after his arrival, he had bought one of the rough ugly little ponies of the country. Those who, for some reason or another, strayed from the beaten paths usually frequented by foreign residents at Yokohama, declared that they had met Young, the pony, and Fred in the most unlooked-for places. The lonely rider, the horse, and the dog appeared, they said, equally lost in deep reverie. Young smoked; the pony, with the reins hanging loose on its neck, walked with his head down, as though it were studying that road of which its master took no heed; while Fred followed close behind, with his dreamy half-closed eyes fixed on the horse's hoofs. Young never addressed anybody, but returned every salute politely, and, so to speak, gratefully. The Europeans at Yokohama wondered at their quiet fellow-exile; and the Japanese called him *kitchingay*—crazy.

Young rarely remained in town when the weather was fine. He would leave the settlement in the early morning with his two four-footed companions, and not return from his ride till dusk. But if it rained and blew hard, one might be sure to meet him on the *bund*—the street which leads from the European quarter to the harbour. On such occasions Sandy, with his hands behind his back, walked slowly up and down the broad road, with Fred at his heels as usual; though it was evident that the poor drenched animal did not share his master's enjoyment of bad weather. At intervals Sandy would stop in his walk and watch with apparent interest the boisterous sea and the vessels that were tossing on it. Whenever this happened, Fred immediately sat upon his haunches and fixed his blinking eyes on his master's countenance, as though he were trying to discover some indication that he was going to exchange the impassable street for the comfortable shelter of his lodgings. If Young stayed too long, Fred pushed him gently with his nose as if to wake him out of his day-dream. Sandy would then move on again; but he never went home till the storm had abated or night had set in. This strange aimless walking up and down gave him the appearance of a man who has missed his railway train, and who, at some strange uninteresting station, seeks to while away the time till the next departure.

Young must have brought some money with him to Yokohama, for he lived on for several weeks without seeking employment. At the end of that time, however, he advertised in the 'Japan Times' to the effect that he had set up in business as public accountant. In this capacity he soon got some employment. He was a steady, conscientious worker, rather slow at his work, and evidently not caring to earn more than was required for his wants. In this way he became acquainted with Mr James Webster, the head of an important American firm, who, after employing Young on several occasions, at last offered him an excellent situation as assistant bookkeeper in his house. This offer Sandy declined with thanks.

"I do not know how long I may remain out here," he said. "I expect letters from home which may oblige me to leave at once."

Those letters never came, and Sandy grew paler and sadder every day. One evening he went to call on James Webster. A visit from Sandy Young was such an unusual occurrence that Webster, who, as a rule, did not like to be disturbed, came forward to greet his visitor. But Sandy would not come in; he remained at the entrance, leaning against the open door. His speech and manner were calm and even careless; and Webster was consequently somewhat surprised to hear that he had come to take leave.

"Sit down, man," said Webster, "and take a soda-and-brandy and a cheroot."

"No, thank you," replied Young. "I leave

early to-morrow morning; and I have only just time to get my things ready."

"So you are really going away?" said Webster. "Well, I am sorry you would not stay with us. As it is, I can only wish you good luck and a prosperous voyage."

He held out his hand, which Young pressed so warmly that Webster looked at him with some surprise; and as he looked, it seemed to him that there was moisture in Sandy Young's eyes.

"Why won't you stay?" continued Webster, who felt a curious interest in the sad, quiet man. "The place I offered you the other day is still there."

Young remained silent for a few moments. Then he shook his head, and said gently, "No, thanks. You are very kind, but I had better go. . . . What should I do here? Japan is a fine country; but it is so very small—always the same blue sea, the same white Fusyyama, and the same people riding the same horses and followed by the same dogs. I am tired of it all. . . . You must admit, Mr Webster, that life is not highly amusing out here."

There was a short pause, after which Sandy

resumed, but speaking more slowly and in still lower tones, "I think there must be a typhoon in the air; I feel so weary. . . . I do not think, Mr Webster, that you can ever have felt as tired as I do. I thought we were going to have a storm this morning. It would perhaps have done me good. This has been a very close, heavy day. . . . Well, good-night. I did not like to leave Yokohama without bidding you good-bye, and thanking you for all your friendliness."

He moved away with hesitating steps; and when he had gone a few paces he turned round and waved his hand to Webster, who was following him with his eye.

"I thank you again, Mr Webster," he repeated with almost pathetic earnestness. "I wish you a *very* good-night." And so he disappeared into the darkness.

That night a terrific storm burst over Yokohama, but it came too late to revive poor weary Sandy. He was found dead in his bedroom the next morning, having hanged himself during the night. On the table lay a large sheet of paper with the following words, written in a bold hand, "Please take care of Fred."

Nothing was found in Sandy's trunk but some shabby clothes and a bundle of old letters which had evidently been read over and over again. They were without envelopes, dated from Limerick, 1855 and 1856, and merely signed "Louisa." They were examined carefully in the hope that they might furnish some clue to Sandy's parentage and connections; but they were love-letters—mere love-letters—and contained nothing that could interest any one but poor Sandy himself. There was frequent mention of a father and a mother in these letters, and it was clear that they had not been favourable to the lovers; but who this father and mother were did not appear. Other persons were mentioned, as "Charles," "Edward," "Mary," and "Florence," but their Christian names only were given. In the last letters of October, November, and December 1856, there was constant reference to a certain Fredrick Millner, a friend of Sandy's, whom he had, apparently, introduced to his cousin and lady-love. In the first of these letters, Louisa wrote that her mother was much pleased with Mr Millner, who was a most agreeable and charming companion. In course of time, Mr Millner became "Frederick Millner," then "Fred Millner,"

"F. M.," and at last he was simply "Fred." Fred had accompanied Louisa and her mother to Dublin, where they had all been much amused. Fred was a capital rider, and at the last meet he had taken the big stone wall behind Hrachan Park, in a style which had excited the admiration of all present. Fred accompanied Louisa frequently on horseback, and she had never had such capital riding-lessons as from him: he understood horses better than anybody, and that ill-tempered "Blackbird" that Sandy had never dared to ride, was as gentle as a lamb with Fred. At the last athletic sports, got up by the officers of the 19th, Fred had thrown the hammer farther than anybody; and would certainly have won the foot hurdle-race likewise, if he had not fallen at the last hurdle. Fred had a beautiful voice; Fred danced well;—Fred here, Fred there, Fred everywhere. In the last letter it was said how "poor daring Fred had fallen with 'Blackbird' at the last steeple-chase and had broken his collar-bone. Yet he did not give up the race, and came in third! Mother has insisted on his remaining here to be nursed by us till he gets well. He sends his best love, and will write as soon as he is able."

These letters were sealed up and deposited in the archives of the British consulate at Yokohama. Inquiry was made officially at Limerick whether a Mr Alexander Young and a Mr Frederick Millner had been known there in 1855 and 1856. In due course of time the reply came, but brought no satisfactory answer to the questions. Alexander Young was quite unknown. A young man, called Frederick Millner, had lived at Limerick at the date mentioned. After bringing shame and sorrow to the daughter of an honoured family, he had left the town in secret and had never been heard of since.

As Alexander Young left no property of any value, no further inquiries were made, and he was soon forgotten. He was buried very quietly; and James Webster, the constable of the English consulate, and Fred, alone accompanied him to the grave.

After the funeral the dog returned to Yokohama. For several days he searched anxiously for his master in his old lodgings and near the new-made grave; but he soon became convinced of the fruitlessness of his endeavours, and thenceforward he became, as a Californian called him, "an institution of Yokohama."

Saudy's last wish, "Please take care of Fred," was faithfully attended to. Many of the residents of Yokohama showed themselves ready to adopt the dog; but Fred did not seem inclined to acknowledge a new master, and testified little gratitude for the caresses bestowed on him. He visited first one and then another of his numerous patrons, and did not object to accompany any of them in turn during a walk or a ride; but no one could boast that Fred was *his* dog. His favourite resort was the club, where, in the evening, all his friends met, and where he usually remained till the last guest left. Then he took up his quarters for the night with one or other of his friends; and hospitality was readily extended to him, for he was both watchful and well-behaved.

A year had thus gone by, when the Georgina once more arrived in Yokohama harbour. The captain walking on the *bund* one day, recognised his former passenger Fred, and called to the dog. Fred snuffed at him deliberately, drooped his head, and appeared for a few moments to meditate profoundly. But suddenly he showed the wildest delight, leaped up at the captain and licked his hands, barking and smiling; then started down the street at full speed, and at last returned to take his old place at the heels of his new master. The captain, we have said, was a philosopher: he accepted the adoption as a decree of fate to which he bowed submissively.

One evening, not long after this, the captain was attacked by a party of drunken Japanese officers. Fred sprang at the throat of one of the assailants and would have strangled him, if another of the Japanese had not cut him down with a stroke of his sword. The captain escaped with a slight wound and took refuge in the club, from whence he sallied forth with a party of friends to give chase to his foes and try to save his dog. But his brave friend and defender was dead. He was buried in the yard of the club-house of Yokohama, where a stone, with the inscription, "Fred, 1863," still marks the place where poor Sandy's faithful companion lies.

THE END.

PRINTED BY WILLIAM BLACKWOOD AND SONS.

CATALOGUE

OF

MESSRS BLACKWOOD & SONS'

PUBLICATIONS.

CATALOGUE

OF

MESSRS BLACKWOOD & SONS'

PUBLICATIONS.

ALISON. History of Europe. By Sir ARCHIBALD ALISON, Bart., D.C.L.

1. From the Commencement of the French Revolution to the Battle of Waterloo.
   LIBRARY EDITION, 14 vols., with Portraits. Demy 8vo, £10, 10s.
   ANOTHER EDITION, in 20 vols. crown 8vo, £6.
   PEOPLE'S EDITION, 13 vols. crown 8vo, £2, 11s.
2. Continuation to the Accession of Louis Napoleon.
   LIBRARY EDITION, 8 vols. 8vo, £6, 7s. 6d.
   PEOPLE'S EDITION, 8 vols. crown 8vo, 34s.
3. Epitome of Alison's History of Europe. Twenty-ninth Thousand, 7s. 6d.
4. Atlas to Alison's History of Europe. By A. Keith Johnston.
   LIBRARY EDITION, demy 4to, £3, 3s.
   PEOPLE'S EDITION, 31s. 6d.

—— Some Account of my Life and Writings: an Autobiography of the late Sir Archibald Alison, Bart., D.C.L. Edited by his Daughter-in-law, LADY ALISON. New and Cheaper Edition, with Portrait engraved on Steel. *[In the Press.*

—— Life of John Duke of Marlborough. With some Account of his Contemporaries, and of the War of the Succession. Third Edition, 2 vols. 8vo. Portraits and Maps, 30s.

—— Essays: Historical, Political, and Miscellaneous. 3 vols. demy 8vo, 45s.

—— Lives of Lord Castlereagh and Sir Charles Stewart, Second and Third Marquesses of Londonderry. From the Original Papers of the Family. 3 vols. 8vo, £2, 2s.

ALIRABI; or, The Banks and Bankers of the Nile. By a HADJI OF HYDE PARK. Crown 8vo, 7s. 6d.

ADAMS. Great Campaigns. A Succinct Account of the Principal Military Operations which have taken place in Europe from 1796 to 1870. By Major C. ADAMS, Professor of Military History at the Staff College. Edited by Captain C. COOPER KING, R.M. Artillery, Instructor of Tactics, Royal Military College. 8vo, with Maps. 16s.

AIRD. Poetical Works of Thomas Aird. Fifth Edition, with Memoir of the Author by the Rev. JARDINE WALLACE, and Portrait. Crown 8vo, 7s. 6d.

ALFORD. The Romance of Coombehurst. By E. M. ALFORD. Author of 'Honor,' 'Netherton-on-Sea,' 'The Fair Maid of Taunton,' &c In 2 vols., post 8vo. *[In the Press.*

ALLARDYCE. The City of Sunshine. By ALEXANDER ALLARDYCE. Three vols. post 8vo, £1, 5s. 6d.

ALLARDYCE. Memoir of the Honourable George Keith Elphinstone, K.B., Viscount Keith of Stonehaven Marischal, Admiral of the Red. One vol. 8vo, with Portrait, Illustrations, and Maps. 21s.

ANCIENT CLASSICS FOR ENGLISH READERS. Edited by Rev. W. LUCAS COLLINS, M.A. Complete in 28 vols., cloth, 2s. 6d. each; or in 14 vols., tastefully bound, with calf or vellum back, £3, 10s.

Contents of the Series.

HOMER: THE ILIAD. By the Editor.
HOMER: THE ODYSSEY. By the Editor.
HERODOTUS. By George C. Swayne, M.A.
XENOPHON. By Sir Alexander Grant, Bart., LL.D.
EURIPIDES. By W. B. Donne
ARISTOPHANES. By the Editor.
PLATO. By Clifton W. Collins, M.A.
LUCIAN. By the Editor.
ÆSCHYLUS. By the Right Rev. the Bishop of Colombo.
SOPHOCLES. By Clifton W. Collins, M.A.
HESIOD AND THEOGNIS. By the Rev. J. Davies, M.A.
GREEK ANTHOLOGY. By Lord Neaves.
VIRGIL. By the Editor.
HORACE. By Sir Theodore Martin, K.C.B.
JUVENAL. By Edward Walford, M.A.
PLAUTUS AND TERENCE. By the Editor.
THE COMMENTARIES OF CÆSAR. By Anthony Trollope.
TACITUS. By W. B. Donne.
CICERO. By the Editor.
PLINY'S LETTERS. By the Rev. Alfred Church, M.A., and the Rev. W. J. Brodribb, M.A.
LIVY. By the Editor.
OVID. By the Rev. A. Church, M.A.
CATULLUS, TIBULLUS, AND PROPERTIUS. By the Rev. Jas. Davies, M.A.
DEMOSTHENES. By the Rev. W. J. Brodribb, M.A.
ARISTOTLE. By Sir Alexander Grant, Bart., LL.D.
THUCYDIDES. By the Editor.
LUCRETIUS. By W. H. Mallock, M.A.
PINDAR. By the Rev. F. D. Morice, M.A.

AYLWARD. The Transvaal of To-day: War, Witchcraft, Sports, and Spoils in South Africa. By ALFRED AYLWARD, Commandant, Transvaal Republic; Captain (late) Lydenberg Volunteer Corps. Second Edition. Crown 8vo, with a Map, 6s.

AYTOUN. Lays of the Scottish Cavaliers, and other Poems. By W. EDMONDSTOUNE AYTOUN, D.C.L., Professor of Rhetoric and Belles-Lettres in the University of Edinburgh. Twenty-eighth Edition. Fcap. 8vo, 7s. 6d.

—— An Illustrated Edition of the Lays of the Scottish Cavaliers. From designs by Sir NOEL PATON. Small 4to, 21s., in gilt cloth.

—— Bothwell: a Poem. Third Edition. Fcap., 7s. 6d.

—— Firmilian; or, The Student of Badajoz. A Spasmodic Tragedy. Fcap., 5s.

—— Poems and Ballads of Goethe. Translated by Professor AYTOUN and Sir THEODORE MARTIN, K.C.B. Third Edition. Fcap., 6s.

—— Bon Gaultier's Book of Ballads. By the SAME. Thirteenth Edition. With Illustrations by Doyle, Leech, and Crowquill. Post 8vo, gilt edges, 8s. 6d.

—— The Ballads of Scotland. Edited by Professor AYTOUN. Fourth Edition. 2 vols. fcap. 8vo, 12s.

—— Memoir of William E. Aytoun, D.C.L. By Sir THEODORE MARTIN, K.C.B. With Portrait. Post 8vo, 12s.

BACH. On Musical Education and Vocal Culture. By ALBERTO B. BACH. Third Edition, Revised and greatly Enlarged. 8vo, 7s. 6d.

BAGOT. The Art of Poetry of Horace. Free and Explanatory Translations in Prose and Verse. By the Very Rev. DANIEL BAGOT, D.D. Third Edition, Revised, printed on *papier vergé*, square 8vo, 5s.

BATTLE OF DORKING. Reminiscences of a Volunteer. From 'Blackwood's Magazine.' Second Hundredth Thousand. 6d.

BY THE SAME AUTHOR.

The Dilemma. Cheap Edition. Crown 8vo, 6s.

BEDFORD. The Regulations of the Old Hospital of the Knights of St John at Valetta. From a Copy Printed at Rome, and preserved in the Archives of Malta; with a Translation, Introduction, and Notes Explanatory of the Hospital Work of the Order. By the Rev. W. K. R. BEDFORD, one of the Chaplains of the Order of St John in England. Royal 8vo, with Frontispiece, Plans, &c., 7s. 6d.

BESANT. The Revolt of Man. By WALTER BESANT, M.A. Sixth Edition. Crown 8vo, 3s. 6d.

——— Readings from Rabelais. In one volume, post 8vo. [*In the Press.*

BLACKIE. Lays and Legends of Ancient Greece. By JOHN STUART BLACKIE, Emeritus Professor of Greek in the University of Edinburgh. Second Edition. Fcap. 8vo. 5s.

——— The Wisdom of Goethe. Crown 8vo. Cloth, extra gilt, 6s.

BLACKWOOD'S MAGAZINE, from Commencement in 1817 to December 1882. Nos. 1 to 806, forming 132 Volumes.

——— Index to Blackwood's Magazine. Vols. 1 to 50. 8vo, 15s.

——— Tales from Blackwood. Forming Twelve Volumes of Interesting and Amusing Railway Reading. Price One Shilling each in Paper Cover. Sold separately at all Railway Bookstalls.

They may also be had bound in cloth, 18s., and in half calf, richly gilt, 30s. or 12 volumes in 6, Roxburghe, 21s., and half red morocco, 28s.

——— Tales from Blackwood. New Series. Complete in Twenty-four Shilling Parts. Handsomely bound in 12 vols., cloth, 30s. In leather back, Roxburghe style, 37s. 6d. In half calf, gilt, 52s. 6d. In half morocco, 55s.

——— Standard Novels. Uniform in size and legibly Printed. Each Novel complete in one volume.

Florin Series, Illustrated Boards.

TOM CRINGLE'S LOG. By Michael Scott.
THE CRUISE OF THE MIDGE. By the Same.
CYRIL THORNTON. By Captain Hamilton.
ANNALS OF THE PARISH. By John Galt.
THE PROVOST, &c. By John Galt.
SIR ANDREW WYLIE. By John Galt.
THE ENTAIL. By John Galt.
MISS MOLLY. By Beatrice May Butt.
REGINALD DALTON. By J. G. Lockhart.
PEN OWEN. By Dean Hook.
ADAM BLAIR. By J. G. Lockhart.
LADY LEE'S WIDOWHOOD. By General Sir E. B. Hamley.
SALEM CHAPEL. By Mrs Oliphant.
THE PERPETUAL CURATE. By Mrs Oliphant
MISS MARJORIBANKS. By Mrs Oliphant.
JOHN: A Love Story. By Mrs Oliphant.

Or in Cloth Boards, 2s. 6d.

Shilling Series, Illustrated Cover.

THE RECTOR, and THE DOCTOR'S FAMILY. By Mrs Oliphant.
THE LIFE OF MANSIE WAUCH. By D. M. Moir.
PENINSULAR SCENES AND SKETCHES. By F. Hardman.
SIR FRIZZLE PUMPKIN, NIGHTS AT MESS, &c.
THE SUBALTERN.
LIFE IN THE FAR WEST. By G. F. Ruxton.
VALERIUS: A Roman Story. By J. G. Lockhart.

Or in Cloth Boards, 1s. 6d.

BLACKMORE. The Maid of Sker. By R. D. BLACKMORE, Author of 'Lorna Doone,' &c. Ninth Edition. Crown 8vo, 7s. 6d.

BOSCOBEL TRACTS. Relating to the Escape of Charles the Second after the Battle of Worcester, and his subsequent Adventures. Edited by J. HUGHES, Esq., A.M. A New Edition, with additional Notes and Illustrations, including Communications from the Rev. R. H. BARHAM, Author of the 'Ingoldsby Legends.' 8vo, with Engravings, 16s.

BRACKENBURY. A Narrative of the Ashanti War. Prepared from the official documents, by permission of Major-General Sir Garnet Wolseley. K.C.B., K.C.M.G. By Major H. BRACKENBURY, R.A., Assistant Military Secretary to Sir Garnet Wolseley. With Maps from the latest Surveys made by the Staff of the Expedition. 2 vols. 8vo, 25s.

BROADLEY. Tunis, Past and Present. With a Narrative of the French Conquest of the Regency. By A. M. BROADLEY. With numerous Illustrations and Maps. 2 vols. post 8vo. 25s.

BROOKE, Life of Sir James, Rajah of Sarāwak. From his Personal Papers and Correspondence. By SPENSER ST JOHN, H.M.'s Minister-Resident and Consul-General Peruvian Republic; formerly Secretary to the Rajah. With Portrait and a Map. Post 8vo, 12s. 6d.

BROUGHAM. Memoirs of the Life and Times of Henry Lord Brougham. Written by HIMSELF. 3 vols. 8vo, £2, 8s. The Volumes are sold separately, price 16s. each.

BROWN. The Forester: A Practical Treatise on the Planting, Rearing, and General Management of Forest-trees. By JAMES BROWN, LL.D., Inspector of and Reporter on Woods and Forests, Benmore House, Port Elgin, Ontario. Fifth Edition, revised and enlarged. Royal 8vo, with Engravings. 36s.

BROWN. The Ethics of George Eliot's Works. By JOHN CROMBIE BROWN. Third Edition. Crown 8vo, 2s. 6d.

BROWN. A Manual of Botany, Anatomical and Physiological. For the Use of Students. By ROBERT BROWN, M.A., Ph.D. Crown 8vo, with numerous Illustrations, 12s. 6d.

BUCHAN. Introductory Text-Book of Meteorology. By ALEXANDER BUCHAN, M.A., F.R.S.E., Secretary of the Scottish Meteorological Society, &c. Crown 8vo, with 8 Coloured Charts and other Engravings, pp. 218. 4s. 6d.

BURBIDGE. Domestic Floriculture, Window Gardening, and Floral Decorations. Being practical directions for the Propagation, Culture, and Arrangement of Plants and Flowers as Domestic Ornaments. By F. W. BURBIDGE. Second Edition. Crown 8vo, with numerous Illustrations, 7s. 6d.

——— Cultivated Plants: Their Propagation and Improvement. Including Natural and Artificial Hybridisation, Raising from Seed, Cuttings, and Layers, Grafting and Budding, as applied to the Families and Genera in Cultivation. Crown 8vo, with numerous Illustrations, 12s. 6d.

BURN. Handbook of the Mechanical Arts Concerned in the Construction and Arrangement of Dwelling-Houses and other Buildings; with Practical Hints on Road-making and the Enclosing of Land. By ROBERT SCOTT BURN, Engineer. Second Edition. Crown 8vo, 6s. 6d.

BURTON. The History of Scotland: From Agricola's Invasion to the Extinction of the last Jacobite Insurrection. By JOHN HILL BURTON, D.C.L., Historiographer-Royal for Scotland. New and Enlarged Edition, 8 vols., and Index. Crown 8vo, £3, 3s.

——— History of the British Empire during the Reign of Queen Anne. In 3 vols. 8vo. 36s.

——— The Scot Abroad. Second Edition. Complete in One volume. Crown 8vo, 10s. 6d.

——— The Book-Hunter. A New and Choice Edition. With a Memoir of the Author, a Portrait etched by Mr Hole, A.R.S.A., and other Illustrations. In small 4to, on hand-made paper.

BUTE. The Roman Breviary: Reformed by Order of the Holy Œcumenical Council of Trent; Published by Order of Pope St Pius V.; and Revised by Clement VIII. and Urban VIII.; together with the Offices since granted. Translated out of Latin into English by JOHN, Marquess of Bute, K.T. In 2 vols. crown 8vo, cloth boards, edges uncut. £2, 2s.

BUTE. The Altus of St Columba. With a Prose Paraphrase and Notes. In paper cover, 2s. 6d.

BUTT. Miss Molly. By BEATRICE MAY BUTT. Cheap Edition, 2s.

—— Delicia. By the Author of 'Miss Molly.' Fourth Edition. Crown 8vo, 7s. 6d.

—— Geraldine Hawthorne: A Sketch. By the Author of 'Miss Molly.' Crown 8vo, 7s. 6d.

CAIRD. Sermons. By JOHN CAIRD, D.D., Principal of the University of Glasgow. Fourteenth Thousand. Fcap. 8vo, 5s.

—— Religion in Common Life. A Sermon preached in Crathie Church, October 14, 1855, before Her Majesty the Queen and Prince Albert. Published by Her Majesty's Command. Cheap Edition, 3d.

CAMERON. Gaelic Names of Plants (Scottish and Irish). Collected and Arranged in Scientific Order, with Notes on their Etymology, their Uses, Plant Superstitions, &c., among the Celts, with copious Gaelic, English, and Scientific Indices. By JOHN CAMERON, Sunderland. 8vo, 7s. 6d.

CAMPBELL, Life of Colin, Lord Clyde. *See* General SHADWELL, at page 20.

CAMPBELL. Sermons Preached before the Queen at Balmoral. By the Rev. A. A. CAMPBELL, Minister of Crathie. Published by Command of Her Majesty. Crown 8vo, 4s. 6d.

CARLYLE. Autobiography of the Rev. Dr Alexander Carlyle, Minister of Inveresk. Containing Memorials of the Men and Events of his Time. Edited by JOHN HILL BURTON. 8vo. Third Edition, with Portrait, 14s.

CARRICK. Koumiss; or, Fermented Mare's Milk: and its Uses in the Treatment and Cure of Pulmonary Consumption, and other Wasting Diseases. With an Appendix on the best Methods of Fermenting Cow's Milk. By GEORGE L. CARRICK, M.D., L.R.C.S.E. and L.R.C.P.E., Physician to the British Embassy, St Petersburg, &c. Crown 8vo, 10s. 6d.

CAUVIN. A Treasury of the English and German Languages. Compiled from the best Authors and Lexicographers in both Languages. Adapted to the Use of Schools, Students, Travellers, and Men of Business; and forming a Companion to all German-English Dictionaries. By JOSEPH CAUVIN, LL.D. & Ph.D., of the University of Göttingen, &c. Crown 8vo, 7s. 6d.

CAVE-BROWN. Lambeth Palace and its Associations. By J. CAVE-BROWN, M.A., Vicar of Detling, Kent, and for many years Curate of Lambeth Parish Church. With an Introduction by the Archbishop of Canterbury. Second Edition, containing an additional Chapter on Medieval Life in the Old Palaces. 8vo, with Illustrations. [*In the Press.*

CHARTERIS. Canonicity; or, Early Testimonies to the Existence and Use of the Books of the New Testament. Based on Kirchhoffer's 'Quellensammlung.' Edited by A. H. CHARTERIS, D.D., Professor of Biblical Criticism in the University of Edinburgh. 8vo, 18s.

CHEVELEY NOVELS, THE.

I. A MODERN MINISTER. 2 vols. bound in cloth, with Twenty-six Illustrations. 17s.

II. SAUL WEIR. 2 vols. bound in cloth. With Twelve Illustrations by F. Barnard. 16s.

III. DORA DORÉE. [*In Preparation.*

CHIROL. 'Twixt Greek and Turk. By M. VALENTINE CHIROL. Post 8vo. With Frontispiece and Map, 10s. 6d.

CHURCH SERVICE SOCIETY. A Book of Common Order: Being Forms of Worship issued by the Church Service Society. Fourth Edition, 5s.

COLQUHOUN. The Moor and the Loch. Containing Minute Instructions in all Highland Sports, with Wanderings over Crag and Corrie, Flood and Fell. By JOHN COLQUHOUN. Fifth Edition, greatly enlarged. With Illustrations. 2 vols. post 8vo, 26s.

COTTERILL. The Genesis of the Church. By the Right. Rev. HENRY COTTERILL, D.D., Bishop of Edinburgh. Demy 8vo, 16s.

CRANSTOUN. The Elegies of Albius Tibullus. Translated into English Verse, with Life of the Poet, and Illustrative Notes. By JAMES CRANSTOUN, LL.D., Author of a Translation of 'Catullus.' Crown 8vo, 6s. 6d.

——— The Elegies of Sextus Propertius. Translated into English Verse, with Life of the Poet, and Illustrative Notes. Crown 8vo, 7s. 6d.

CRAWFORD. The Doctrine of Holy Scripture respecting the Atonement. By the late THOMAS J. CRAWFORD, D.D., Professor of Divinity in the University of Edinburgh. Third Edition. 8vo, 12s.

——— The Fatherhood of God, Considered in its General and Special Aspects, and particularly in relation to the Atonement, with a Review of Recent Speculations on the Subject. Third Edition, Revised and Enlarged. 8vo, 9s.

———. The Preaching of the Cross, and other Sermons. 8vo, 7s. 6d.

——— The Mysteries of Christianity. Being the Baird Lecture for 1874. Crown 8vo, 7s. 6d.

DE AINSLIE. Life as I have Found It. By General DE AINSLIE. Post 8vo, 12s. 6d.

DESCARTES. The Method, Meditations, and Principles of Philosophy of Descartes. Translated from the Original French and Latin. With a New Introductory Essay, Historical and Critical, on the Cartesian Philosophy. By JOHN VEITCH, LL.D., Professor of Logic and Rhetoric in the University of Glasgow. A New Edition, being the Eighth. Price 6s. 6d.

DU CANE. The Odyssey of Homer, Books I.-XII. Translated into English Verse. By Sir CHARLES DU CANE, K.C.M.G. 8vo, 10s. 6d.

DUDGEON. History of the Edinburgh or Queen's Regiment Light Infantry Militia, now 3rd Battalion The Royal Scots; with an Account of the Origin and Progress of the Militia, and a Brief Sketch of the old Royal Scots. By Major R. C. DUDGEON, Adjutant 3rd Battalion The Royal Scots. Post 8vo, with Illustrations, 10s. 6d.

ELIOT. Impressions of Theophrastus Such. By GEORGE ELIOT. New and cheaper Edition. Crown 8vo, 5s.

——— Adam Bede. Illustrated Edition. 3s. 6d., cloth.

——— The Mill on the Floss. Illustrated Edition. 3s. 6d., cloth.

——— Scenes of Clerical Life. Illustrated Edition. 3s., cloth.

——— Silas Marner: The Weaver of Raveloe. Illustrated Edition. 2s. 6d., cloth.

——— Felix Holt, the Radical. Illustrated Edition. 3s. 6d., cloth.

——— Romola. With Vignette. 3s. 6d., cloth.

——— Middlemarch. Crown 8vo, 7s. 6d.

——— Daniel Deronda. Crown 8vo, 7s. 6d.

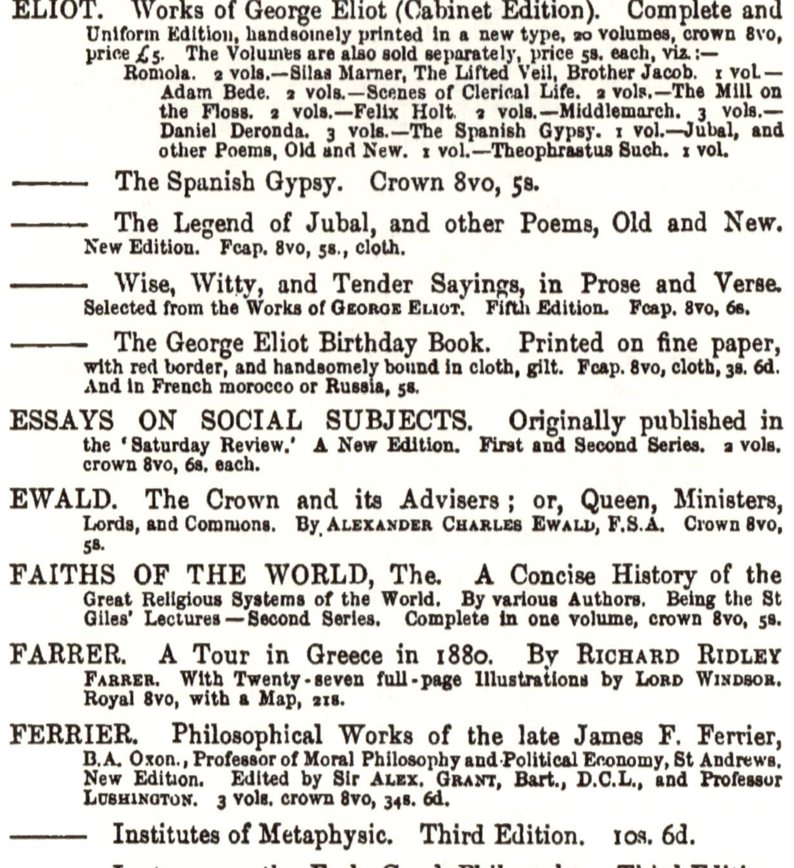

ELIOT. Works of George Eliot (Cabinet Edition). Complete and Uniform Edition, handsomely printed in a new type, 20 volumes, crown 8vo, price £5. The Volumes are also sold separately, price 5s. each, viz.:—
Romola. 2 vols.—Silas Marner, The Lifted Veil, Brother Jacob. 1 vol.—Adam Bede. 2 vols.—Scenes of Clerical Life. 2 vols.—The Mill on the Floss. 2 vols.—Felix Holt. 2 vols.—Middlemarch. 3 vols.—Daniel Deronda. 3 vols.—The Spanish Gypsy. 1 vol.—Jubal, and other Poems, Old and New. 1 vol.—Theophrastus Such. 1 vol.

——— The Spanish Gypsy. Crown 8vo, 5s.

——— The Legend of Jubal, and other Poems, Old and New. New Edition. Fcap. 8vo, 5s., cloth.

——— Wise, Witty, and Tender Sayings, in Prose and Verse. Selected from the Works of George Eliot. Fifth Edition. Fcap. 8vo, 6s.

——— The George Eliot Birthday Book. Printed on fine paper, with red border, and handsomely bound in cloth, gilt. Fcap. 8vo, cloth, 3s. 6d. And in French morocco or Russia, 5s.

ESSAYS ON SOCIAL SUBJECTS. Originally published in the 'Saturday Review.' A New Edition. First and Second Series. 2 vols. crown 8vo, 6s. each.

EWALD. The Crown and its Advisers; or, Queen, Ministers, Lords, and Commons. By Alexander Charles Ewald, F.S.A. Crown 8vo, 5s.

FAITHS OF THE WORLD, The. A Concise History of the Great Religious Systems of the World. By various Authors. Being the St Giles' Lectures—Second Series. Complete in one volume, crown 8vo, 5s.

FARRER. A Tour in Greece in 1880. By Richard Ridley Farrer. With Twenty-seven full-page Illustrations by Lord Windsor. Royal 8vo, with a Map, 21s.

FERRIER. Philosophical Works of the late James F. Ferrier, B.A. Oxon., Professor of Moral Philosophy and Political Economy, St Andrews. New Edition. Edited by Sir Alex. Grant, Bart., D.C.L., and Professor Lushington. 3 vols. crown 8vo, 34s. 6d.

——— Institutes of Metaphysic. Third Edition. 10s. 6d.

——— Lectures on the Early Greek Philosophy. Third Edition. 10s. 6d.

——— Philosophical Remains, including the Lectures on Early Greek Philosophy. 2 vols., 24s.

FISH AND FISHERIES. A Selection from the Prize Essays of the International Fisheries Exhibition, Edinburgh, 1882. Edited by David Herbert, M.A. With Maps and Illustrations. 8vo, 7s. 6d.

FLINT. The Philosophy of History in Europe. Vol. I., containing the History of that Philosophy in France and Germany. By Robert Flint, D.D., LL.D., Professor of Divinity, University of Edinburgh. 8vo, 15s.

——— Theism. Being the Baird Lecture for 1876. Third Edition. Crown 8vo, 7s. 6d.

——— Anti-Theistic Theories. Being the Baird Lecture for 1877. Second Edition. Crown 8vo, 10s. 6d.

FORBES. The Campaign of Garibaldi in the Two Sicilies: A Personal Narrative. By Charles Stuart Forbes, Commander, R.N. Post 8vo, with Portraits, 12s.

FOREIGN CLASSICS FOR ENGLISH READERS. Edited by Mrs OLIPHANT. Price 2s. 6d.

Now published:—

DANTE. By the Editor.
VOLTAIRE. By Major-General Sir E. B. Hamley, K.C.M.G.
PASCAL. By Principal Tulloch.
PETRARCH. By Henry Reeve, C.B.
GOETHE. By A. Hayward, Q.C.
MOLIÈRE. By the Editor and F. Tarver, M.A.
MONTAIGNE. By Rev. W. L. Collins, M.A.
RABELAIS. By Walter Besant, M.A.
CALDERON. By E. J. Hasell.
SAINT SIMON. By Clifton W. Collins, M.A.
CERVANTES. By the Editor.
CORNEILLE AND RACINE. By Henry M. Trollope.
MADAME DE SÉVIGNÉ. By Miss Thackeray.
LA FONTAINE, AND OTHER FRENCH FABULISTS. By Rev. W. L. Collins, M.A.
SCHILLER. By James Sime, M.A., Author of 'Lessing: his Life and Writings.'
TASSO. By E. J. Hasell.
ROUSSEAU. By Henry Grey Graham.

In preparation—LEOPARDI, by the Editor. ALFRED DE MUSSET, by C. F. Oliphant.

FRANZOS. The Jews of Barnow. Stories by KARL EMIL FRANZOS. Translated by M. W. MACDOWALL. Crown 8vo, 6s.

GALT. Annals of the Parish. By JOHN GALT. Fcap. 8vo, 2s.

——— The Provost. Fcap. 8vo, 2s.

——— Sir Andrew Wylie. Fcap. 8vo, 2s.

——— The Entail; or, The Laird of Grippy. Fcap. 8vo, 2s.

GENERAL ASSEMBLY OF THE CHURCH OF SCOTLAND.

——— Family Prayers. Authorised by the General Assembly of the Church of Scotland. A New Edition, crown 8vo, in large type, 4s. 6d. Another Edition, crown 8vo, 2s.

——— Prayers for Social and Family Worship. For the Use of Soldiers, Sailors, Colonists, and Sojourners in India, and other Persons at home and abroad, who are deprived of the ordinary services of a Christian Ministry. Cheap Edition, 1s. 6d.

——— The Scottish Hymnal. Hymns for Public Worship. Published for Use in Churches by Authority of the General Assembly. Various sizes—viz.: 1. Large type, for pulpit use, cloth, 3s. 6d. 2. Longprimer type, cloth, red edges, 1s. 6d.; French morocco, 2s. 6d.; calf, 6s. 3. Bourgeois type, cloth, red edges, 1s.; French morocco, 2s. 4. Minion type, limp cloth, 6d.; French morocco, 1s. 6d. 5. School Edition, in paper cover, 2d. 6. Children's Hymnal, paper cover, 1d. No. 2, bound with the Psalms and Paraphrases, cloth, 3s.; French morocco, 4s. 6d.; calf, 7s. 6d. No. 3, bound with the Psalms and Paraphrases, cloth, 2s.; French morocco, 3s.

——— The Scottish Hymnal, with Music. Selected by the Committees on Hymns and on Psalmody. The harmonies arranged by W. H. Monk. Cloth, 1s. 6d.; French morocco, 3s. 6d. The same in the Tonic Sol-fa Notation, 1s. 6d. and 3s. 6d.

——— The Scottish Hymnal, with Fixed Tune for each Hymn. Longprimer type, 3s. 6d.

GERARD. Reata: What's in a Name? By E. D. GERARD. New Edition. In one volume, crown 8vo, 6s.

——— Beggar my Neighbour. A Novel. New Edition, complete in one volume, crown 8vo, 6s.

GLEIG. The Subaltern. By G. R. GLEIG, M.A., late Chaplain-General of Her Majesty's Forces. Originally published in 'Blackwood's Magazine.' Library Edition. Revised and Corrected, with a New Preface. Crown 8vo, 7s. 6d.

GOETHE'S FAUST. Translated into English Verse by Sir THEODORE MARTIN, K.C.B. Second Edition, post 8vo, 6s. Cheap Edition, fcap., 3s. 6d.

GOETHE. Poems and Ballads of Goethe. Translated by Professor AYTOUN and Sir THEODORE MARTIN, K.C.B. Third Edition, fcap. 8vo, 6s.

GORDON CUMMING. At Home in Fiji. By C. F. GORDON CUMMING, Author of 'From the Hebrides to the Himalayas.' Fourth Edition, complete in one volume post 8vo. With Illustrations and Map. 7s. 6d.

—— A Lady's Cruise in a French Man-of-War. New and Cheaper Edition. In one volume, 8vo. With Illustrations and Map. 12s. 6d.

—— Fire-Fountains. The Kingdom of Hawaii: Its Volcanoes, and the History of its Missions. With Map and numerous Illustrations. In two vols. 8vo, 25s.

GRANT. Bush-Life in Queensland. By A. C. GRANT. New Edition. In one volume crown 8vo, 6s.

HAMERTON. Wenderholme: A Story of Lancashire and Yorkshire Life. By PHILIP GILBERT HAMERTON, Author of 'A Painter's Camp.' A New Edition. Crown 8vo, 6s.

HAMILTON. Lectures on Metaphysics. By Sir WILLIAM HAMILTON, Bart., Professor of Logic and Metaphysics in the University of Edinburgh. Edited by the Rev. H. L. MANSEL, B.D., LL.D., Dean of St Paul's; and JOHN VEITCH, M.A., Professor of Logic and Rhetoric, Glasgow. Sixth Edition. 2 vols. 8vo, 24s.

—— Lectures on Logic. Edited by the SAME. Third Edition. 2 vols., 24s.

—— Discussions on Philosophy and Literature, Education and University Reform. Third Edition, 8vo, 21s.

—— Memoir of Sir William Hamilton, Bart., Professor of Logic and Metaphysics in the University of Edinburgh. By Professor VEITCH of the University of Glasgow. 8vo, with Portrait, 18s.

—— Sir William Hamilton: The Man and his Philosophy. Two Lectures Delivered before the Edinburgh Philosophical Institution, January and February 1883. By the SAME. Crown 8vo, 2s.

HAMILTON. Annals of the Peninsular Campaigns. By Captain THOMAS HAMILTON. Edited by F. Hardman. 8vo, 16s. Atlas of Maps to illustrate the Campaigns, 12s.

HAMLEY. The Operations of War Explained and Illustrated. By Major-General Sir EDWARD BRUCE HAMLEY, K.C.M.G. Fourth Edition, revised throughout. 4to, with numerous Illustrations, 30s.

—— Thomas Carlyle: An Essay. Second Edition. Crown 8vo. 2s. 6d.

—— The Story of the Campaign of Sebastopol. Written in the Camp. With Illustrations drawn in Camp by the Author. 8vo, 21s.

—— On Outposts. Second Edition. 8vo, 2s.

—— Wellington's Career; A Military and Political Summary. Crown 8vo, 2s.

—— Lady Lee's Widowhood. Crown 8vo, 2s. 6d.

—— Our Poor Relations. A Philozoic Essay. With Illustrations, chiefly by Ernest Griset. Crown 8vo, cloth gilt, 3s. 6d.

HAMLEY. Guilty, or Not Guilty? A Tale. By Major-General W. G. HAMLEY, late of the Royal Engineers. New Edition. Crown 8vo, 3s. 6d.

—— The House of Lys: One Book of its History. A Tale. Second Edition. 2 vols. crown 8vo. 17s.

—— Traseaden Hall. "When George the Third was King." New and Cheaper Edition, crown 8vo, 6s.

HANDY HORSE-BOOK; or, Practical Instructions in Riding, Driving, and the General Care and Management of Horses. By 'MAGENTA.' Ninth Edition, with 6 Engravings, 4s. 6d.

BY THE SAME.

Our Domesticated Dogs: their Treatment in reference to Food, Diseases, Habits, Punishment, Accomplishments. Crown 8vo, 2s. 6d.

HARBORD. Definitions and Diagrams in Astronomy and Navigation. By the Rev. J. B. HARBORD, M.A., Assistant Director of Education, Admiralty. 1s.

——— Short Sermons for Hospitals and Sick Seamen. Fcap. 8vo, cloth, 4s. 6d.

HARDMAN. Scenes and Adventures in Central America. Edited by FREDERICK HARDMAN. Crown 8vo. 6s.

HASELL. Bible Partings. By E. J. HASELL. Crown 8vo. [*In the Press.*

HAY. The Works of the Right Rev. Dr George Hay, Bishop of Edinburgh. Edited under the Supervision of the Right Rev. Bishop STRAIN. With Memoir and Portrait of the Author. 5 vols. crown 8vo, bound in extra cloth, £1, 1s. Or, sold separately—viz.:

The Sincere Christian Instructed in the Faith of Christ from the Written Word. 2 vols., 8s.—The Devout Christian Instructed in the Law of Christ from the Written Word. 2 vols., 8s.—The Pious Christian Instructed in the Nature and Practice of the Principal Exercises of Piety. 1 vol., 4s.

HEATLEY. The Horse-Owner's Safeguard. A Handy Medical Guide for every Man who owns a Horse By G. S. HEATLEY, M.R.C., V.S. Crown 8vo, 5s.

——— The Stock-Owner's Guide. A Handy Medical Treatise for every Man who owns an Ox or a Cow. Crown 8vo, 4s. 6d.

HEMANS. The Poetical Works of Mrs Hemans. Copyright Editions.

One Volume, royal 8vo, 5s.

The Same, with Illustrations engraved on Steel, bound in cloth, gilt edges, 7s. 6d.

Six Volumes in Three, fcap., 12s. 6d.

SELECT POEMS OF MRS HEMANS. Fcap., cloth, gilt edges, 3s.

HOLE. A Book about Roses: How to Grow and Show Them. By the Rev. Canon HOLE. With coloured Frontispiece by the Hon. Mrs Francklin. Seventh Edition, revised. Crown 8vo, 7s. 6d.

HOME PRAYERS. By Ministers of the Church of Scotland and Members of the Church Service Society. Second Edition. Fcap. 8vo, 3s.

HOMER. The Odyssey. Translated into English Verse in the Spenserian Stanza. By PHILIP STANHOPE WORSLEY. Third Edition, 2 vols. fcap., 12s.

——— The Iliad. Translated by P. S. WORSLEY and Professor CONINGTON. 2 vols. crown 8vo, 21s.

HOSACK. Mary Queen of Scots and Her Accusers. Containing a Variety of Documents never before published. By JOHN HOSACK, Barrister-at-Law. A New and Enlarged Edition, with a Photograph from the Bust on the Tomb in Westminster Abbey. 2 vols. 8vo, £1, 1s.

INDEX GEOGRAPHICUS: Being a List, alphabetically arranged, of the Principal Places on the Globe, with the Countries and Subdivisions of the Countries in which they are situated, and their Latitudes and Longitudes. Applicable to all Modern Atlases and Maps. Imperial 8vo, pp. 676, 21s.

JAMIESON. The Laird's Secret. By J. H. JAMIESON. In 2 vols. crown 8vo, 17s.

JEAN JAMBON. Our Trip to Blunderland; or, Grand Excursion to Blundertown and Back. By JEAN JAMBON. With Sixty Illustrations designed by CHARLES DOYLE, engraved by DALZIEL. Fourth Thousand. Handsomely bound in cloth, gilt edges, 6s. 6d. Cheap Edition, cloth, 3s. 6d. In boards, 2s. 6d.

JOHNSON. The Scots Musical Museum. Consisting of upwards of Six Hundred Songs, with proper Basses for the Pianoforte. Originally published by JAMES JOHNSON; and now accompanied with Copious Notes and Illustrations of the Lyric Poetry and Music of Scotland, by the late WILLIAM STENHOUSE; with additional Notes and Illustrations, by DAVID LAING and C. K. SHARPE. 4 vols. 8vo, Roxburghe binding, £2, 12s. 6d.

JOHNSTON. The Chemistry of Common Life. By Professor J. F. W. JOHNSTON. New Edition, Revised, and brought down to date. By ARTHUR HERBERT CHURCH, M.A. Oxon.; Author of 'Food: its Sources, Constituents, and Uses;' 'The Laboratory Guide for Agricultural Students;' 'Plain Words about Water,' &c. Illustrated with Maps and 102 Engravings on Wood. Complete in one volume, crown 8vo, pp. 618, 7s. 6d.

——— Elements of Agricultural Chemistry and Geology. Thirteenth Edition, Revised, and brought down to date. By CHARLES A. CAMERON, M.D., F.R.C.S.I., &c. Fcap. 8vo, 6s. 6d.

——— Catechism of Agricultural Chemistry and Geology. An entirely New Edition, revised and enlarged, by CHARLES A. CAMERON, M.D., F.R.C.S.I., &c. Eighty-first Thousand, with numerous Illustrations, 1s.

JOHNSTON. Patrick Hamilton: a Tragedy of the Reformation in Scotland, 1528. By J. P. JOHNSTON. Crown 8vo, with Two Etchings by the Author, 5s.

KEITH ELPHINSTONE. Memoir of the Honourable George Keith Elphinstone, K.B., Viscount Keith of Stonehaven Marischal, Admiral of the Red.—*See* ALEXANDER ALLARDYCE, at page 4.

KING. The Metamorphoses of Ovid. Translated in English Blank Verse. By HENRY KING, M.A., Fellow of Wadham College, Oxford, and of the Inner Temple, Barrister-at-Law. Crown 8vo, 10s. 6d.

KINGLAKE. History of the Invasion of the Crimea. By A. W. KINGLAKE. Cabinet Edition. Seven Volumes, crown 8vo, at 6s. each. The Volumes respectively contain:—

I. THE ORIGIN OF THE WAR between the Czar and the Sultan.
II. RUSSIA MET AND INVADED. With 4 Maps and Plans.
III. THE BATTLE OF THE ALMA. With 14 Maps and Plans.
IV. SEBASTOPOL AT BAY. With 10 Maps and Plans.
V. THE BATTLE OF BALACLAVA. With 10 Maps and Plans.
VI. THE BATTLE OF INKERMAN. With 11 Maps and Plans.
VII. WINTER TROUBLES. With Map.

——— History of the Invasion of the Crimea. Vol. VI. Winter Troubles. Demy 8vo, with a Map, 16s.

——— Eothen. A New Edition, uniform with the Cabinet Edition of the 'History of the Crimean War,' price 6s.

KNOLLYS. The Elements of Field-Artillery. Designed for the Use of Infantry and Cavalry Officers. By HENRY KNOLLYS, Captain Royal Artillery; Author of 'From Sedan to Saarbrück,' Editor of 'Incidents in the Sepoy War,' &c. With Engravings. Crown 8vo, 7s. 6d.

LAVERGNE. The Rural Economy of England, Scotland, and Ireland. By LEONCE DE LAVERGNE. Translated from the French. With Notes by a Scottish Farmer. 8vo, 12s.

LEE. Lectures on the History of the Church of Scotland, from the Reformation to the Revolution Settlement. By the late Very Rev. JOHN LEE, D.D., LL.D., Principal of the University of Edinburgh. With Notes and Appendices from the Author's Papers. Edited by the Rev. WILLIAM LEE, D.D. 2 vols. 8vo, 21s.

LEE-HAMILTON. Poems and Transcripts. By EUGENE LEE-HAMILTON. Crown 8vo, 6s.

LEES. A Handbook of Sheriff Court Styles. By J. M. LEES, M.A., LL.B., Advocate, Sheriff-Substitute of Lanarkshire. In 1 vol. 8vo. [*In the Press.*

LEWES. The Physiology of Common Life. By GEORGE H. LEWES, Author of 'Sea-side Studies,' &c. Illustrated with numerous Engravings. 2 vols., 12s.

LOCKHART. Doubles and Quits. By Laurence W. M. LOCKHART. With Twelve Illustrations. Third Edition. Crown 8vo, 6s.

——— Fair to See: a Novel. Seventh Edition, crown 8vo, 6s.

——— Mine is Thine: a Novel. Seventh Edition, crown 8vo, 6s.

LORIMER. The Institutes of Law: A Treatise of the Principles of Jurisprudence as determined by Nature. By JAMES LORIMER, Regius Professor of Public Law and of the Law of Nature and Nations in the University of Edinburgh. New Edition, revised throughout, and much enlarged. 8vo, 18s.

——— The Institutes of the Law of Nations. A Treatise of the Jural Relation of Separate Political Communities. In 2 vols. 8vo. Volume I., price 16s. Volume II. in preparation.

LYON. History of the Rise and Progress of Freemasonry in Scotland. By DAVID MURRAY LYON, Secretary to the Grand Lodge of Scotland. In small quarto. Illustrated with numerous Portraits of Eminent Members of the Craft, and Facsimiles of Ancient Charters and other Curious Documents. £1, 11s. 6d.

MACDOWALL. The Jews of Barnow. *See* FRANZOS, at page 10.

M'COMBIE. Cattle and Cattle-Breeders. By WILLIAM M'COMBIE, Tillyfour. A New and Cheaper Edition, 2s. 6d., cloth.

MACRAE. A Handbook of Deer-Stalking. By ALEXANDER MACRAE, late Forester to Lord Henry Bentinck. With Introduction by HORATIO ROSS, Esq. Fcap. 8vo, with two Photographs from Life. 3s. 6d.

M'CRIE. Works of the Rev. Thomas M'Crie, D.D. Uniform Edition. Four vols. crown 8vo, 24s.

——— Life of John Knox. Containing Illustrations of the History of the Reformation in Scotland. Crown 8vo, 6s. Another Edition, 3s. 6d.

——— Life of Andrew Melville. Containing Illustrations of the Ecclesiastical and Literary History of Scotland in the Sixteenth and Seventeenth Centuries. Crown 8vo, 6s.

——— History of the Progress and Suppression of the Reformation in Italy in the Sixteenth Century. Crown 8vo, 4s.

——— History of the Progress and Suppression of the Reformation in Spain in the Sixteenth Century. Crown 8vo, 3s. 6d.

——— Sermons, and Review of the 'Tales of My Landlord.' Crown 8vo, 6s.

——— Lectures on the Book of Esther. Fcap. 8vo, 5s.

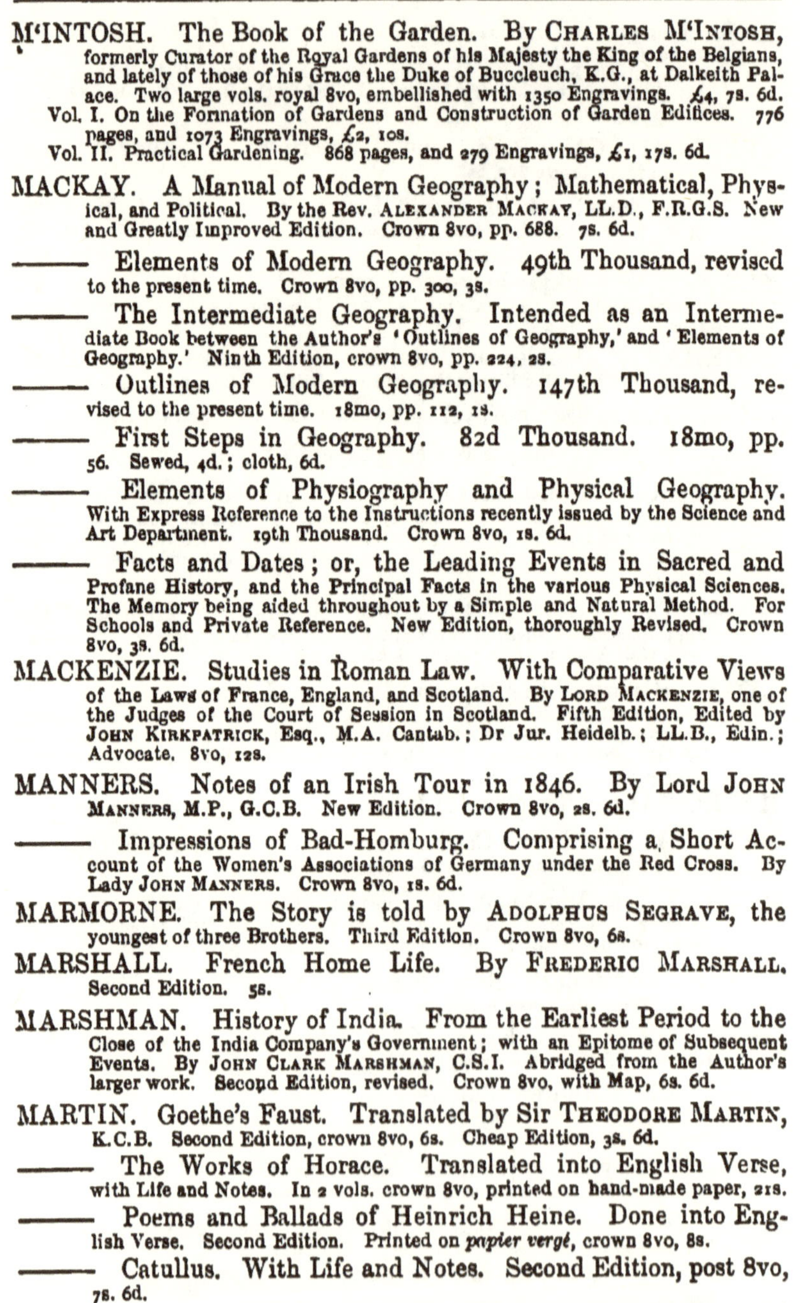

M'INTOSH. The Book of the Garden. By CHARLES M'INTOSH, formerly Curator of the Royal Gardens of his Majesty the King of the Belgians, and lately of those of his Grace the Duke of Buccleuch, K.G., at Dalkeith Palace. Two large vols. royal 8vo, embellished with 1350 Engravings. £4, 7s. 6d.
Vol. I. On the Formation of Gardens and Construction of Garden Edifices. 776 pages, and 1073 Engravings, £2, 10s.
Vol. II. Practical Gardening. 868 pages, and 279 Engravings, £1, 17s. 6d.

MACKAY. A Manual of Modern Geography; Mathematical, Physical, and Political. By the Rev. ALEXANDER MACKAY, LL.D., F.R.G.S. New and Greatly Improved Edition. Crown 8vo, pp. 688. 7s. 6d.

—— Elements of Modern Geography. 49th Thousand, revised to the present time. Crown 8vo, pp. 300, 3s.

—— The Intermediate Geography. Intended as an Intermediate Book between the Author's 'Outlines of Geography,' and 'Elements of Geography.' Ninth Edition, crown 8vo, pp. 224, 2s.

—— Outlines of Modern Geography. 147th Thousand, revised to the present time. 18mo, pp. 112, 1s.

—— First Steps in Geography. 82d Thousand. 18mo, pp. 56. Sewed, 4d.; cloth, 6d.

—— Elements of Physiography and Physical Geography. With Express Reference to the Instructions recently issued by the Science and Art Department. 19th Thousand. Crown 8vo, 1s. 6d.

—— Facts and Dates; or, the Leading Events in Sacred and Profane History, and the Principal Facts in the various Physical Sciences. The Memory being aided throughout by a Simple and Natural Method. For Schools and Private Reference. New Edition, thoroughly Revised. Crown 8vo, 3s. 6d.

MACKENZIE. Studies in Roman Law. With Comparative Views of the Laws of France, England, and Scotland. By LORD MACKENZIE, one of the Judges of the Court of Session in Scotland. Fifth Edition, Edited by JOHN KIRKPATRICK, Esq., M.A. Cantab.; Dr Jur. Heidelb.; LL.B., Edin.; Advocate. 8vo, 12s.

MANNERS. Notes of an Irish Tour in 1846. By Lord JOHN MANNERS, M.P., G.C.B. New Edition. Crown 8vo, 2s. 6d.

—— Impressions of Bad-Homburg. Comprising a Short Account of the Women's Associations of Germany under the Red Cross. By Lady JOHN MANNERS. Crown 8vo, 1s. 6d.

MARMORNE. The Story is told by ADOLPHUS SEGRAVE, the youngest of three Brothers. Third Edition. Crown 8vo, 6s.

MARSHALL. French Home Life. By FREDERIC MARSHALL. Second Edition. 5s.

MARSHMAN. History of India. From the Earliest Period to the Close of the India Company's Government; with an Epitome of Subsequent Events. By JOHN CLARK MARSHMAN, C.S.I. Abridged from the Author's larger work. Second Edition, revised. Crown 8vo, with Map, 6s. 6d.

MARTIN. Goethe's Faust. Translated by Sir THEODORE MARTIN, K.C.B. Second Edition, crown 8vo, 6s. Cheap Edition, 3s. 6d.

—— The Works of Horace. Translated into English Verse, with Life and Notes. In 2 vols. crown 8vo, printed on hand-made paper, 21s.

—— Poems and Ballads of Heinrich Heine. Done into English Verse. Second Edition. Printed on *papier vergé*, crown 8vo, 8s.

—— Catullus. With Life and Notes. Second Edition, post 8vo, 7s. 6d.

—— The Vita Nuova of Dante. With an Introduction and Notes. Second Edition, crown 8vo, 5s.

MARTIN. Aladdin: A Dramatic Poem. By ADAM OEHLENSCHLAEGER. Fcap. 8vo, 5s.

—— Correggio: A Tragedy. By OEHLENSCHLAEGER. With Notes. Fcap. 8vo, 3s.

—— King Rene's Daughter: A Danish Lyrical Drama. By HENRIK HERTZ. Second Edition, fcap., 2s. 6d.

MEIKLEJOHN. An Old Educational Reformer—Dr Bell. By J. M. D. MEIKLEJOHN, M.A., Professor of the Theory, History, and Practice of Education in the University of St Andrews. Crown 8vo, 3s. 6d.

MICHEL. A Critical Inquiry into the Scottish Language. With the view of Illustrating the Rise and Progress of Civilisation in Scotland. By FRANCISQUE-MICHEL, F.S.A. Lond. and Scot., Correspondant de l'Institut de France, &c. In One handsome Quarto Volume, printed on hand-made paper, and appropriately bound in Roxburghe style. Price 66s.

MICHIE. The Larch: Being a Practical Treatise on its Culture and General Management. By CHRISTOPHER YOUNG MICHIE, Forester, Cullen House. Crown 8vo, with Illustrations. 7s. 6d.

MINTO. A Manual of English Prose Literature, Biographical and Critical: designed mainly to show Characteristics of Style. By W. MINTO, M.A., Professor of Logic in the University of Aberdeen. Second Edition, revised. Crown 8vo, 7s. 6d.

—— Characteristics of English Poets, from Chaucer to Shirley. Crown 8vo, 9s.

MITCHELL. Biographies of Eminent Soldiers of the last Four Centuries. By Major-General JOHN MITCHELL, Author of 'Life of Wallenstein.' With a Memoir of the Author. 8vo, 9s.

MOIR. Poetical Works of D. M. MOIR (Delta). With Memoir by THOMAS AIRD, and Portrait. Second Edition, 2 vols. fcap. 8vo, 12s.

—— Domestic Verses. New Edition, fcap. 8vo, cloth gilt, 4s. 6d.

—— Lectures on the Poetical Literature of the Past Half-Century. Third Edition, fcap. 8vo, 5s.

—— Life of Mansie Wauch, Tailor in Dalkeith. With 8 Illustrations on Steel, by the late GEORGE CRUIKSHANK. Crown 8vo, 3s. 6d. Another Edition, fcap. 8vo, 1s. 6d.

MOMERIE. Defects of Modern Christianity, and other Sermons. By the Rev. A. W. MOMERIE, M.A., D.Sc., Professor of Logic and Metaphysics in King's College, London. Crown 8vo, 5s.

—— The Basis of Religion. Being an Examination of Natural Religion. Crown 8vo, 2s. 6d.

MONTAGUE. Campaigning in South Africa. Reminiscences of an Officer in 1879. By Captain W. E. MONTAGUE, 94th Regiment, Author of 'Claude Meadowleigh,' &c. 8vo, 10s. 6d.

MONTALEMBERT. Count de Montalembert's History of the Monks of the West. From St Benedict to St Bernard. Translated by Mrs OLIPHANT. 7 vols. 8vo, £3, 17s. 6d.

—— Memoir of Count de Montalembert. A Chapter of Recent French History. By Mrs OLIPHANT, Author of the 'Life of Edward Irving,' &c. 2 vols. crown 8vo, £1, 4s.

MORE THAN KIN. By M. P. Crown 8vo, 7s. 6d.

MURDOCH. Manual of the Law of Insolvency and Bankruptcy: Comprehending a Summary of the Law of Insolvency, Notour Bankruptcy, Composition-contracts, Trust-deeds, Cessios, and Sequestrations; and the Winding-up of Joint-Stock Companies in Scotland; with Annotations on the various Insolvency and Bankruptcy Statutes; and with Forms of Procedure applicable to these Subjects. By JAMES MURDOCH, Member of the Faculty of Procurators in Glasgow. Fourth Edition, Revised and Enlarged, 8vo, £1.

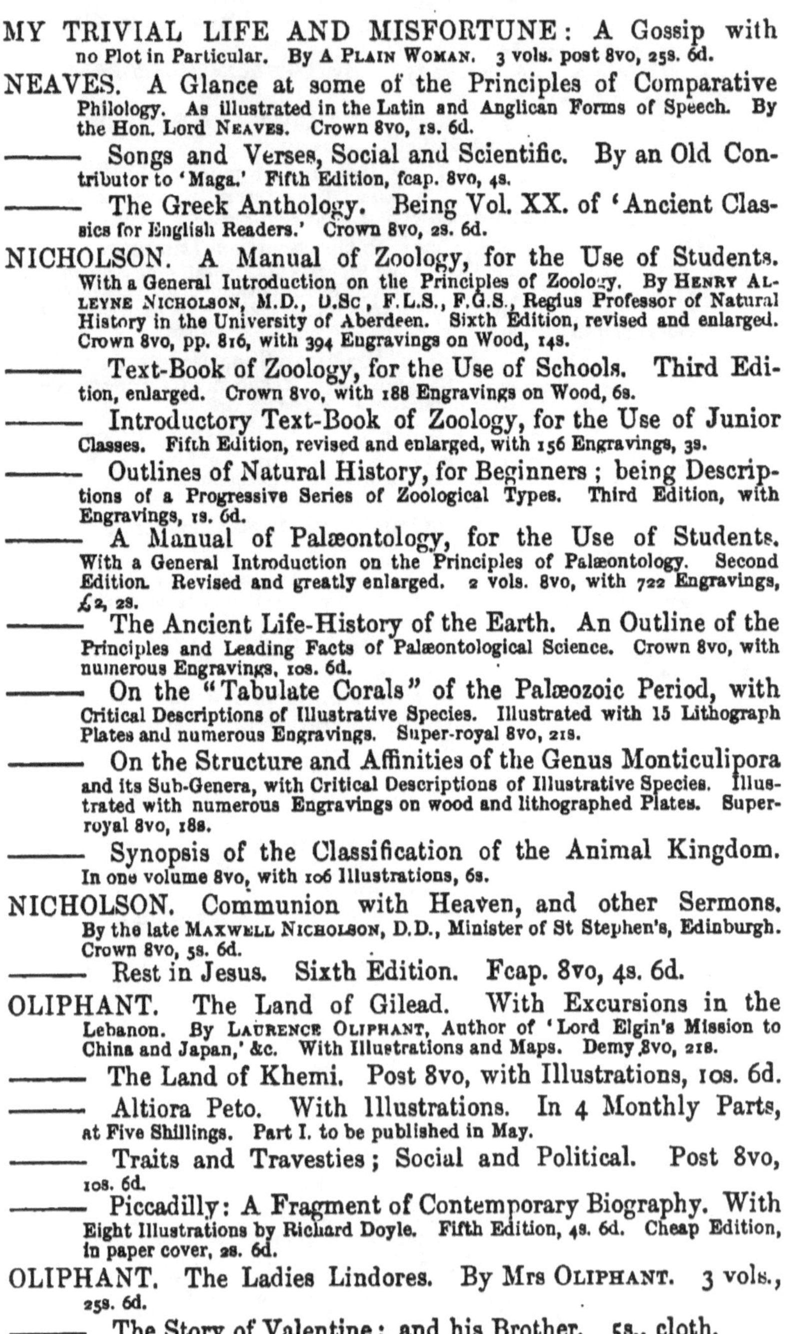

MY TRIVIAL LIFE AND MISFORTUNE: A Gossip with no Plot in Particular. By A PLAIN WOMAN. 3 vols. post 8vo, 25s. 6d.

NEAVES. A Glance at some of the Principles of Comparative Philology. As illustrated in the Latin and Anglican Forms of Speech. By the Hon. Lord NEAVES. Crown 8vo, 1s. 6d.

——— Songs and Verses, Social and Scientific. By an Old Contributor to 'Maga.' Fifth Edition, fcap. 8vo, 4s.

——— The Greek Anthology. Being Vol. XX. of 'Ancient Classics for English Readers.' Crown 8vo, 2s. 6d.

NICHOLSON. A Manual of Zoology, for the Use of Students. With a General Introduction on the Principles of Zoology. By HENRY ALLEYNE NICHOLSON, M.D., D.Sc., F.L.S., F.G.S., Regius Professor of Natural History in the University of Aberdeen. Sixth Edition, revised and enlarged. Crown 8vo, pp. 816, with 394 Engravings on Wood, 14s.

——— Text-Book of Zoology, for the Use of Schools. Third Edition, enlarged. Crown 8vo, with 188 Engravings on Wood, 6s.

——— Introductory Text-Book of Zoology, for the Use of Junior Classes. Fifth Edition, revised and enlarged, with 156 Engravings, 3s.

——— Outlines of Natural History, for Beginners; being Descriptions of a Progressive Series of Zoological Types. Third Edition, with Engravings, 1s. 6d.

——— A Manual of Palæontology, for the Use of Students. With a General Introduction on the Principles of Palæontology. Second Edition. Revised and greatly enlarged. 2 vols. 8vo, with 722 Engravings, £2, 2s.

——— The Ancient Life-History of the Earth. An Outline of the Principles and Leading Facts of Palæontological Science. Crown 8vo, with numerous Engravings, 10s. 6d.

——— On the "Tabulate Corals" of the Palæozoic Period, with Critical Descriptions of Illustrative Species. Illustrated with 15 Lithograph Plates and numerous Engravings. Super-royal 8vo, 21s.

——— On the Structure and Affinities of the Genus Monticulipora and its Sub-Genera, with Critical Descriptions of Illustrative Species. Illustrated with numerous Engravings on wood and lithographed Plates. Super-royal 8vo, 18s.

——— Synopsis of the Classification of the Animal Kingdom. In one volume 8vo, with 106 Illustrations, 6s.

NICHOLSON. Communion with Heaven, and other Sermons. By the late MAXWELL NICHOLSON, D.D., Minister of St Stephen's, Edinburgh. Crown 8vo, 5s. 6d.

——— Rest in Jesus. Sixth Edition. Fcap. 8vo, 4s. 6d.

OLIPHANT. The Land of Gilead. With Excursions in the Lebanon. By LAURENCE OLIPHANT, Author of 'Lord Elgin's Mission to China and Japan,' &c. With Illustrations and Maps. Demy 8vo, 21s.

——— The Land of Khemi. Post 8vo, with Illustrations, 10s. 6d.

——— Altiora Peto. With Illustrations. In 4 Monthly Parts, at Five Shillings. Part I. to be published in May.

——— Traits and Travesties; Social and Political. Post 8vo, 10s. 6d.

——— Piccadilly: A Fragment of Contemporary Biography. With Eight Illustrations by Richard Doyle. Fifth Edition, 4s. 6d. Cheap Edition, in paper cover, 2s. 6d.

OLIPHANT. The Ladies Lindores. By Mrs OLIPHANT. 3 vols., 25s. 6d.

——— The Story of Valentine; and his Brother. 5s., cloth.

OLIPHANT. Katie Stewart. 2s. 6d.

—— Salem Chapel. 2s. 6d., cloth.

—— The Perpetual Curate. 2s. 6d., cloth.

—— Miss Marjoribanks. 2s. 6d., cloth.

—— The Rector, and the Doctor's Family. 1s. 6d., cloth.

—— John: A Love Story. 2s. 6d., cloth.

OSBORN. Narratives of Voyage and Adventure. By Admiral SHERARD OSBORN, C.B. 3 vols. crown 8vo, 12s.

OSSIAN. The Poems of Ossian in the Original Gaelic. With a Literal Translation into English, and a Dissertation on the Authenticity of the Poems. By the Rev. ARCHIBALD CLERK. 2 vols. imperial 8vo, £1, 11s. 6d.

OSWALD. By Fell and Fjord; or, Scenes and Studies in Iceland. By E. J. OSWALD. Post 8vo, with Illustrations. 7s. 6d.

PAGE. Introductory Text-Book of Geology. By DAVID PAGE, LL.D., Professor of Geology in the Durham University of Physical Science, Newcastle. With Engravings on Wood and Glossarial Index. Eleventh Edition, 2s. 6d.

—— Advanced Text-Book of Geology, Descriptive and Industrial. With Engravings, and Glossary of Scientific Terms. Sixth Edition, revised and enlarged, 7s. 6d.

—— Geology for General Readers. A Series of Popular Sketches in Geology and Palæontology. Third Edition, enlarged, 6s.

—— Chips and Chapters. A Book for Amateurs and Young Geologists. 5s.

—— Economic Geology; or, Geology in its relation to the Arts and Manufactures. With Engravings, and Coloured Map of the British Islands. Crown 8vo, 7s. 6d.

—— Introductory Text-Book of Physical Geography. With Sketch-Maps and Illustrations. Edited by CHARLES LAPWORTH, F.G.S., &c., Professor of Geology and Mineralogy in the Mason Science College, Birmingham. 11th Edition. 2s. 6d.

—— Advanced Text-Book of Physical Geography. Third Edition, Revised and Improved. With Engravings. 5s.

PAGET. Paradoxes and Puzzles: Historical, Judicial, and Literary. Now for the first time published in Collected Form. By JOHN PAGET, Barrister-at-Law. 8vo, 12s.

PATON. Spindrift. By Sir J. NOEL PATON. Fcap., cloth, 5s.

—— Poems by a Painter. Fcap., cloth, 5s.

PATTERSON. Essays in History and Art. By R. HOGARTH PATTERSON. 8vo, 12s.

—— The New Golden Age, and Influence of the Precious Metals upon the World. 2 vols. 8vo, 31s. 6d.

PAUL. History of the Royal Company of Archers, the Queen's Body-Guard for Scotland. By JAMES BALFOUR PAUL, Advocate of the Scottish Bar. Crown 4to, with Portraits and other Illustrations. £2, 2s.

PAUL. Analysis and Critical Interpretation of the Hebrew Text of the Book of Genesis. Preceded by a Hebrew Grammar, and Dissertations on the Genuineness of the Pentateuch, and on the Structure of the Hebrew Language. By the Rev. WILLIAM PAUL, A.M. 8vo, 18s.

PETTIGREW. The Handy Book of Bees, and their Profitable Management. By A. PETTIGREW. Fourth Edition, Enlarged, with Engravings. Crown 8vo, 3s. 6d.

PHILLIMORE. Uncle Z. By GREVILLE PHILLIMORE, Rector of Henley-on-Thames. Crown 8vo, 7s. 6d.

—— Only a Black Box; Or, A Passage in the Life of a Curate. Crown 8vo, 7s. 6d.

PHILOSOPHICAL CLASSICS FOR ENGLISH READERS. Companion Series to Ancient and Foreign Classics for English Readers. Edited by WILLIAM KNIGHT, LL.D., Professor of Moral Philosophy, University of St Andrews. In crown 8vo volumes, with portraits, price 3s. 6d.

1. DESCARTES. By Professor Mahaffy, Dublin.
2. BUTLER. By the Rev. W. Lucas Collins, M.A., Honorary Canon of Peterborough.
3. BERKELEY. By Professor A. Campbell Fraser, Edinburgh.
4. FICHTE. By Professor Adamson, Owens College, Manchester.
5. KANT. By William Wallace, M.A., LL.D., Merton College, Oxford.
6. HAMILTON. By Professor Veitch, Glasgow.
7. HEGEL. By Professor Edward Caird, Glasgow.

POLLOK. The Course of Time: A Poem. By ROBERT POLLOK, A.M. Small fcap. 8vo, cloth gilt, 2s. 6d. The Cottage Edition, 32mo, sewed, 8d. The Same, cloth, gilt edges, 1s. 6d. Another Edition, with Illustrations by Birket Foster and others, fcap., gilt cloth, 3s. 6d., or with edges gilt, 4s.

PORT ROYAL LOGIC. Translated from the French: with Introduction, Notes, and Appendix. By THOMAS SPENCER BAYNES, LL.D., Professor in the University of St Andrews. Eighth Edition, 12mo, 4s.

POST-MORTEM. Third Edition, 1s.

BY THE SAME AUTHOR.

The Autobiography of Thomas Allen. 3 vols. post 8vo, 25s. 6d.

POTTS AND DARNELL. Aditus Faciliores: An easy Latin Construing Book, with Complete Vocabulary. By A. W. POTTS, M.A., LL.D., Head-Master of the Fettes College, Edinburgh, and sometime Fellow of St John's College, Cambridge; and the Rev. C. DARNELL, M.A., Head-Master of Cargilfield Preparatory School, Edinburgh, and late Scholar of Pembroke and Downing Colleges, Cambridge. Seventh Edition, fcap. 8vo, 3s. 6d.

—— Aditus Faciliores Graeci. An easy Greek Construing Book, with Complete Vocabulary. Third Edition, fcap. 8vo, 3s.

PRINGLE. The Live-Stock of the Farm. By ROBERT O. PRINGLE. Third Edition, crown 8vo. [*In the Press.*

PUBLIC GENERAL STATUTES AFFECTING SCOTLAND, from 1707 to 1847, with Chronological Table and Index. 3 vols. large 8vo, £3, 3s.

PUBLIC GENERAL STATUTES AFFECTING SCOTLAND, COLLECTION OF. Published Annually with General Index.

RAMSAY. Rough Recollections of Military Service and Society. By Lieut.-Col. BALCARRES D. WARDLAW RAMSAY. Two vols. post 8vo, 21s.

REID. A Handy Manual of German Literature. By M. F. REID. For Schools, Civil Service Competitions, and University Local Examinations. Fcap. 8vo, 3s.

RIMMER. The Early Homes of Prince Albert. By ALFRED RIMMER, Author of 'Our Old Country Towns,' &c. Beautifully Illustrated with Tinted Plates and numerous Engravings on Wood. One volume 8vo, 21s.

ROBERTSON. Orellana, and other Poems. By J. LOGIE ROBERTSON. Fcap. 8vo. Printed on hand-made paper. 6s.

—— Our Holiday Among the Hills. By JAMES and JANET LOGIE ROBERTSON. Fcap. 8vo, 3s. 6d.

ROSSLYN. Sonnets. By the EARL OF ROSSLYN. Crown 8vo. [*In the Press.*

RUSSELL. The Haigs of Bemersyde. A Family History. By JOHN RUSSELL. Large octavo, with Illustrations. 21s.

RUSTOW. The War for the Rhine Frontier, 1870: Its Political and Military History. By Col. W. RUSTOW. Translated from the German, by JOHN LAYLAND NEEDHAM, Lieutenant R.M. Artillery. 3 vols. 8vo, with Maps and Plans, £1, 11s. 6d.

SANDERS. Matthew Dale, Farmer. By Mrs SANDERS (A. L. O. S.) 2 vols. post 8vo, 17s.

SCHETKY. Ninety Years of Work and Play. Sketches from the Public and Private Career of JOHN CHRISTIAN SCHETKY, late Marine Painter in Ordinary to the Queen. By his DAUGHTER. Crown 8vo, 7s. 6d.

SCOTCH LOCH FISHING. By "Black Palmer." Crown 8vo, interleaved with blank pages, 4s.

SELLAR. Manual of the Education Acts for Scotland. By ALEXANDER CRAIG SELLAR, Advocate. Seventh Edition, greatly enlarged, and revised to the present time. 8vo, 15s.

SELLER AND STEPHENS. Physiology at the Farm; in Aid of Rearing and Feeding the Live Stock. By WILLIAM SELLER, M.D., F.R.S.E., Fellow of the Royal College of Physicians, Edinburgh, formerly Lecturer on Materia Medica and Dietetics; and HENRY STEPHENS, F.R.S.E., Author of 'The Book of the Farm,' &c. Post 8vo, with Engravings, 16s.

SETON. Memoir of Alexander Seton, Earl of Dunfermline, Seventh President of the Court of Session, and Lord Chancellor of Scotland. By GEORGE SETON, M.A. Oxon.; Author of the 'Law and Practice of Heraldry in Scotland,' &c. Crown 4to, 21s.

SHADWELL. The Life of Colin Campbell, Lord Clyde. Illustrated by Extracts from his Diary and Correspondence. By Lieutenant-General SHADWELL, C.B. 2 vols. 8vo. With Portrait, Maps, and Plans. 36s.

SIM. Margaret Sim's Cookery. With an Introduction by L. B. WALFORD, Author of 'Mr Smith: A Part of His Life,' &c. Crown 8vo, 5s.

SIME. King Capital. By WILLIAM SIME. 2 vols. post 8vo, 17s.

SIMPSON. Dogs of other Days: Nelson and Puck. By EVE BLANTYRE SIMPSON. Fcap. 8vo, with Illustrations, 4s. 6d.

SMITH. The Pastor as Preacher; or, Preaching in connection with Work in the Parish and the Study; being Lectures delivered at the Universities of Edinburgh, Aberdeen, and Glasgow. By HENRY WALLIS SMITH, D.D., Minister of Kirknewton and East Calder; one of the Lecturers on Pastoral Theology appointed by the General Assembly of the Church of Scotland. Crown 8vo, 5s.

SMITH. Italian Irrigation: A Report on the Agricultural Canals of Piedmont and Lombardy, addressed to the Hon. the Directors of the East India Company; with an Appendix, containing a Sketch of the Irrigation System of Northern and Central India. By Lieut.-Col. R. BAIRD SMITH, F.G.S., Captain, Bengal Engineers. Second Edition. 2 vols. 8vo, with Atlas in folio, 30s.

SMITH. Thorndale; or, The Conflict of Opinions. By WILLIAM SMITH, Author of 'A Discourse on Ethics,' &c. A New Edition. Crown 8vo, 10s. 6d.

——— Gravenhurst; or, Thoughts on Good and Evil. Second Edition, with Memoir of the Author. Crown 8vo, 8s.

——— A Discourse on Ethics of the School of Paley. 8vo, 4s.

SMITH. Dramas. 1. Sir William Crichton. 2. Athelwold. 3. Guidone. 24mo, boards, 3s.

SOUTHEY. The Birthday, and other Poems. Second Edition, 5s.

——— Chapters on Churchyards. Fcap., 2s. 6d.

SPEKE. What led to the Discovery of the Nile Source. By John Hanning Speke, Captain H.M. Indian Army. 8vo, with Maps, &c., 14s.

——— Journal of the Discovery of the Source of the Nile. By J. H. Speke, Captain H.M. Indian Army. With a Map of Eastern Equatorial Africa by Captain Speke; numerous illustrations, chiefly from Drawings by Captain Grant; and Portraits, engraved on Steel, of Captains Speke and Grant. 8vo, 21s.

SPROTT. The Worship and Offices of the Church of Scotland; or, the Celebration of Public Worship, the Administration of the Sacraments, and other Divine Offices, according to the Order of the Church of Scotland. By George W. Sprott, D.D., Minister of North Berwick. Crown 8vo, 6s.

STARFORTH. Villa Residences and Farm Architecture: A Series of Designs. By John Starforth, Architect. 102 Engravings. Second Edition, medium 4to, £2, 17s. 6d.

STATISTICAL ACCOUNT OF SCOTLAND. Complete, with Index, 15 vols. 8vo, £16, 16s.

Each County sold separately, with Title, Index, and Map, neatly bound in cloth, forming a very valuable Manual to the Landowner, the Tenant, the Manufacturer, the Naturalist, the Tourist, &c.

STEPHENS. The Book of the Farm; detailing the Labours of the Farmer, Farm-Steward, Ploughman, Shepherd, Hedger, Farm-Labourer, Field-Worker, and Cattleman. By Henry Stephens, F.R.S.E. Illustrated with Portraits of Animals painted from the life; and with 557 Engravings on Wood, representing the principal Field Operations, Implements, and Animals treated of in the Work. A New and Revised Edition, the third, in great part Rewritten. 2 vols. large 8vo, £2, 10s.

——— The Book of Farm-Buildings; their Arrangement and Construction. By Henry Stephens, F.R.S.E., Author of 'The Book of the Farm;' and Robert Scott Burn. Illustrated with 1045 Plates and Engravings. Large 8vo, uniform with 'The Book of the Farm,' &c. £1, 11s. 6d.

——— The Book of Farm Implements and Machines. By J. Slight and R. Scott Burn, Engineers. Edited by Henry Stephens. Large 8vo, uniform with 'The Book of the Farm,' £2, 2s.

——— Catechism of Practical Agriculture. With Engravings. 1s.

STEWART. Advice to Purchasers of Horses. By John Stewart, V.S. Author of 'Stable Economy.' 2s. 6d.

——— Stable Economy. A Treatise on the Management of Horses in relation to Stabling, Grooming, Feeding, Watering, and Working. Seventh Edition, fcap. 8vo, 6s. 6d.

STIRLING. Missing Proofs: a Pembrokeshire Tale. By M. C. Stirling, Author of 'The Grahams of Invermoy.' 2 vols. crown 8vo, 17s.

——— The Minister's Son; or, Home with Honours. 3 vols. post 8vo, 25s. 6d.

STORMONTH. Etymological and Pronouncing Dictionary of the English Language. Including a very Copious Selection of Scientific Terms. For Use in Schools and Colleges, and as a Book of General Reference. By the Rev. James Stormonth. The Pronunciation carefully Revised by the Rev. P. H. Phelp, M.A. Cantab. Seventh Edition, Revised throughout, containing many words not to be found in any other Dictionary. Crown 8vo, pp. 800. 7s. 6d.

STORMONTH. The School Etymological Dictionary and Word-Book. Combining the advantages of an ordinary pronouncing School Dictionary and an Etymological Spelling-book. Fcap. 8vo, pp. 254. 2s.

STORY. Graffiti D'Italia. By W. W. STORY, Author of 'Roba di Roma.' Second Edition, fcap. 8vo, 7s. 6d.

—— Nero; A Historical Play. Fcap. 8vo, 6s.

—— Vallombrosa. Post 8vo, 5s.

STRICKLAND. Lives of the Queens of Scotland, and English Princesses connected with the Regal Succession of Great Britain. By AGNES STRICKLAND. With Portraits and Historical Vignettes. 8 vols. post 8vo, £4, 4s.

STURGIS. John-a-Dreams. A Tale. By JULIAN STURGIS. New Edition, crown 8vo, 3s. 6d.

—— Little Comedies, Old and New. Crown 8vo, 7s. 6d.

—— Dick's Wandering. 3 vols., post 8vo, 25s. 6d.

SUTHERLAND. Handbook of Hardy Herbaceous and Alpine Flowers, for general Garden Decoration. Containing Descriptions, in Plain Language, of upwards of 1000 Species of Ornamental Hardy Perennial and Alpine Plants, adapted to all classes of Flower-Gardens, Rockwork, and Waters; along with Concise and Plain Instructions for their Propagation and Culture. By WILLIAM SUTHERLAND, Gardener to the Earl of Minto; formerly Manager of the Herbaceous Department at Kew. Crown 8vo, 7s. 6d.

TAYLOR. Destruction and Reconstruction: Personal Experiences of the Late War in the United States. By RICHARD TAYLOR, Lieutenant-General in the Confederate Army. 8vo, 10s. 6d.

TAYLOR. The Story of My Life. By the late Colonel MEADOWS TAYLOR, Author of 'The Confessions of a Thug,' &c. &c. Edited by his Daughter. New and cheaper Edition, being the Fourth. Crown 8vo, 6s.

THOLUCK. Hours of Christian Devotion. Translated from the German of A. Tholuck, D.D., Professor of Theology in the University of Halle. By the Rev. ROBERT MENZIES, D.D. With a Preface written for this Translation by the Author. Second Edition, crown 8vo, 7s. 6d.

THOMSON. Handy Book of the Flower-Garden: being Practical Directions for the Propagation, Culture, and Arrangement of Plants in Flower-Gardens all the year round. Embracing all classes of Gardens, from the largest to the smallest. With Engraved and Coloured Plans, illustrative of the various systems of Grouping in Beds and Borders. By DAVID THOMSON, Gardener to his Grace the Duke of Buccleuch, K.G., at Drumlanrig. Third Edition, crown 8vo, 7s. 6d.

—— The Handy Book of Fruit-Culture under Glass: being a series of Elaborate Practical Treatises on the Cultivation and Forcing of Pines, Vines, Peaches, Figs, Melons, Strawberries, and Cucumbers. With Engravings of Hothouses, &c., most suitable for the Cultivation and Forcing of these Fruits. Second Edition. Crown 8vo, with Engravings, 7s. 6d.

THOMSON. A Practical Treatise on the Cultivation of the Grape-Vine. By WILLIAM THOMSON, Tweed Vineyards. Ninth Edition, 8vo, 5s.

TOM CRINGLE'S LOG. A New Edition, with Illustrations. Crown 8vo, cloth gilt, 5s. Cheap Edition, 2s.

TRAILL. Recaptured Rhymes. Being a Batch of Political and other Fugitives arrested and brought to Book. By H. D. TRAILL. Crown 8vo, 5s.

TRANSACTIONS OF THE HIGHLAND AND AGRICULTURAL SOCIETY OF SCOTLAND. Published annually, price 5s.

TROLLOPE. The Fixed Period. By ANTHONY TROLLOPE. 2 vols., fcap. 8vo, 12s.

TULLOCH. Rational Theology and Christian Philosophy in England in the Seventeenth Century. By JOHN TULLOCH, D.D., Principal of St Mary's College in the University of St Andrews; and one of her Majesty's Chaplains in Ordinary in Scotland. Second Edition. 2 vols. 8vo, 28s.

—— The Christian Doctrine of Sin; being the Croall Lecture for 1876. Crown 8vo, 6s.

—— Theism. The Witness of Reason and Nature to an All-Wise and Beneficent Creator. 8vo, 10s. 6d.

TYTLER. The Wonder-Seeker; or, The History of Charles Douglas. By M. FRASER TYTLER, Author of 'Tales of the Great and Brave,' &c. A New Edition. Fcap., 3s. 6d.

VIRGIL. The Æneid of Virgil. Translated in English Blank Verse by G. K. RICKARDS, M.A., and Lord RAVENSWORTH. 2 vols. fcap. 8vo, 10s.

WALFORD. Mr Smith: A Part of his Life. By L. B. WALFORD. Cheap Edition, 3s. 6d.

—— Pauline. Fifth Edition. Crown 8vo, 6s.

—— Cousins. Fourth Edition. Crown 8vo, 6s.

—— Troublesome Daughters. Third Edition. Crown 8vo, 6s.

—— Dick Netherby. Crown 8vo, 7s. 6d.

WARREN'S (SAMUEL) WORKS. People's Edition, 4 vols. crown 8vo, cloth, 18s. Or separately:—

Diary of a Late Physician. 3s. 6d. Illustrated, crown 8vo, 7s. 6d.

Ten Thousand A-Year. 5s.

Now and Then. The Lily and the Bee. Intellectual and Moral Development of the Present Age. 4s. 6d.

Essays: Critical, Imaginative, and Juridical. 5s.

WARREN. The Five Books of the Psalms. With Marginal Notes. By Rev. SAMUEL L. WARREN, Rector of Esher, Surrey; late Fellow, Dean, and Divinity Lecturer, Wadham College, Oxford. Crown 8vo, 5s.

WATSON. Christ's Authority; and other Sermons. By the late ARCHIBALD WATSON, D.D., Minister of the Parish of Dundee, and one of Her Majesty's Chaplains for Scotland. With Introduction by the Very Rev. Principal Caird, Glasgow. Crown 8vo, 7s. 6d.

WELLINGTON. Wellington Prize Essays on "the System of Field Manœuvres best adapted for enabling our Troops to meet a Continental Army. Edited by Major-General Sir EDWARD BRUCE HAMLEY, K.C.M.G. 8vo, 12s. 6d.

WESTMINSTER ASSEMBLY. Minutes of the Westminster Assembly, while engaged in preparing their Directory for Church Government, Confession of Faith, and Catechisms (November 1644 to March 1649). Printed from Transcripts of the Originals procured by the General Assembly of the Church of Scotland. Edited by the Rev. ALEX. T. MITCHELL, D.D., Professor of Ecclesiastical History in the University of St Andrews, and the Rev. JOHN STRUTHERS, LL.D., Minister of Prestonpans. With a Historical and Critical Introduction by Professor Mitchell. 8vo, 15s.

WHITE. The Eighteen Christian Centuries. By the Rev. JAMES WHITE, Author of 'The History of France.' Seventh Edition, post 8vo, with Index, 6s.

——— History of France, from the Earliest Times. Sixth Thousand, post 8vo, with Index, 6s.

WHITE. Archæological Sketches in Scotland—Kintyre and Knapdale. By Captain T. P. WHITE, R.E., of the Ordnance Survey. With numerous Illustrations. 2 vols. folio, £4, 4s. Vol. I., Kintyre, sold separately, £2, 2s.

WILLS AND GREENE. Drawing-room Dramas for Children. By W. G. WILLS and the Hon. Mrs GREENE. Crown 8vo, 6s.

WILSON. Works of Professor Wilson. Edited by his Son-in-Law, Professor FERRIER. 12 vols. crown 8vo, £2, 8s.

——— Christopher in his Sporting-Jacket. 2 vols., 8s.

——— Isle of Palms, City of the Plague, and other Poems. 4s.

——— Lights and Shadows of Scottish Life, and other Tales. 4s.

——— Essays, Critical and Imaginative. 4 vols., 16s.

——— The Noctes Ambrosianæ. Complete, 4 vols., 14s.

——— The Comedy of the Noctes Ambrosianæ. By CHRISTOPHER NORTH. Edited by JOHN SKELTON, Advocate. With a Portrait of Professor Wilson and of the Ettrick Shepherd, engraved on Steel. Crown 8vo, 7s. 6d.

——— Homer and his Translators, and the Greek Drama. Crown 8vo, 4s.

WINGATE. Annie Weir, and other Poems. By DAVID WINGATE. Fcap. 8vo, 5s.

——— Lily Neil. A Poem. Crown 8vo, 4s. 6d.

WORDSWORTH. The Historical Plays of Shakespeare. With Introductions and Notes. By CHARLES WORDSWORTH, D.C.L., Bishop of S. Andrews. 3 vols. post 8vo, each price 7s. 6d.

——— A Discourse on Scottish Church History. From the Reformation to the Present Time. With Prefatory Remarks on the St Giles' Lectures, and Appendix of Notes and References. Crown 8vo, cloth, 2s. 6d.

WORSLEY. Poems and Translations. By PHILIP STANHOPE WORSLEY, M.A. Edited by EDWARD WORSLEY. Second Edition, enlarged. Fcap. 8vo, 6s.

WYLDE. A Dreamer. By KATHARINE WYLDE. In 3 vols., post 8vo, 25s. 6d.

YOUNG. Songs of Béranger done into English Verse. By WILLIAM YOUNG. New Edition, revised. Fcap. 8vo, 4s. 6d.

YULE. Fortification: for the Use of Officers in the Army, and Readers of Military History. By Col. YULE, Bengal Engineers. 8vo, with numerous Illustrations, 10s. 6d.